Flash MX Most Wanted Effects & Movies

Sham Bhangal
Chad Corbin
David Doull
Keith Peters
Adam Phillips
Jordan Stone
Todd Yard
WideGroup :: Digital Motion

Flash MX Most Wanted Effects & Movies

© 2002 friends of ED

First Printed December 2002

Trademark Acknowledgements

friends of ED has endeavored to provide trademark information about all the companies and products mentioned in this book by the appropriate use of capitals. However, friends of ED cannot guarantee the accuracy of this information.

Published by friends of ED

30-32 Lincoln Road, Olton, Birmingham.
B27 6PA. UK.
Printed in USA

ISBN 1-903450-94-2

Credits

Authors
Sham Bhangal
Chad Corbin
David Doull
Keith Peters
Adam Phillips
Jordan Stone
Todd Yard
WideGroup :: Digital Motion

Reviewers
Sally Cruikshank
Ola Bergner
Chris Crane
Michael Pearce

Graphic Editors
Chantal Hepworth
Ty Bhogal

Editors
Dan Britton
Gavin Wray

Indexer
Fiona Murray
Simon Collins

Proof Reader
Helena Sharman

Project Manager
Jenni Harvey

Managing Editor
Sonia Mullineux

Original Concept
Matt Knight

Special Thanks to
MirCorp for the use of their images

Introduction

It's fast; it's fun; it's design dynamite. The aim of this book is to provide you with the **most wanted** effects in Flash.

We've done extensive research, scouring the Flash community and its forums, to find out exactly what it is that people are craving to build in Flash. We've taken these topics and crafted chapters designed to give you what you want. We've noted common problems that hit Flash users time and time again, and we've sought out the best people to provide simple solutions to those problems.

With each topic, we've looked at what solutions, if any, are currently available to the community. We've considered if they meet the standard Flash user's needs. And finally, we've crafted our own solution, using authors who are experts in each field.

For the first, time you'll find the solutions to the most frequent problems and most wanted features in one book.

Each chapter will guide you through the most wanted effects in a series of stepped tutorials, giving you tips and tricks along the way from our expert authors. Maybe once you've finished this book, you'll be the one answering the questions in the forums, and providing that most wanted knowledge to others.

figure 1a
the wonder of existence

Layout conventions

We want this book to be as clear and easy to use as possible, so we've introduced a number of layout styles that we've used throughout.

- Instructions in exercises appear as numbered steps.
- We'll use different styles to emphasize things that appear on the screen.
- Hyperlinks will take the following format: www.friendsofed.com.
- Code will appear in `this style`, and code we want to emphasize will be like **`this`**. You'll also see input information and element names in the `same style`.
- Keyboard shortcuts are written out like this: CTRL+A. PC users should press the CTRL (Control) key and the S key at the same time, while Mac users the ⌘ (Command) key and S key. All shortcuts are in the PC format.
- If we introduce a new **important term**, then these will be in bold.
- When we want you to click on a menu, and then through subsequent sub-menus, we will indicate to like so: Text>Style>Bold (see picture).

Download files

Throughout each of the chapters, you'll see references to download files. These are the completed files for everything you will build throughout the book, and also extra files to help you along the way. These files can be downloaded from the link on the friends of ED homepage (www.friendsofed.com).

Support – we're here to help

All books from friends of ED should be easy to follow and error-free. However, if you do run into problems, don't hesitate to get in touch – our support is fast, friendly and free.

You can reach us at support@friendsofed.com, quoting the last for digits of the ISBN in the subject of the e-mail (that's 0942), and even if our dedicated support team are unable to solve your problem immediately, your queries will be passed onto the people who put the book together, the editors and authors, to solve. All our authors help with the support on their books, and will either directly mail people with answers, or (more usually) send their response to an editor to pass on.

We'd love to hear from you, even if it's just to request future books, ask about friends of ED, or tell us how much you loved *Flash MX Most Wanted!*

> *To tell us a bit about yourself and make comments about the book, why not fill out the reply card at the back and send it to us!*

If your enquiry concerns an issue not directly concerned with book content, then the best place for these types of questions is our message boards at http://www.friendsofed.com/forums. Here, you'll find a variety of designers talking about what they do, who should be able to provide some ideas and solutions.

For news, more books, sample chapters, downloads, author interviews and more, send your browser to www.friendsofed.com. To take a look at the brand new friends of ED Flash MX bookshelf from which this book comes, take a look at flashmxlibrary.com.

About the Author
Todd Yard

After studying theatre in London, and then working for several years as an actor in the US, Todd was introduced to Flash in 2000. Hw was quickly taken by how it allowed for both stunning creativity and programmatic logic application – a truly left brain, right brain approach to production – and has not looked back. He now works as Creative Director for Daedalus Media in New York City, which specializes in the creation of Flash-based corporate presentations, primarily for clients in the investment banking industry. His more frivolous work and experimentation can be found at his personal Website, www.27Bobs.com.

Preloaders and Player Detection

Todd Yard

About the Effect

Preloaders are *the* most requested effect on Flash forums. To many they are just the mechanics that occur while you wait for the main action, but this needn't be the case. Until Internet connections are instantaneous, and no download times are required (which is a long way off), preloaders are a necessity.

By making a preloader visually impressive, you are almost guaranteeing that the user will be prepared to wait while your main content loads in. A dull preloader, or even worse, none at all, will usually result in most users leaving the site straight away – you've lost the chance to get your message across.

Player detection is equally important. It's all very well having a high-tech impressive site, but if a user can't view it you've wasted your time.

By the end of this chapter, you'll have enough expertise to ensure that users are kept at your site, or at least until they've got to the main section.

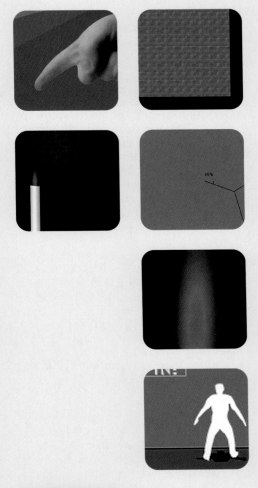

Something's coming...

Please wait, the actual chapter text is coming...

Could you imagine if we were made to wait for other types of media in our lives? You turn on the television for your favorite show at 8pm, and then have to sit and watch a blank screen for five minutes while wondering what the delay is. You flip on the radio and are treated to a long dead silence before music starts to come out. Unthinkable.

The thing is, we are used to immediate feedback with most aspects of our modern lives. Unfortunately, this doesn't yet apply to the Internet. There is an amazing amount of information out there being passed across a limited bandwidth, and until the day arrives when that bandwidth isn't a concern (and don't hold your breath!), we as developers need to consider the problems that can arise.

One thing we can do for the user is inform them of why they are being made to wait for their instant gratification. It's important to give some kind of feedback as your content loads. This is where preloaders come in.

When I speak of preloaders, I am not referring to Flash intro animations. That is a different kind of animal entirely, as you'll see in the chapter by WideGroup. No, a preloader is a way to keep the user informed of the loading progress of content. They can also be an entertaining diversion while the main content loads, such as a small animation or a game, with 'small' being the operative word. However, the projects in this chapter will concentrate on offering the user feedback. Of course, you can do that in an entertaining way as well!

Flash Player detection

Before we can offer any feedback to the user, we need to make sure they have the necessary player to view the content. Browser detection can be a fairly tricky procedure, stemming from the number of browsers and version numbers out there. Depending on the browser of an individual user, you might want to load a different page for them to view. Thankfully, one of the great benefits of Flash is that it doesn't really matter which browser a Flash movie is viewed in. As long as the proper plug-in is installed in the browser, everything will more or less appear the same. So, how do you ensure that the plug-in is installed, and if so, the proper version? In this tutorial, we are going to create a simple HTML and Flash file that will take care of all that for us.

Player detection

This is an extremely easy way to detect whether a user has a version of the player plug-in or not. It doesn't require any JavaScript, so is a safe and easy option to utilize for both Navigator and Explorer.

1.   Create a new Flash MX movie, simply leaving the default stage set-up for the time being. Save it as `sniffer.fla`.

2. Go into the Publish Settings dialog box (File>Publish Settings/CTRL+SHIFT+F12) and its HTML tab. Change Dimensions to Percent. Publish the movie.

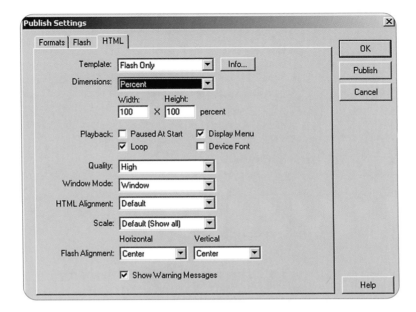

3. In a simple text or code editor, such as Notepad or Dreamweaver, open the new `sniffer.html` file that you just created. You'll find it in the same folder that you saved the FLA in. You'll notice a `<meta>` tag with a few attributes in the `<HEAD>` tag at the top:

```
<meta http-equiv=Content-Type content="text/html;  charset=ISO-8859-1">
```

4. Add an additional `<meta>` tag right after the tag listed above:

```
<meta http-equiv="refresh" content="5;URL=http://www.macromedia.com/shockwave
/download/download.cgi?P1_Prod_Version=ShockwaveFlash&P5_Language=English">
```

Here, the `http-equiv` attribute of the `<meta>` tag is asking the browser to refresh after five seconds (the number specified in the `content` attribute). However, we have set the URL to the download page on the Macromedia site, so when the browser refreshes, it actually acts as if the specified URL is the page to refresh. This, in effect, sends the user to the download page.

5. Open the HTML file in a web browser, and watch the redirection take place after five seconds.

You might think it a bit presumptuous to redirect the user in this way, so perhaps you might send them to another HTML page in your domain that you have designed to inform them that they need the plug-in, or perhaps to an HTML alternative to your site.

6. Return to `sniffer.fla`, open up the Actions panel (F9), and add the following line of code in the first frame:

```
getURL("http://www.friendsofed.com", "_self");
```

What are we doing? Well, as soon as the sniffer movie loads, the Flash Player will execute a `getURL` command and load the specified page into the same browser window as the `sniffer.html` file, *overwriting it before it can refresh*. However, if the player plug-in is not installed, the new home page obviously won't load. Five seconds would then pass and the user would be redirected to the Macromedia download page. Simple!

7. Drop a simple logo onto the stage in the FLA. Make the background colors fit in with the color scheme of your site. Hopefully, this page will only appear for a few seconds for most of the users, but there's no reason why we can't make it something other than a flash of white!

8. Publish the SWF by pressing CTRL+ENTER. Be sure *not* to choose the main publish option (File>Publish/SHIFT+F12), as this would republish the HTML page and remove our code modification. Test the movie by opening `sniffer.html` in a browser.

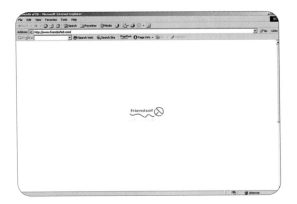

Version detection

Once we have determined whether the user has the Flash Player plug-in, and so sent them to the appropriate page, we need to ensure that they have the proper version of the plug-in for the site we've produced. This is actually very easy to take care of in the Flash movie itself. You see, if the user's browser has a previous version of the Flash Player, it will still read a SWF produced in Flash MX. However, if you have used ActionScript that is only available for the current version of the Player (at the time of this writing, build 6,0,47,0), then that code will not be run by the older Player plug-in, and things can start to go haywire.

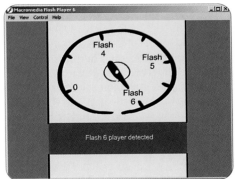

We can use this to our advantage, though. By testing the Player with commands that are from the more recent versions of the Player, we can determine the version installed in the user's browser. We'll even build an animation to inform the user if they have the correct version installed, or if they need to upgrade. Open up `versionMeter.swf` to see the finished movie.

Meter graphics

1. Create a new movie and save it as `versionMeter.fla`. Change the background color to #666666 (Modify>Document/CTRL+J), but leave the rest of the movie parameters at their default settings.

2. Create six layers in all (Insert>Layer), naming them (from top to bottom) code, peg, spinner, meter, textfield and box. Make each layer 45 frames long, by pressing F5 at frame 45 of each layer.

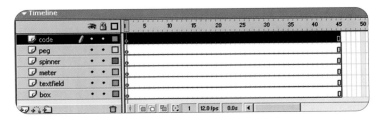

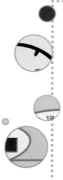

3. Draw three background rectangle graphics for our meter on the `box` layer. I drew the top and bottom boxes with a `#E6E6E6` fill, and the middle box (which will be behind the text) with a `#683517` fill. I also added a 4 point black stroke to the sides of the gray rectangles.

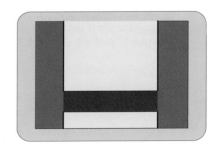

4. In the `meter` layer, draw a black circle with no fill for the meter itself. I chose to use a stylus for a sloppier feel, but you can also just use the Oval tool (O), if you like. Center this circle in the top rectangle. Convert it into a movie clip named `circle` (F8), and then copy and paste it in place (CTRL+C, then CTRL+SHIFT+V). Scale the duplicate down to about 20% of the original, and center it inside the larger circle. You may find the Align panel useful for organizing objects on the stage (CTRL+K).

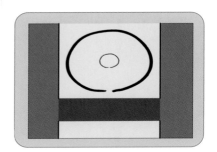

5. Still in the `meter` layer, draw an individual tick mark for the meter, and convert it into a movie clip symbol named `tick`. Anything you reuse in Flash should be made into a symbol, as that will keep the file size down. Once you have a tick symbol, drag multiple instances onto your stage from the Library, and place them on the inside of the circle at equal degrees around its face. Use as many as you like to achieve your desired look for the meter, and rotate them so they are facing inwards.

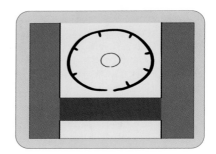

6. The final step for the `meter` layer is to add labels for the versions of Flash, using the Text tool (T). Choose any font you like, but remember to embed fonts that may not be on the user's computer. Arrange the labels around the meter in sequential order.

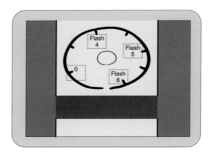

7. On the `textfield` layer, create a **dynamic** text field over the middle box, giving it the **variable** name `message` (versions before MX won't recognize an instance name). Choose center alignment and give it a white font color to make it stand out from the dark rectangle background. Type 'testing for plug-in' in the text field.

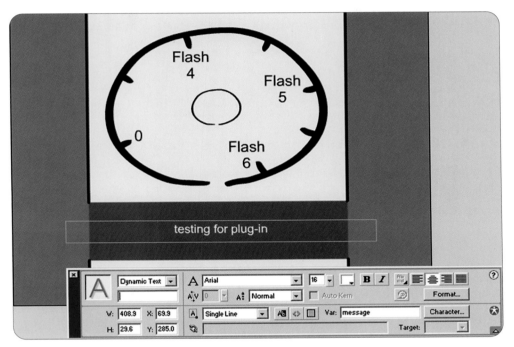

8. We now need a spinner to point to the detected version. On the `spinner` layer, make a simple graphic that is wider at one end than the other. I used the stylus again for this, but using the Rectangle tool and adjusting one side would work just as well. Convert this graphic into a movie clip named `innerSpinner` (F8). Once you have done this, convert that instance of `innerSpinner` into another movie clip called `spinner` (F8 again), which should leave you with an `innerSpinner` instance nested inside `spinner`. The reason we nest this will become apparent when we add some code to make the spinner 'jitter' as it moves about the meter.

9. Go into Symbol Editing mode for `innerSpinner`. Place the graphic so that the point you want the spinner to revolve around is over the registration point. Then return to Scene 1 and place the `spinner` instance in the center of the meter.

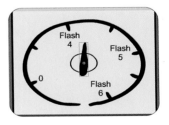

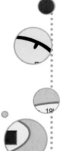

10. Finally, on the `peg` layer of the main timeline, draw a small ellipse with a #E6E6E6 colored fill and place it over the point around which you've set the spinner to spin. This is the peg holding the spinner down.

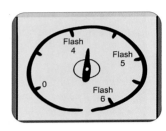

Version-checking code

Now that we have our graphics finished, it's time to write a small bit of code to test the version number of the user's plug-in player.

1. Make keyframes (F6) in the `code` layer on the main timeline at frames 5, 20, 35 and 45.

2. Open up the Actions panel (F9) in frame 5 and type the code:

```
message = "you need to upgrade to the Flash 6 plug-in";
stop();
if (true) {
    message = "testing for plug-in";
    play();
}
```

The `if` statement was introduced in Flash Player 4, so if the player recognizes the statement, the spinner will continue its spin. Otherwise, the playhead is stopped, and you could then inform the user of their options, (I'll leave that to you).

3. Now, at frame 20 of the `code` layer, type the following code:

```
if (!Array) {
    message = "you need to upgrade to the Flash 6 plug-in";
    stop();
}
```

`Array` is an object that was introduced in Flash 5. The same logic applies here as in the previous step, but in reverse. If the player doesn't recognize the object, it stops the playhead. If the user's player isn't stopped here, we know they have at least version 5 of the Player.

4. In frame 35, add the following code:

```
if (!System) {
    message = "you need to upgrade to the Flash 6 plug-in";
    stop();
}
```

Flash MX has introduced the new `System` object, so we can use that here to check for the Flash Player 6. If you wanted to bypass the previous steps at frames 5 and 20, and simply check to see if your newly-designed Flash MX project is viewable for the user, this code shows you how you could do it.

5. At frame 45, type the following code into the Actions panel:

```
message = "Flash 6 player detected";
stop();
```

If the user has made it to this frame, we know they have the proper player, and you can proceed to whatever page or scene that you wish. Understand that for your projects, all of this code can be behind the scenes and contained in a single frame. For purposes of this demonstration, we are letting the users glimpse what is happening backstage! To do that, we need some animation.

Animating the meter

Now that the code is ready to test, we need to animate our meter to show us if the code is working. We will do this by spinning it to point at the version we are currently checking for.

1. On the `spinner` layer, rotate the spinner on the stage using the Free Transform tool (Q), so that it is pointing at the 0. Then make a keyframe at frame 5 (F6), and another at frame 15. In frame 15, rotate the meter so that it is pointing at Flash 4. With any of the spinner frames selected in between 5 and 15, go to the Property inspector and select Motion from the Tween drop-down menu. Scrub your timeline to see the spinner spin into position.

2. Make a new keyframe at frame 20, and a further one at frame 30. In frame 30, rotate the spinner to point at Flash 5. Create a motion tween between the two frames.

3. Finally, make keyframes at frames 35 and 45. In frame 45, rotate the spinner to point at Flash 6. Create a motion tween between these two frames as well.

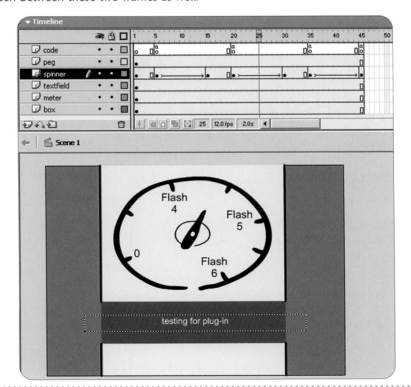

If you test your movie now (CTRL+ENTER), you should see the spinner smoothly going from point to point, stopping briefly at each one. We can add a little bit of code to make it more jittery as it progresses about the meter.

4. In the Property inspector, give the `spinner` clip an instance name of `spinner`. Double-click on the `spinner` instance to go into it, then select `innerSpinner` clip and give it an instance name of `innerspinner`.

5. Now go to frame 1 of Scene 1's `code` layer and open up the Actions panel. Add the following code:

```
spinner.innerspinner.onEnterFrame = function() {
    this._rotation = Math.random()*10-5;
};
```

Here, we've used dot syntax to reference the `innerspinner` instance and create an `onEnterFrame` handler for it. Pretty easy for such an effective addition, isn't it? Here we set a new rotation for `innerSpinner` each frame within a range of –5 and 5. `Math.random()` returns a number between 0 and 1, which we multiply by 10 to give us a range from 0 to 10. Subtracting 5 gives us an equal range on either side of 0.

We needed to nest the spinners so that we could tween the outer symbol while using code to rotate the inner symbol. You could do the entire thing with code, but that is for another tutorial! Here, we were concentrating on how to determine the existence and the specs of a user's Player, and I think we've succeeded admirably. Again, you could (and most likely will) do all of this behind the scenes, invisibly redirecting the user based on what they can or can't view. The same concepts apply, but maybe aren't as graphically fun!

Textual preloader

Great! Now we know that a user can view all of our hard work, we send them to our site. They start loading all of the JPEGs, MP3s and 3D animations, having no idea what excitement is in store! Of course, we didn't plan on them getting bored waiting and heading elsewhere...

Wait a minute! Of course we planned for it! Not only did we consider how to split the site up to load only what the user was ready for, but we created a nifty preloader to inform them of what was coming and how long they would have to wait.

Preloaders come in all shapes and sizes, but pretty much all that provide feedback do so in a similar manner. It's how developers take that data and display it that differs. In this first tutorial, we'll cover the basics of how to get the relevant data and show it to the user. The result will be a field of information about the loading progress. Open up `textFeedback.swf` to see the end result of the next exercise.

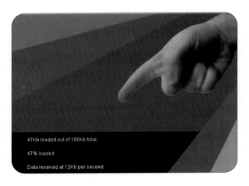

47Kb loaded out of 100Kb total.

47% loaded.

Data received at 12Kb per second.

The graphical point

Since a field of numbers isn't the most interesting thing in the world, I decided to spice things up a bit with a Monty Python-esque hand from the Man upstairs.

1. Create a new movie and save it as `textFeedback.fla`. Keep the default movie settings, but change the movie's background color to `#064847`, which matches the background color of the hand.

2. Create five layers named (from top to bottom) code, rays, textfield, ground and hand.

3. On the ground layer, draw a horizontal black rectangle across the bottom of the stage.

4. On the textfield layer, create a text field large enough to hold five lines of text. Make it Dynamic Text, and Multiline. Give the text field an instance name of info in the Property inspector. Set a _sans font, a color of white and a point size of 12. You should try to use device fonts as often as you can in your preloaders, as it will help to keep your file sizes down. If you choose to use a special font, be sure only to embed what you need to.

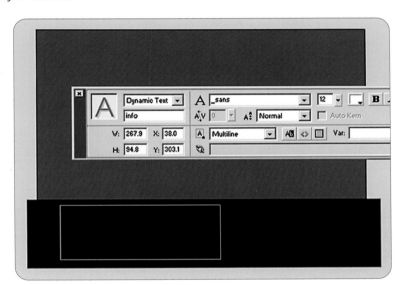

5. Create a new movie clip (CTRL+F8), and call it hand. Import hand.jpg from the download files into this symbol (CTRL+R). This is a shot of my own hand, filtered a bit in Photoshop and saved as a JPEG. Although it is a fairly large graphic, I was able to export it at 7Kb, thanks to a fair amount of blurring. If you use bitmaps in your preloaders, concentrate on making them as small as possible. With the JPEG image selected, press F8 to convert it into a movie clip symbol called innerHand. The new movie clip will be nested inside the hand clip.

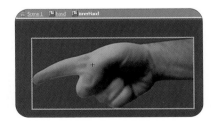

6. While still inside the hand movie clip, create a new keyframe at frame 10, and another at frame 20. Create motion tweens between all three keyframes, and then move the innerHand at frame 10 to the left by about 70 pixels. Scrubbing the timeline should show the hand moving to the right and to the left on the stage.

7. Back on the main timeline, drop an instance of hand onto the hand layer. Set it up in the upper right corner of the stage, and rotate it using the Free Transform tool (Q), so that it points down towards the text field.

8. Finally, draw several trapezoidal rays of varying colors on the rays layer. I actually worked with only one, converted it into a symbol, and then used the tinting effects. Anything and everything to keep the file size down!

Test your movie (CTRL+ENTER), and you should see the hand from heaven pointing down to earth!

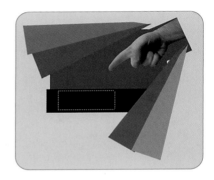

Assessing the load

Almost all preloaders work by comparing the number of bytes loaded against the total number of bytes to load, and ours will be no different. In fact, that will be the basic foundation of all of the preloaders in this chapter. In this text feedback preloader, almost all of the work will be taken care of with a single function that will be called regularly, assessLoad().

1. With frame 1 of the code layer selected, type the following, which is the start of a function, into the Actions panel (F9):

```
assessLoad = function (clip, endPreloadFunc) {
    var kbLoaded = clip.getBytesLoaded()/1024;
    var kbTotal = clip.getBytesTotal()/1024;
    var percent = Math.floor(kbLoaded/kbTotal*100);
```

When we call this function, we will send two parameters: clip will be the movie clip that we are assessing (whether it be the main timeline, an individual movie clip, or a level) and endPreloadFunc will be the function we want called when a load is complete (possibly to send the playhead to the loaded frame).

Inside the function, we declare three variables. `kbLoaded` is the number of kilobytes that have loaded into `clip`, while `kbTotal` is the total number of kilobytes to load. `getBytesLoaded()` and `getBytesTotal()` actually return bytes, so we divide by 1024 to convert the value into kilobytes. Using these two variables, we can find a percent of the kilobytes loaded. Multiplying by 100 gives us a percent between 0 and 100, and using `Math.floor` leaves us with an integer.

2. Add the following lines after those you typed in the last step:

```
if (clip.secondCount>=1) {
    clip.rate = Math.floor(kbLoaded-previousKb);
    clip.previousKb = kbLoaded;
    clip.secondCount = 0;
} else {
    clip.secondCount += .1;
}
```

We are going to determine how quickly the data is being transferred, and to do this we will run a test every second. How will we know when a second has passed? Well, we could use `getTimer()`, but since we will use the new `setInterval` to call this function every tenth of a second, I decided to run the test every tenth time this function is called. `clip.secondCount` holds the current count, which we add .1 to every function call. As soon as that value reaches 1, we find the rate, which is the previous amount of kilobytes loaded subtracted from the current amount. Once we have determined the rate, we set the `previousKb` to equal the current amount and reinitialize the `secondCount`.

Now that we have the amount of kilobytes loaded, the total amount to load, the percent that has loaded, and the rate of transfer, we need to display it for the user. We do that in the next lines.

3. Place these lines after the `if` conditional:

```
info.text = Math.floor(kbLoaded)+"Kb loaded out of "+Math.floor
➥(kbTotal)+"Kb total.";
info.text += newline+newline;
info.text += percent+"% loaded.";
info.text += newline+newline;
info.text += "Data received at "+clip.rate+"Kb per second.";
```

Here, we simply place all of the data into the text field on stage (`info`). I used `newline` to add blank lines in between (you can also use `\n`).

4. Finish the `assessLoad()` function with the following lines:

```
if ((kbLoaded/kbTotal == 1) && kbLoaded>1) {
    endPreloadFunc();
}
};
```

Finally, if the number of kilobytes loaded equals the number to load, we call the function stored in the `endPreloadFunc` argument sent to `assessLoad` (the second condition of `kbLoaded>1` is just a safety check to ensure that *some* content has loaded).

That's it for `assessLoad()`, and remember that the concepts discussed in it will apply to all of our remaining preloaders as well. Now, let's write a function to call when the load is over.

5. Type the following code after the `assessLoad` function:

```
endPreload = function () {
    clearInterval(preload);
};
```

This is where you would put any code you want run when the load is over. Perhaps it is as simple as `_root.play()`, or you might want to start some movie clips animating. Whatever you need to have happen would be placed in this function. The single line I've included clears the interval call that will be calling `assessLoad()` every tenth of a second. We'll write that next.

6. Add the following line to the end of the code:

```
preload = setInterval(assessLoad, 100, this, endPreload);
```

`preload` is the interval ID that we give to a new interval that will call the function `assessLoad` (first parameter) every 100 milliseconds (second parameter). We can send the `assessLoad` function the parameters of `this` and `endPreload` (which correspond to `clip` and `endPreloadFunc` in the arguments of `assessLoad`), and all in one line of code! So, now `assessLoad` will be called every 100 milliseconds, assessing the load of the main timeline (`this`) and calling `endPreload` once the load is complete.

If you test you movie now, you won't see the numbers change since everything loads instantaneously. To simulate a load in the testing environment, add the following lines to the beginning of `assessLoad`:

```
var kbLoaded = clip.getBytesLoaded()/1024;
var kbTotal = clip.getBytesTotal()/1024;
kbLoaded = i++;
kbTotal = 100;
var percent = Math.floor(kbLoaded/kbTotal*100);
```

Test your movie again and see the load in progress!

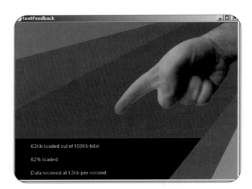

Loading bar preloader

The most common form of preloader that you'll find is the loading or progress bar. In this type of preloader, a graphic bar is drawn to show the percent of the data loaded. In the previous exercise, we looked at how to get the necessary information about a load. Here, we will look at how to display that information graphically. Open up `loadingBar.swf` to see the final result.

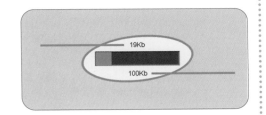

Bar graphics

1. Create a new movie and save it as `loadingBar.fla`. I'll let you choose your own colors for this one. Go crazy!

2. Create five layers (Insert>Layer) named (from top to bottom) `code`, `lines`, `bar`, `well` and `ellipse`.

3. With the Rectangle tool (R), draw a horizontal rectangular bar in the center of your stage on the `bar` layer. Convert it into a movie clip named `bar` (F8), and make sure that the registration point is set at the left middle of the graphic. This is necessary in order for the scaling to work properly. Name the instance of the movie clip `bar`.

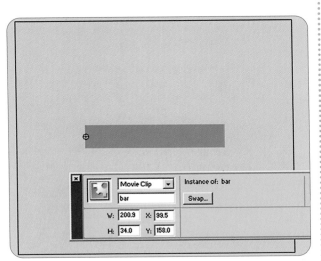

4. Add two text fields to the `textfields` layer, placing one above the bar in the center of the stage, and the other below the bar in the center of the stage. Name the top text field `loaded` and the bottom text field `total`, in the Instance Name field of the Property inspector. Make both the text fields Dynamic Text, with _sans as the font and choose center alignment.

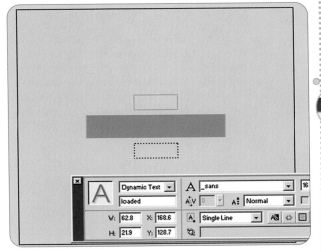

17

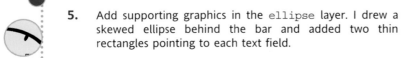

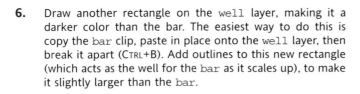

5. Add supporting graphics in the `ellipse` layer. I drew a skewed ellipse behind the bar and added two thin rectangles pointing to each text field.

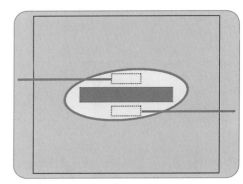

6. Draw another rectangle on the `well` layer, making it a darker color than the bar. The easiest way to do this is copy the `bar` clip, paste in place onto the `well` layer, then break it apart (CTRL+B). Add outlines to this new rectangle (which acts as the well for the `bar` as it scales up), to make it slightly larger than the `bar`.

Bar code

The code for this example should look very familiar to you, as it hasn't changed much from the last example. In fact, there's actually less of it, so I'll give it to you all in one go!

1. Type the following into the Actions panel on frame 1 of the `code` layer:

```
assessLoad = function (clip, endPreloadFunc) {
    var kbLoaded = clip.getBytesLoaded()/1024;
    var kbTotal = clip.getBytesTotal()/1024;
    var percent = Math.floor(kbLoaded/kbTotal*100);
    loaded.text = Math.floor(kbLoaded)+"Kb";
    total.text = Math.floor(kbTotal)+"Kb";
    bar._xscale = percent;
    if ((kbLoaded/kbTotal == 1) && kbLoaded>1) {
        endPreloadFunc();
    }
};
endPreload = function () {
    clearInterval(preload);
};
preload = setInterval(assessLoad, 100, this, endPreload);
bar._xscale = 0;
```

The only difference in this code from the previous exercise is that we are no longer looking for the rate of data transfer. Instead, we populate our two text fields with their appropriate values, and then we scale the `bar` movie clip up to the current percent loaded. Because we set the registration point at the left side of bar, it will scale towards the right as the percent increases. Everything else remains the same, including using a `setInterval` to call our `assessLoad` function every 100 milliseconds.

2. Now, of course, we need to set our `bar` down to 0 at the start of the loading process, so add this final line at the end of our code:

```
bar._xscale = 0;
```

If you'd like to now test your movie, add the following lines to your code (for the same reason as in the last exercise – to actually see something!):

```
var kbLoaded = clip.getBytesLoaded()/1024;
var kbTotal = clip.getBytesTotal()/1024;
kbLoaded = i++;
kbTotal = 100;
```

Pretty snazzy loading bar! Be sure to check on the download files for a variation on this code that uses the drawing API to create the bar graphic. Plus, because it's set up as a component, you can just drag and drop it onto your stage for whatever project, without having to reinvent the wheel when you don't need to. And the best part – you already know most of the code!

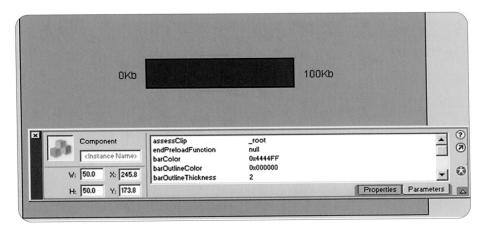

Code animated preloader

We have used the `percent` variable in our `assessLoad` function to scale a bar, but there's no reason why you can't use this value to alter any number of properties in order to animate. In this next exercise, we'll move a masked candle's position so that it looks as if it is melting as the site loads. Once the load is complete, the candle will go out, and we'll fade up into the site. Open up `candle.swf` to see the final effect.

Candle graphics

There are considerably more graphics to create for this effect, so let's break it down into a number of sections. First, we'll set up our layer and frame structure on the main stage. Then we'll take care of the candle and flame graphics. After that, we'll need to look at the brick wall and the flickering light on the wall. Finally, we'll bring everything together on the stage and set up the mask for the candle, which allows for the melting effect.

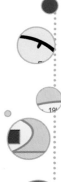

The main timeline

1. Create a new movie and save it as `candle.fla`. Make the background black, and then create eight layers and name them (from top to bottom) `code`, `blackOut`, `content`, `candleMask`, `candle`, `textfield`, `flicker` and `wall`.

2. On the `blackOut` layer, draw a black box with the Rectangle tool to cover the entire stage. Convert it into a movie clip named `blackOut` (F8), and name the instance on stage `blackOut` as well. We'll use this for the fading out and fading in of the stage. In the Property inspector, set its alpha to 0 so it is unseen at the start of the movie.

3. Make a new keyframe in frame 2 of the `content` layer (F6). Next, add a new frame (but not a keyframe) to the `blackOut` layer in frame 2 (F5). None of the other layers should extend to the second frame.

4. You now need to add some content to the `content` layer for when the loading ends and the stage fades up. This would be your main site if you were using this as your site's preloader. I just added some colored rectangles to the stage so I could see the effect. Do the same, or add whatever you'd like as your content.

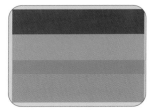

Creating fire and wax

1. Create a new movie clip called `candle` (CTRL+F8). In the new symbol, and with the Rectangle tool, draw a very tall, vertical rectangle and fill it with a horizontal linear gradient, going from #B6B692 to #FFFFB9 back to #B6B692. Play with the gradient and the colors until you get a nice rounded illusion for the candle. You can also adjust the top of the candle shape to make it less even. Don't worry about the bottom of the candle, as that will be masked.

2. Name the layer containing this new graphic as `candleBase`, and then create a new layer below it called `flames`. While in this new layer, draw a tall ellipse with a solid fill at the top of the candle (don't worry about the color right now). Convert it into a movie clip called `flames`. Name the instance in that stage `flames` in the Property inspector, as well.

3. Double-click on `flames` to enter its Symbol Editing mode. We're going to create a nested symbol, so select the ellipse graphic and convert it into a movie clip called `flame`. You should now have a move clip instance of `flame` inside the movie clip `flames`.

4. Double-click on the instance of the `flame` clip to enter its Symbol Editing mode. It's here that we will create the animated effect. Select a radial gradient in the Color Mixer panel. Give it three color stops placed at about 0%, 30% and 100%, with the following values for each (in order from left to right):

   - color: #C96B6B, alpha: 39%

   - color: #BF4C4C, alpha: 48%

   - color: #BF4C4C, alpha: 0%

Apply this gradient to the ellipse, and then use the Fill Transform tool to resize the gradient, squashing it horizontally and setting its center point near the bottom of the ellipse.

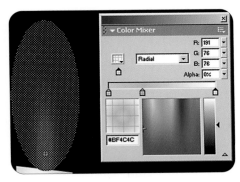

5. Create keyframes (F6) for `flame` every five or so frames (you don't need to be exact), until frame 37. In each keyframe, alter the gradient values slightly, perhaps increasing or decreasing alpha. You can also use the Fill Transform tool to rotate and scale the gradient at each keyframe. The trick is to only do slight adjustments – anything more will be distracting and won't look right. Also, keep the first and last frame identical, so that the animation loops seamlessly.

6. Once you have made all of the adjustments to the gradients, make shape tweens between all of the keyframes. Then scrub the timeline to see the results of the effect.

7. With the single flame complete, return to its parent timeline, the `flames` movie clip. Create two new layers, giving three in total, and name them (top to bottom) `blue`, `orange` and `red`. Extend each layer to frame 37 (using the F5 keyboard shortcut), which is the number of frames inside the individual `flame` movie clip (we need to do this because we are going to give the flame instances Graphic behaviors).

8. The instance of `flame` already on stage in flames should be in the `red` layer. Give it a Graphic behavior, with a Loop option in the Property inspector, and set its first frame to frame 1. Copy and paste this instance into each of the `blue` and `orange` layers. Set each instance to start at a different frame in the Property inspector.

9. Scale the instance in the `orange` layer up slightly, and then access its advanced color effects in the Property inspector. Make it slightly more orange in hue. The values I used were:

- R: 83%, 0

- G: 100%, 0

- B: 18%, 0

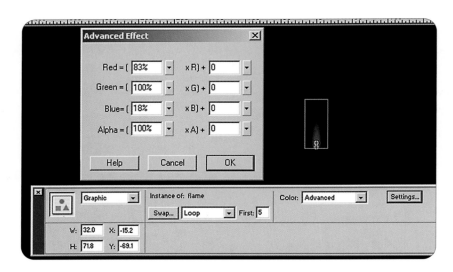

10. Scale the instance in the `blue` layer down until it's about a quarter of the size of the red. Access its advanced color properties to make it blue, and lower its alpha. My values were:

   - R: -80%, 0
   - G: 38%, 0
   - B: 100%, 157
   - alpha: 34%, 0

Scrub your timeline to see the effect, then tweak to your heart's content.

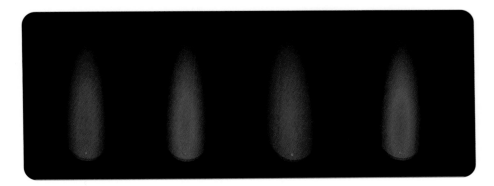

Lighting a brick wall

Here, we take advantage of a tileable bitmap in order to keep our file size down. Even though the brick wall is fairly large, the image that makes it up is only 50x50 pixels.

1. Import to your Library the file `bricks.jpg` from the download files (File>Import to Library). This image was created completely in Photoshop, using its feature such as Filter>Offset in order to create a tileable image.

2. On the main timeline, select the `wall` layer and draw a solid-filled rectangle on it that covers the entire left half of the stage, leaving just a little room at the bottom for an imagined floor.

3. Select the rectangle, and then go to the Color Mixer (SHIFT+F9) and select Bitmap as the fill option. The bricks appear in your graphic, but they fill the entire rectangle. Select the Transform Fill tool and scale the bitmap on the stage down to give you a nice sized brick. Next, use the Eyedropper tool (I) to select the scaled – down fill. Finally, fill the rectangle with the Paint Bucket tool (K).

   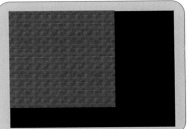

   That's the wall taken care of. Now we take care of the flickering light effect that the candle casts upon it.

4. On the `flicker` layer, draw a rectangle with a solid black fill that is the same width as the wall, but is about twice as tall. Convert this shape into a movie clip named `flicker`. Name the instance on stage `flicker` in the Property inspector, as well.

23

5. Double-click on `flicker` to enter its edit mode. We are going to set this up in a similar fashion to the way we set up `flame`. Create a radial gradient that goes from black with an alpha of 67% to black with an alpha of 100%. The center of the gradient will be where the wall should be visible. Apply this gradient to the rectangle. Use the Transform Fill tool if the gradient extends beyond the boundaries of the rectangle.

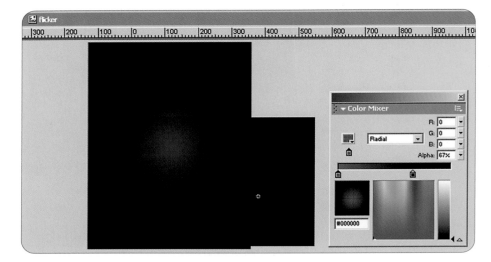

6. Create keyframes every 10 frames or so until frame 50. At each keyframe, adjust the alpha of the center color, stop slightly and use the Transform Fill tool to scale the gradient up or down slightly. Once you have adjusted all of the keyframes (remembering to keep the first and last the same), create shape tweens between them all. Now return to the main timeline – it's time to put everything together!

Putting it together

With all of our graphics drawn, it's simply a matter of assembling everything on the main timeline.

1. Drag an instance of `candle` from your Library into the `candle` layer. Set it at the left side of the stage. Name the instance `candle` in the Property inspector.

2. On the `textfield` layer, add a new Dynamic Text text field to the bottom left of the stage, just to the right of the base of the candle. Give it the instance name `loaded`, with a font of _sans and a color of white. Type in some text so that you can see how it will look on the stage (remember that it will be filled dynamically at runtime).

3. On the `candleMask` layer, draw a rectangle to cover all the candle, except for the very bottom. Round the bottom of this rectangle slightly (this will make the bottom of the candle appear rounded once it is masked). The melting candle effect works by moving the candle down the stage, but masking it at the bottom. Because the mask is static, and because the candle is simply a linear gradient that is consistent for its entire height, the illusion works.

4. Right click, or command click, on the `candleMask` layer and select Mask from the drop-down menu. This should successfully mask your candle, and that means we are done with the graphics!

Candle code

There is only a little bit more code in this example than our previous examples, but it all builds on the same foundation, so most of it should be familiar to you. Open up your Actions panel in the first frame of the `code` layer.

1. Type the following at the top of your code:

```
candleStartY = candle._y;
candleEndY = 500;
candleRange = candleEndY - candleStartY;

flickerStartY = flicker._y;
flickerEndY = 375;
flickerRange = flickerEndY - flickerStartY;
```

The animation works by moving the candle and the flicker effect down the stage, based on the percentage loaded. In order to do this, we need to work within a set range and move each movie clip a percentage of the distance in that range. Each start position is the movie clip's actual placement on the stage. The end position is a hard-coded number that I got from actually moving the clips on the stage, and deciding where a good stopping place would be for each. Therefore, your values might differ from mine for the end positions, so play with the numbers and enter those that work for you. The range for each clip is then the start position subtracted from the end position.

2. The `assessLoad()` function should be like an old friend to you now. Add this after the previous code:

```
assessLoad = function (clip, endPreloadFunc) {
    var kbLoaded = clip.getBytesLoaded()/1024;
    var kbTotal = clip.getBytesTotal()/1024;
    var percent = Math.floor(kbLoaded/kbTotal*100);
    loaded.text = percent+"% loaded";
    candle._y = percent/100*candleRange+candleStartY;
    flicker._y = percent/100*flickerRange+flickerStartY;
    if ((kbLoaded/kbTotal == 1) && kbLoaded>1) {
        endPreloadFunc();
    }
};
```

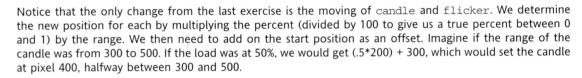

Notice that the only change from the last exercise is the moving of `candle` and `flicker`. We determine the new position for each by multiplying the percent (divided by 100 to give us a true percent between 0 and 1) by the range. We then need to add on the start position as an offset. Imagine if the range of the candle was from 300 to 500. If the load was at 50%, we would get (.5*200) + 300, which would set the candle at pixel 400, halfway between 300 and 500.

3. Our `endPreload()` function is a bit more substantial this time around:

```
endPreload = function () {
    clearInterval(preload);
    blackOut.onEnterFrame = function() {
        this._alpha += 5;
        candle.flames._xscale = candle.flames._yscale -= 5;
        candle.flames._alpha -= 5;
        if (this._alpha>=100) {
            delete this.onEnterFrame;
            this._alpha = 100;
            this._parent.gotoAndStop(2);
            fadeUpInt = setInterval(this._parent, "fadeUp", 1000);
        }
    };
};
```

First, we clear the interval just as we have done before. Then, we give a new `onEnterFrame` handler to `blackOut` (the large black box that covers the stage). Every frame that follows will add 5 to its alpha (fading it up) and scale down the `candle.flames` clip, as well as fade it out (making it look as if the fire is going out). Once the `blackOut` clip is fully visible (meaning it is pitch black on stage, of course!), the main timeline is sent to frame 2 and a new interval is set up.

There are two ways to call `setInterval`. We have been using one in all of our preloaders so far, and this is an example of the other method. Here, we first specify the object where a function resides (`this._parent` or the main timeline). Then, the function name is sent as a string. Finally, we send the number of milliseconds before each interval call. I am using this interval to create a delay time before a function is called. In this case, the function `fadeUp()` on the main timeline will be called after one second has passed, which will give us one second of darkness before the main stage fades up. We'll take care of that function now.

4. Add the following function after `endPreload()`:

```
fadeUp = function () {
    clearInterval(fadeUpInt);
    blackOut.onEnterFrame = function() {
        this._alpha -= 5;
        if (this._alpha<=0) {
            delete this.onEnterFrame;
            this._visible = 0;
        }
    };
};
```

This is pretty much the reverse of the previous `onEnterFrame` function. In this one, we lower `blackOut`'s alpha instead of raising it. The effect of `blackOut` fading out is actually that it seems as if the lights on the main stage are fading up. Once `blackOut` is completely faded out, it deletes its `onEnterFrame` and makes itself invisible.

5.   One last thing to take care of. Add these lines to your code:

```
preload = setInterval(assessLoad, 100, this,
➥endPreload);
stop();
```

38% loaded

Nothing surprising there, right? We set up our `assessLoad` call every 100 milliseconds, and we're good to go! Remember to add the following lines to `assessLoad()`, in order to test:

```
var kbLoaded = clip.getBytesLoaded()/1024;
var kbTotal = clip.getBytesTotal()/1024;
kbLoaded = i++;
kbTotal = 100;
```

Test it out and watch as the candle informs the user graphically how much time is remaining, then offers a nice smooth transition to the content. Nice!

Frame animated preloader

In the last example, we used the percent variable to alter the properties of movie clips in order to animate. If you are more of a frame-by-frame animator, there's no reason why you can't use the same concepts to create your own frame-based animated preloaders. The idea is to use the percent variable to send the playhead of the main timeline, or a movie clip, to a specified frame in a range. Open up the file `crack_in_the_wall.swf` to see the result of this tutorial. Click on the man or the text to begin the simulated load animation.

Although we still need to use code to find out the status of the load, the actual animation is driven by frame-by-frame animation and tweens. Let's look and see how it was done.

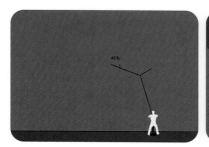

Cracking graphics

What a poser

1. Open up the file `crack_in_the_wall_start.fla`, and save it locally on your computer. We'll be recreating everything you saw in the final movie, except for the man animation. This animation was created using Poser 5, a 3D character animation tool that is a very fun and intuitive program to play around in. It actually exports to the SWF format, but I've found the files are usually huge, and so difficult to use online. However, by exporting as silhouettes (two colors including the shadow) at a low resolution, you get workable files that you can use to great effect. Add to that a pass through Optimaze, a Flash optimization tool, and this 22 frame 3D animation was reduced to a tiny 8Kb.

I have set up all of the layers on the main timeline in this file, but have yet to add any content. If you open the Library (F11), you will see some symbols for a chainsaw, and three further movie clips: `manPrepare`, `manStruggle` and `manOpen`. The struggling clip is what will appear during the actual load sequence. `manPrepare` will play before the sequence begins, and `manOpen` will play after the sequence concludes.

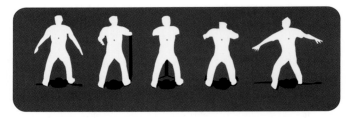

2. Drop an instance of `manPrepare` in frame 1 of the `man` layer. Reduce his scale in the Transform panel to 43% (CTRL+T). Place the instance in the lower right area of the stage.

3. In frame 11, create a keyframe in the man layer (F6). Select the manPrepare instance on the new keyframe, and swap it in the Property inspector for manStruggle. Name the instance manStruggle in the Property inspector.

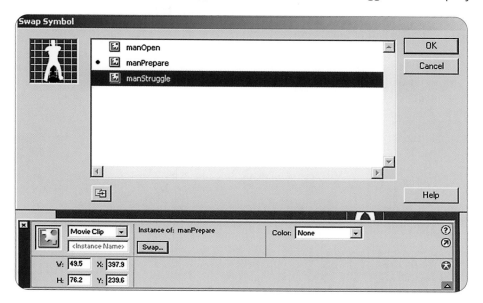

4. Then go back to frame 1 and select the manPrepare instance. Change its behavior to Graphic in the Property inspector, with the option of Play Once.

5. Create a new keyframe at frame 111 of the man layer. Swap the manStruggle instance with a manOpen instance, in the Property inspector. Change the manOpen instance's behavior to Graphic, with the option of Play Once.

6. Once more, select manStruggle in frame 11. With it selected, open up the Actions panel and type the following, ensuring that it is attached to the clip, and not the timeline:

```
onClipEvent(load) {
    this.stop();
}

onClipEvent(enterFrame) {
    if (this._currentframe == 0) {
        this.nextFrame();
    } else if (this._currentframe == this._totalframes) {
        this.prevFrame();
    } else if (Math.random() > .5) {
        this.nextFrame();
    } else {
        this.prevFrame();
    }
}
```

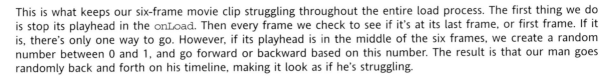

This is what keeps our six-frame movie clip struggling throughout the entire load process. The first thing we do is stop its playhead in the `onLoad`. Then every frame we check to see if it's at its last frame, or first frame. If it is, there's only one way to go. However, if its playhead is in the middle of the six frames, we create a random number between 0 and 1, and go forward or backward based on this number. The result is that our man goes randomly back and forth on his timeline, making it look as if he's struggling.

"Tear down the wall!"

1. Before we can make the wall crumble, we need to build it up. Go to the first frame of the `wall` layer, select #536642 for a fill color, and draw a rectangle to cover all but the very bottom of the stage. If you go to frame 11 and look where the man's shadow meets the wall, you can see how far down to place it.

2. In frame 11, select the `crack` layer. With a hairline black stroke, use the Line tool to draw a crack coming from the area of the man's chest up to the top of the stage. Draw some offshooting cracks as well. If you wish to keep my layer structure and follow what I did exactly, make sure the final crack divides the wall into four portions (I had left, right, top, with a top fragment as well).

The crack, as you have now seen, is fully drawn at the beginning. We, in fact, use a mask to slowly reveal the crack throughout the loading process.

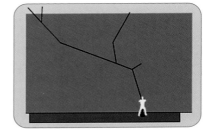

3. In frame 11 of the `mask` layer, draw a solid-filled rectangle, the width and height of the cracked area of the stage. Convert it into a movie clip called `mask` (F8), and then set it so that its top is just below where the line starts at the man's chest. We don't want any of the line showing at the start, so make sure the mask isn't covering any portion of it.

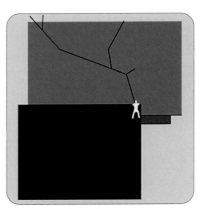

4. Create a new keyframe for the `mask` layer at frame 110. Move it so that it covers the whole of the crack on the stage, and then create a motion tween between frames 11 and 110. If you test the movie now, you should see the man struggling and the crack slowly forming. Not bad!

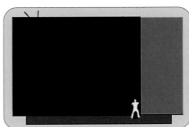

5. Once the man throws open his arms, the wall should crumble, not disappear entirely. To achieve this, we need to create separate movie clips for each portion of the wall. Copy and paste in place the wall graphic onto frame 111 of the `rightWall` layer. Then, copy and paste in place the crack onto the same layer. The crack copy should cut into the wall copy, allowing you to select each individual wall portion and turn it into a movie clip (extend and close the crack where needed to achieve this). Once you have converted all the wall portions into movie clips, delete the crack copy and move each wall portion to its own layer in frame 111 (they shouldn't exist before frame 111). The four layers I've already created are `rightWall`, `leftWall`, `topWall` and `topFragment`. If you have additional wall portions, add the layers as needed.

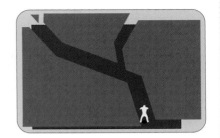

6. With all of the separate portions as movie clips on their own layers, we can tween them off as the man throws open his arms. Create new keyframes in each of the fragment layers at frame 117. Rotate and move each wall fragment off the stage in the direction it would be thrown. Create motion tweens for each.

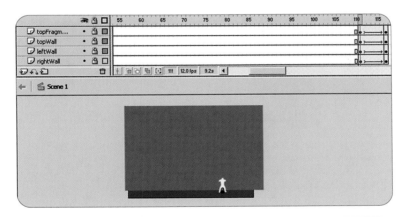

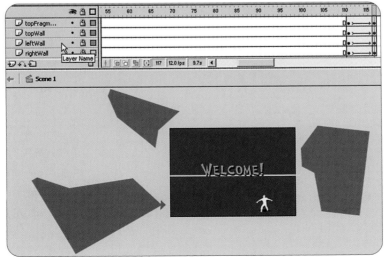

Test your movie to see how it's all working. The man animates to a starting position, struggles over 100 frames as the crack slowly forms, then throws the wall open, sending it in fragments off the stage. Almost there!

Climbing percent

In case the graphic isn't enough of a clue for the user about what's going on, we're going to add a percent text field that follows the crack up the stage.

1. In frame 16 of the `percent` layer, create a keyframe and make a new Dynamic Text text field, with the instance name `percentLoaded`. Convert it into a movie clip (so we can do some tweening) named `percentHolder`. Give the `percentHolder` clip on the stage an instance name of `percentHolder` in the Property inspector as well. Place the clip as shown below:

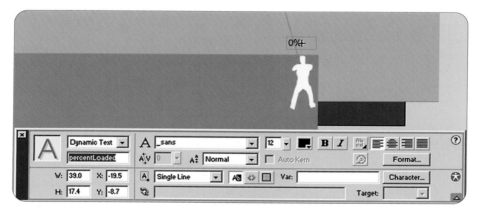

2. With the `mask` layer locked so that the effect can be seen, scrub the playhead between frames 16 and 110, and at every frame that the crack comes to a junction or bend, create a keyframe on the `percent` layer. Move the `percentHolder` clip at each keyframe, so it is right where the crack bends in another direction, and then create motion tweens between all of these frames. Scrub the timeline to make sure it moves as you would like it to.

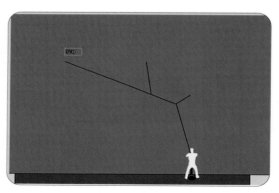

Giving the users what they want

We have pretty much everything but the code for our preloader completed. However, we need some content that we are actually preloading *for*. Plus, let's give the user some chance for interactivity before the animation begins.

1. Go to the `content` layer at frame 111, and add whatever content you would like to be revealed as the wall crumbles. I simply created a welcome message, but you could add whatever you would like.

2. In frame 1 of the `text` layer, create a new text field. Pick a fun font, and type in 'You want in?'. I used the font color #DCEDAF, but pick whatever strikes your fancy.

3. Drag an instance of the `mask` symbol from the Library into the `button` layer at frame 1. Name the instance `invButton` in the Property inspector, and then scale it down so it only covers the man and the text message. In the Property inspector, select Alpha under the Color options and set its value to 0.

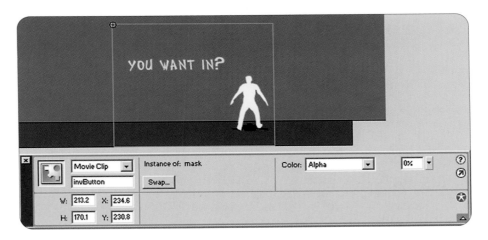

4. I decided that my man was not strong enough to rip the wall apart with his bare hands, so I created a chainsaw to help him on his way. Onto the `chainsaw` layer, drag a copy of `chainsaw_mc` from the Library to frame 1. Double-click on the clip to go into its edit mode. You'll see there is a tween, which shrinks the size of the chain saw. Click on frame 10, the final frame, on the tween layer and position the saw so it is in the man's hand. When this clip is run, the chainsaw will zoom into our man's hand.

5. Back on the main timeline, drag a copy of the `chainsaw` graphic from the Library to frame 2 of the `chainsaw` layer, again positioning it over the man's hand, where the `chainsaw_mc` clip finishes when it's run. On frame 11, place another instance of the graphic, slightly behind the man, at shoulder level. Finish off by creating a motion tween between these two keyframes.

33

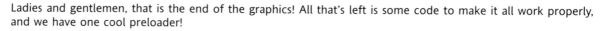

Ladies and gentlemen, that is the end of the graphics! All that's left is some code to make it all work properly, and we have one cool preloader!

Cracking Code

Because of the nature of this preloader, we don't have everything nice and contained in one frame, as in the previous example. There's still very little code to go through, though, since you're now becoming a preloaders expert!

1. Select the code layer and open up your Actions panel. We need the following code at frame 1:

    ```
    stop();
    invButton.onRelease = function() {
        this._parent.play();
    }
    ```

    First, we stop our playhead, of course, and give the user control to start it up again. As soon as they click on the invisible button covering the man, the main timeline will move on.

2. Next go to frame 9 of the code layer, which is two frames before the struggling and cracking begin. Add these lines to the Actions panel. Does this code ring a bell?

    ```
    assessLoad = function (clip, endPreloadFunc) {
        var kbLoaded = clip.getBytesLoaded()/1024;
        var kbTotal = clip.getBytesTotal()/1024;
        var percent = Math.floor(kbLoaded/kbTotal * 100);
        percentHolder.percentLoaded.text = percent + "%";
        if ((kbLoaded/kbTotal == 1) && kbLoaded > 1) {
            endPreloadFunc();
        } else {
            _level0.gotoAndStop(percent + 10);
        }
    };
    endPreload = function () {
        clearInterval(preload);
        _level0.gotoAndPlay("endSequence");
    };
    preload = setInterval(assessLoad, 100, this, endPreload);
    stop();
    ```

Once more, our friend assessLoad takes care of the preloading process. You can see in the if statement that we move our main timeline to a frame based on the percent loaded. I made it easy by having a 100-frame sequence from frame 11 to frame 110. That way, we just take our percent value between 1 and 100 and add 10, and then send the main timeline's playhead there. In the endPreload() function, we send the playhead to endSequence, where the man throws the wall open to reveal the content.

That's it! Of course, by now you know the necessary lines to add for testing:

```
var kbLoaded = clip.getBytesLoaded()/1024;
var kbTotal = clip.getBytesTotal()/1024;
kbLoaded = i++;
kbTotal = 150;
```

Test your movie and watch it all fall down!

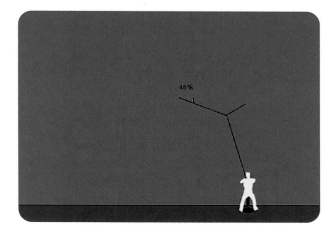

Summary

As users demand more and more content, and as developers create more and more content for those users, providing some form of feedback during the loading process of that content becomes a necessity. In this chapter, we have looked at ways of taking the information we can ascertain about a load and displaying it in entertaining and informative forms for the user. When building your own versions, it's important to remember that the whole point of a preloader is to keep the users from becoming bored or frustrated as they wait for the *main* content. Keep your preloaders small. Keep your preloaders interesting. But most importantly, keep your preloaders coming, because no matter how grand your content, no one will stick around for a blank screen!

About the Author
WideGroup :: Digital Motion

www.widegroup.net

Since their beginning in 1997, up to the present day, WideGroup has been heading the revolution of rich content on the web. Specializing in high impact web sites, and online branding for the entertainment industry and for corporate identities, WideGroup is helping to raise the standard of design to a higher level.

Having served major clients in South America, and due to the demand for high impact and interactive web sites, presentations, broadcasting and CD-ROMs abroad, WideGroup expanded and shifted its base from Cordoba, Argentina to Hollywood, the core of the Entertainment Industry. Concentrating on Macromedia's Flash MX design software gives WideGroup's projects 98% of the total online audience. WideGroup's primary customer base is currently the entertainment industry. Existing clients include DreamWorks SKG, America Online, Showcase Cinemas and MirCorp. WideGroup focuses on quality, as opposed to quantity, when selecting the projects it undertakes. WideGroup positions itself as the "Giorgio Armani" of the digital world. By only accepting the higher-end projects, WideGroup has established a stellar reputation for quality work within the entertainment industry.

WideGroup specializes in creating interfaces, Web Movie Trailers, Teasers and Video games. A range of formats are produced for: web, CD-cards, CD-ROMs, VHS, TV, cinema screenings and corporate identities.

In 2003, WideGroup is looking to position itself as the first interactive agency to expand its focus to include the entertainment industry. As many Studios have tried and failed to capitalize on the interactive end, WideGroup seeks to turn this around, both figuratively and literally by building a State of the art development center, and its own Studio. WideGroup is beginning to converge the mediums and is bringing the future of productions to today's outlets.

High Impact Flash Intros

WideGroup :: Digital Motion

About the Effect

Flash intros are one of he most talked about, and even controversial, topics on the Flash forums. There is a movement that suggests the Flash intro is dead. We'd like these people to take a look at the end product of the tutorial in this chapter.

If people are not watching Flash intros, it's because they've seen it all before; the design techniques have become stale. The answer is not to quit – it is to push the boundaries to new extremes. Innovation is the key here; if people like what they see, they'll forget the skip button exists, and word of a great intro spreads around the web rapidly.

The tutorial in this chapter will introduce you to the techniques that make a successful high impact Flash intro. These movies are more than just an animation; they're full blown cinema-style trailers.

Prepare to be amazed.

Background information

Right, we've got an intro to build. However, before we rush in, let's take a look at who we're actually doing the project for, so that we can get an idea of how the final product fits their requirements.

The Client – about MirCorp

MirCorp is pioneering a new era in commercial – manned Space travel & on orbit destinations. Their successful commercialization of the Russian Mir Space Station marked a revolution in the Space Industry. Followed quickly by the MirCorp-led effort to launch the World's first private citizen explorer, Dennis Tito, MirCorp has changed the face of Space forever. No longer it is it the destination of a privileged few – it is the domain of everyone.

MirCorp was looking to redesign www.mir-corp.com. In line with the refreshed corporate image, MirCorp was seeking to develop a new, interactive and highly captivating website. The primary purpose of the site was to market and sell Space Adventures. The new website needed to also showcase these adventures with high quality and an exciting new look. A new face for space needed to be created, and for that they came to WideGroup. MirCorp is definitely a world changing company, and this means that an out-of-this-world intro is required for their site.

For the intro/transition, we wanted to create the feeling for the viewers that they were traveling in one of their main adventures, which is the Edge of Space. For this, we simulated by means of animation and sounds, a flight on a jet to the edge of space. We encapsulated it to look like a trailer, and gave it an entertainment look. This high speed and high flight animation finally ends in space, where we provide the user with a central command that lets them take over and explore this new experience.

Take a visit to the MirCorp site and get a flavor of what we're trying to achieve in this intro. Before you start, take a look at the finished file, `MirCorp.swf`, and make sure you have your headphones on!

Production

Start by opening the movie `MirCorp_start.fla` from the download files for this chapter. We've set the document properties in this file as follows:

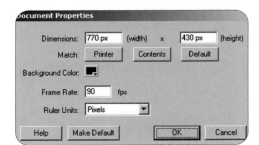

Within the Library, you'll find all the images and sound files needed to complete this project. If at any time you become confused, or aren't sure if you've done something right, take a look in `MirCorp_final.fla` for the finished file. Note that there are a few images at the start of the final FLA file that we don't mention in the tutorial. This is due to them being part of a preloader that isn't built in the chapter. Why not add your own preloader from what you've learnt in Todd Yard's chapter?

> *Note that all symbols created in this chapter should have central registration points.*

Anyway, enough scene setting – on with the movie. In the start file you will find all the layers and keyframes set up on the main timeline.

Elastic screen

1. Let's start with the bottom layer of the timeline, SPACEBG. On this layer, we'll use shape tweening to create an 'elastic screen' effect. On frame 1, use the Rectangle tool (R) to draw a rectangle the same size as the Flash movie dimensions (770x430), and center it on the stage. This rectangle should have a white fill, but no stroke.

2. Create a keyframe at frame 15 of the SPACEBG layer (F6). Up to this point the screen will be static. Make a further keyframe at frame 40, and at this frame reduce the size of the rectangle to 616x344 in the Property inspector. Use the Align panel (CTRL+K) to re-center the new, smaller rectangle on the stage.

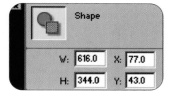

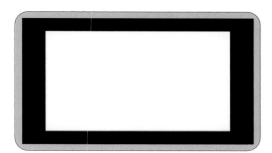

3. Select a frame between frames 15 and 40, and choose Shape from the Tween drop-down menu in the Property inspector. Drag the playhead between these frames and you'll see that we've achieved a transition that smoothly reduces the size of the rectangle – but we're not going to stop at this. Your timeline should look like the screenshot below:

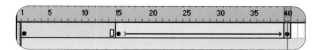

4. Insert a further keyframe at frame 20 of the SPACEBG layer. At this new keyframe, use the Arrow tool to bend each of the four sides of the rectangle inwards from their center point. Note that the rectangle must **not** be selected for you to be able to drag the sides.

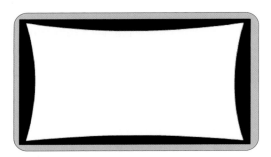

5. Now, at frame 25, add another keyframe, and this time bend the four sides of the rectangle outwards slightly. Take a look at the following transition screenshots to see what we're after.

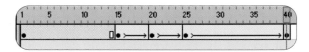

If you scrub the timeline, you'll see the basis of our elastic screen effect:

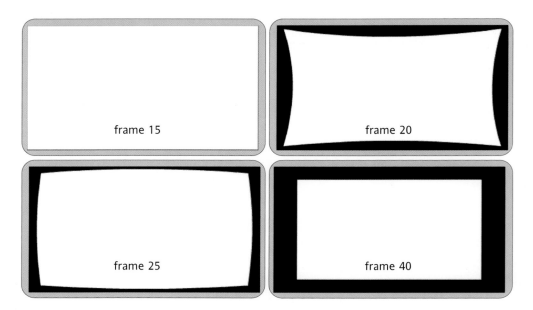

frame 15

frame 20

frame 25

frame 40

6. Click back on frame 15, and change the easing value in the Property inspector to −100. At frame 20, set the easing to 100.

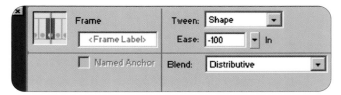

> *Whenever we do shape tweenings in order to create the "elastic page" or "elasticity in shapes" effects, we have to insert the keyframes first, and then apply the transformation we desire to each keyframe.*

7. We'll now add a bit more elasticity to finish off the effect. Add a keyframe at frame 45, and this time bend the two sides outwards, but the top and bottom inwards. Create a shape tween between frames 40 and 45.

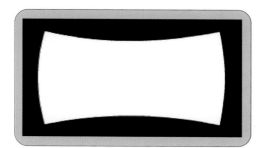

8. Create a final keyframe for this layer at frame 50. Here, bend the top and bottom back outwards, so that you've got the shape similar to that at frame 25. With the shape selected, open the Scale and Rotate panel (Modify>Transform>Scale and Rotate/CTRL+ALT+S), and reduce the size to 20%. Re-center the new small shape on the stage. Apply a final shape tween between frames 45 and 50. Set the easing values for the frames as shown in the table below:

Frame	Easing
25	100
40	0
45	100

9. At frame 51, we want a blank frame, so select this frame on the timeline and then use F7 to insert a blank keyframe. We've now finished on the SPACEBG layer. Drag the playhead back and forth to watch the elastic rectangle do its business and then shrink away.

The flight

Viewing window

After our elastic screen has finished, the next part of the movie will be the 'flight above the ocean' animation. For this animation, we need to create a window that all the content will be viewed within.

1. Find the MASK layer on the timeline. On this layer, we can define the area that will act as our viewing window. This layer has been set as a mask layer (if you right-click on the layer name, you'll see that Mask has been selected from the drop-down menu). All the layers below this, excluding our SPACEBG layer at the bottom, have been set to Masked, so any content on these layers will only appear if it's within the viewing window. (To mask additional layers, you would select the layer and choose Modify>Layer, where you'll find the Masked option.)

2. Select frame 52 of the MASK layer; this frame is just after the elastic animation has finished. With the Rectangle tool, draw a rectangle measuring 650x300 (with a white fill, but no stroke), and center the rectangle on the stage. This rectangle defines the viewing window. A blank keyframe has been inserted on frame 430 of this layer, and the mask will work for every frame up to this point, at which point we'll no longer require the view window.

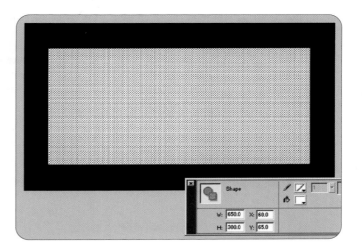

3. Select the white rectangle on the stage and copy it (CTRL+C). Now go to the layer above MASK layer, which is called WHITEANIM. At frame 52 of this layer (a keyframe), paste the rectangle shape in place (CTRL+SHIFT+V). Next, convert the rectangle into a graphic symbol (F8), and call this white. With the new symbol selected, press F8 again, and call the new graphic symbol whiteanim. Double-click into the whiteanim instance, where you'll find the nested white graphic. Create a keyframe at frame 25 of the default layer in the whiteanim graphic. Select the white symbol on the stage at frame 25, and from the Color drop-down menu, select Alpha. Set this alpha value to 0%. Now create a *motion* tween from frame 1 to 25. The whiteanim symbol now becomes transparent as it plays. This little effect helps the transition between one section of the movie and the next, and we'll be reusing it later on.

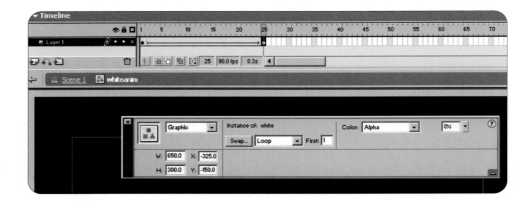

As our naming convention, we add anim *on the end of a symbol name to indicate an animation. This helps us identify relevant animations quickly in the Library. We add* obj *to signify a static object symbol.*

If you now return to the main timeline, you'll see that we've set a blank keyframe at frame 73, as we want the whiteanim graphic to disappear at this point.

4. To finish off the viewer window, we'll add a border to the edge to neaten things up. Select the frame 52 keyframe of the BORDER layer. Draw another centered rectangle measuring 650x300, but this time set the stroke to a gray color (#CCCCCC), with no stroke. Once again there is a blank keyframe at frame 430 in this layer, as we want the border to be visible for the same duration as the mask that creates the viewing area. The border nicely frames the masked area.

Flight sound effects

Our next stage in the creating of the intro is to create the ambience of the flight through the use of sound effects. If you take a look in the Library (F11), you'll find that three sound files that we've imported to use for this section: ambientflying.wav, strongambient.wav, and radio1.wav. Each of these sounds has been edited so that it can be looped seamlessly. We have set aside a layer for each of these sounds, and we'll bring them into the movie now.

1. Select the keyframe at frame 52 of the AMBIENTFLYING layer. In the Property inspector, select ambientflying.wav from the Sound drop-down menu. This brings the appropriate sound onto the timeline. Set the Sync for the sound to Event, and the loop value to 995. From the Effect drop-down, select Custom, and click on the Edit button next to this. In the Edit Envelope, change the horizontal lines so they roughly mirror the screenshot — these lines refer to the volume levels of the left and right channels.

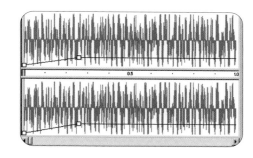

2. At frame 52 on the STRONGAMBIENT layer, select the sound of the same name from the drop-down menu. Once again, we want the effect set to Custom, and the sync to Event. This time leave the number of loops as 0. Set the channel volumes as shown in the screenshot.

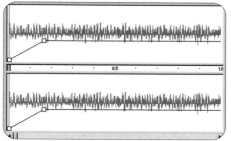

3. Now, on the RADIO layer, bring the radio1.wav file onto timeline at frame 52. The sync is set to Event once more, with no looping. Don't forget to change the effect to Custom and set, as shown.

Now we have three sounds on the timeline — two to create the ambience of the jet flight, and one for the distorted speech between the pilot and his 'central command'.

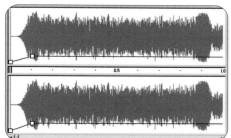

The background

To produce this intro, we needed to give the viewer the feeling of flying above the ocean, and the sensation of advancing speed. This allows us to introduce the viewer to the experience of extreme tourism.

All of the content for this section will appear though the mask, so we put it all on the masked layer we looked at earlier.

The first background image is of the ocean, and was created using Photoshop. We created a document, set to 800x600, and used the gradient tool in two color tones:

- Foreground: #59799F
- Background: #C6D7E7

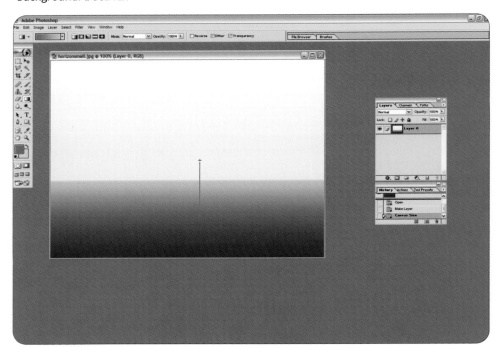

We exported the background from Photoshop in JPEG format, and at the maximum quality. You can find this image in the Library as horizonsmall.jpg.

1. At the bottom of the masked layers on the main timeline, you'll see HORIZON. Drag horizonsmall.jpg from the Library onto the keyframe at frame 52 of this layer. Using the Property inspector, place the image at x=-13, y=-54. Now, convert the image into a movie clip symbol (F8), and name the symbol horizon.

2. Double-click on the `horizon` clip to go into its edit mode, and rename the default layer as `HORIZONBG`. Select the image on this layer, and convert it into a further symbol (this time a graphic called `horizonobj`).

3. Make sure you're still on the `HORIZONBG` layer, and not within the new symbol. We're going to have large gaps between keyframes on this layer, so that when we tween, the movements will be really smooth. Create a keyframe at frame 70 (F6). We'll leave this frame as it is; it's frame 1 we want to change.

4. At frame 1, select the `horizonobj` symbol on the stage. Go to the Property inspector, and change the y position of the graphic from −461.5 to 399.5. In the Color menu, select Brightness, and set the level to 55%. We've done so to create a smooth transition when the `whiteanim` clip we created earlier fades into this. Create a motion tween between frames 1 and 70, which will increase the brightness, and move the symbol upwards as the movie plays. Also, set the easing value of this transition to 100.

5. Next, insert a keyframe at frame 140. At this frame, move the graphic symbol slightly lower, to y=−458.5. Create a motion tween between frames 70 and 140, setting the easing of this tween to −100.

6. Create a further keyframe at frame 217. This time, move the graphic's y position back to −461.5. Create a motion tween from frame 140 to 217, but don't apply any easing this time. The tweens we've used so far will be useful to create a soft vertical movement loop. We'll place the code to create this loop at frame 217. We need the horizon to loop until the titling sequence occurs, which we'll see created later. After the titling, we'll give the flight some rough movements, and then suddenly go up to leave the atmosphere!

7. The timeline for this clip will eventually be 312 frames long, so go to frame 312 and press F5 to make the timeline the correct length. We need five layers in this clip in total, so create four new ones now (Insert>Layer). Name them as shown in the screenshot. All these layers will be 312 frames in length, as this is the length we set the default layer to.

8.   Let's add that code to create the loop now. Insert a keyframe at frame 217 of the ACTIONS layer, and with this frame selected, open the Actions panel (F9). Enter the following code:

```
if (_level0.go == "yes") {
        play();
} else if (_level0.go == "no") {
        gotoAndPlay(70);
}
```

This code refers to a variable that we'll create from the root timeline later. If the variable go, which will live in _level0, is set to "yes", then the horizon movie will play on. If not, we'll loop back to frame 70 and play on again from there. This little section between frames 70 and 217 will keep looping until the variable is set to "yes".

Now, it's time to create the content for when the variable is set to "yes", and we consequently want the movie to play on. We're going to be rotating our background around to simulate the plane moving.

Rotating the background bitmap

Unfortunately, Flash doesn't handle bitmap rotation well. However, don't worry, as we've got a way around this. Above the layer containing the graphic, you'll see a layer called HORIZONLINE. We're going to add a graphic onto this layer that will cover the horizon line of the bitmap. This way we 'hide' the bitmap's rupture, and it'll look good to the eye. This is a great trick to overcome this Flash bug.

9.   On a new keyframe at frame 217 of the HORIZONLINE layer, use the Oval tool to draw a wide, thin shape, which covers the horizon line of the bitmap image. Use no stroke, but a fill that is a gradient mixture of white and transparency. Convert the shape into a graphic symbol called border.

10. Now make a keyframe at frame 218, and drag the border symbol from frame 217 to frame 218. We do this because we don't want this symbol to appear as part of the loop that ends at frame 217. That's our cover up symbol finished, and ready to be used.

11. Create a new keyframe at frame 264 of both the HORIZONBG and HORIZONLINE layers. Click on frame 264 on the HORIZONBG timeline and the bitmap graphic will be selected on the stage. Hold down the SHIFT key, and click on frame 264 of the HORIZONLINE layer, which will select the border graphic *as well*. We can now rotate both of the clips at once!

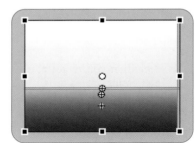

12. Using the Free Transform tool, rotate both symbols counterclockwise, as shown in the screenshot:

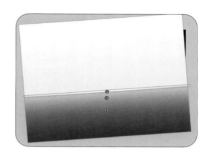

13. Insert another keyframe at frame 281 of each layer, and, using the same technique to select both symbols, rotate the graphic clockwise:

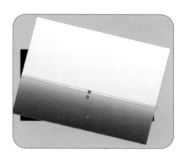

14. Add a further keyframe at frame 299 on both layers. This time, the graphics are rotated counterclockwise again:

15. Finally, at frame 312, we rotate the graphics so they're level again, and also move them slightly downwards to simulate upward movement:

16. Now that you've got all the keyframes for the two layers, join them all together with motion tweens. Set the easing values as in the following table:

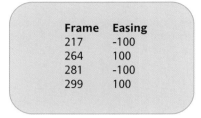

Frame	Easing
217	-100
264	100
281	-100
299	100

The timeline for the two layers should look like so:

That's the rotating done, which is the main effect of the background. However, there are still a few more things that we can add to the horizon clip to add to the realism of the whole experience.

The clouds

To create a realistic final result, we need to have good plane movement, but we also need to simulate other elements such as wind, and the sensation of speed. Adding clouds and a couple of audio effects to our movie will allow is to achieve this, and enhance our imaginary pilot's maneuvers.

1. Take a look in the Library (F11), and you'll see a file called cloud.png. This is our image that will form the basis of the cloud effect. Drag a copy of the image onto frame 231 of the horizon symbol's CLOUDS layer.

2. With the cloud image selected, press F8, and convert it to a graphic symbol called cloud. With the new symbol selected, press F8 again, creating a further graphic symbol, this time called cloudanim. If you remember the naming convention we introduced earlier, you'll realize that we made this second symbol in order to animate the first. This will be the home of our moving clouds. The accompanying screenshot shows the nesting of the symbols, but stay on the horizon timeline for the moment so you don't get lost.

3. Double-click on the `cloudanim` symbol to go into its edit mode. We're going to use tweening to have clouds moving across the stage from right to left, and taking in the clouds of the stage in order to create a loop later. On frame 1 of the default layer, select the `cloud` symbol, and then scale, rotate and position the `cloud` instance so it reflects the information in the screenshot below:

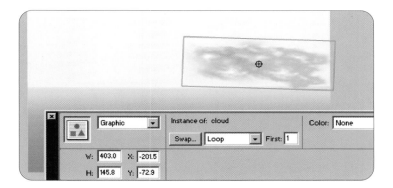

4. Insert a keyframe at frame 6, and move the x position of the clip from −201.5 to −991.5. This moves the cloud nearly off the left edge of the stage. Create a motion tween between frames 1 and 6, and set the easing of the tween to 100. Now select all the frames on the layer (clicking on the layer name once will do this), and copy the frames (Edit>Copy Frames/CTRL+ALT+C).

5. Create a new layer (Insert>Layer), and click on frame 7 of this layer. Now paste the copy of the frames (Edit>Paste Frames/CTRL+ALT+V). Add a blank keyframe to frame 13 of Layer 2 (F7) and an extra frame at frame 14 (F5). We add these extra frames so that the stage is clear for a few frames at the end. Your timeline should look as like the screenshot:

6. There's one more thing we need to do to the complete the cloud effect. For the `cloud` instances at frames 6, 7 and 12, select Advanced from Property inspector's Color drop-down (you need the relevant instance selected on the stage to do this). Click on the Settings button and alter the values to reflect the screenshot. Our clouds will appear white and fluffy at these keyframes.

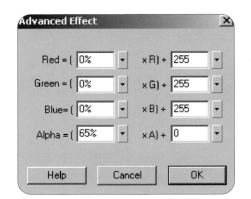

Going back to the `horizon` movie clip's timeline, we'll see something like this:

7. Make a new keyframe at frame 248 of the `horizon` clip's CLOUDS layer (F6), and then a blank keyframe at 260 (F7). At frames 231 and 248, set the graphic to Play Once, in the Property inspector. Ensure you've got the `x` and `y` positions of the graphics at these frames set as in the screenshot as well.

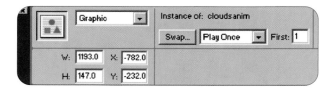

8. If you scrub the playhead, you'll see that our clouds are going from right to left when the background rotates to the left. We want them to go the other way when the background rotates right. There's a little trick we can use to achieve this. Make a new keyframe at frame 265 of the CLOUDS layer; this is just after the background starts rotating to the right. Drop an instance of `cloudsanim` onto this frame. With the instance selected, flip it horizontally (Modify>Transform>Flip Horizontal). Set the graphic to Play Once, and position it with x=-462, y=-172. Finally, insert a blank keyframe at frame 277 (F7). If you now scrub the playhead, you'll see the cloud fly in the opposite direction for this section. Great!

Your clouds should move roughly along the horizon. You can play around with this and see which effect or movement of clouds mixes best with the movement of the horizon, in your opinion.

Horizon sounds

Let's finish off the `horizon` movie clip by adding a few sounds. We'll have one to represent the take off of the plane, one to create a movement sound that accompanies our imaginary pilot's maneuver, and a final one of the pilot's radio conversation.

1. Onto the SOUNDS layer, create a keyframe at frame 217. Attach the sound `takeoff.wav` through the Property inspector, once again using a custom sound effect. This matches the airplane's movement and helps create the sensation of a takeoff.

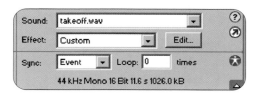

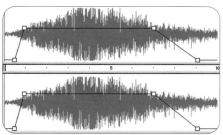

2. At a frame 226 keyframe, bring in the `titling.wav` sound file:

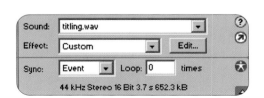
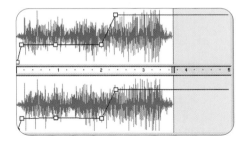

3. And finally, at a keyframe at frame 277, attach `radioconv1` to the timeline. This gives realism to the animation.

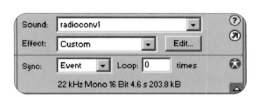
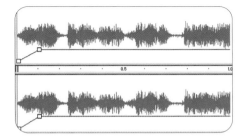

We now do one bit of code to finish off.

4. Create a keyframe at the final frame of the ACTIONS layer, and add the following code to the Actions panel (F9):

```
stop();
_root.play();
```

This code stops the `horizon` timeline, and restarts the main timeline of the movie, which has stopped, while waiting for this clip to complete.

The `horizon` movie clip is now ready!

Back to the main timeline

Let's go back to the main timeline, where we'll create the other effect that will help us simulate forward speed, as if we were traveling rapidly in an airplane. We'll do this by creating a symbol with the shape of a small circle, to which we have applied a 'motion blur' effect. Like we did in the beginning with the background, we edited this new graphic in Photoshop.

You'll find this image in the Library as `minicloud.png`. We've saved the image in PNG format, as this allows high quality transparency.

1. Onto the keyframe at frame 52 of the main timeline's CLOUDZOOM layer, drag a copy of `minicloud.png` onto the stage. Select the image on the stage, and convert it to a graphic symbol called `minicloudobj` (F8). With the new symbol selected, press F8 again and call the new graphic symbol `minicloudsanim`. Repeat this process again, calling the final graphic symbol `miniclouds`. You should have a little nest of clips now.

2. Click into the `minicloudsanim` timeline. We found it easiest to make all the other layers on the main timeline invisible, in order to ensure we entered into the right clip. Select the `minicloudobj` instance on the stage, and resize it in the Property inspector to W=129.1, H=91.3. These precise values aren't really necessary, but they'll help you mirror our effect exactly. Open the Scale and Rotate panel (CTRL+ALT+S), and rotate the symbol –45 degrees. Now reposition the symbol to x=190.2, y=-280.4.

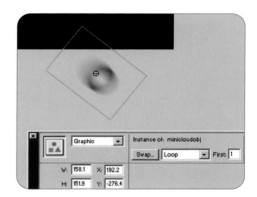

3. Next, create a keyframe at frame 16 of the default layer in `minicloudsanim`. At this frame, select the symbol and choose Brightness from the Color drop-down menu in the Property inspector. Set the values to 81% – this will change the image to white colors. Go back to frame 1 and resize the image to 10% of its current size (CTRL+ALT+S), and center the symbol on the stage using the Align panel (CTRL+K). Use an Advanced color effect on the symbol at this frame, as shown in the screenshot:

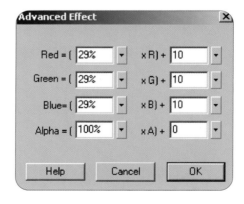

4. Create a motion tween between frames 1 and 16, setting the easing to –100. The graphic will now zoom out from the center, increasing in size and changing color slightly as it goes. Finish of this layer by inserting a blank keyframe at frame 17 (F7), and pressing F5 at frame 39. We want the timeline to be 39 frames long.

5. Next, create three new layers (Insert>Layer). Select frames 1 through 17 on Layer 1, and copy these frames (CTRL+ALT+C). Paste the frames at frame 8 of Layer 2, frame 5 of Layer 3, and frame 11 of Layer 4 (CTRL+ALT+V). Use SHIFT+F5 to remove any spare frames at the end of each layer, so that they're all 39 frames long.

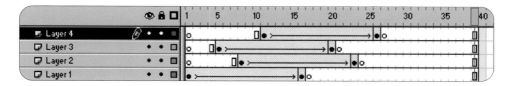

6. We want tweens on the top two layers to move down and right, rather than down and left. By doing this, the end effect is one of zooming through the air. At the start and end keyframes of the tweens on Layer 3 and Layer 4, select the minicloudobj instance on the stage, and flip it horizontally (Modify>Transform>Flip Horizontal). At the end keyframe of both these layers, set the x position of the clip to -395.9. We've now got our zooming in two directions.

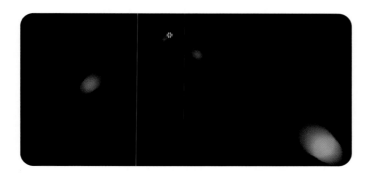

7. Now go up a level to the miniclouds symbol timeline. Rename the default layer to 1, and extend the timeline to frame 129, by pressing F5 at this frame. Add six new layers, and then name and arrange them as show in the screenshot. All these new layers will be 129 frames long by default.

8. Drag a copy of the minicloudsanim symbol onto a new keyframe at the frames highlighted below, and rotate the symbol by the value shown (CTRL+ALT+S). Each instance of the symbol will run for the duration of timeline remaining (as in until frame 129). All of the instances are set to loop in the Property inspector.

Layer	Keyframe	Rotation
2	8	180
3	10	-135
4	25	45
5	18	45
6	15	-45

9. To finish off the symbol, add the following code to a new keyframe at frame 129 of the ACTIONS layer:

```
gotoAndPlay(25);
```

This line creates a loop back to frame 25, which is where the last looping animation starts (on Layer 4).

10. Return to the movie's root timeline and select the miniclouds instance on frame 52 of the CLOUDZOOM layer. From the Color drop-down, select Brightness, and set this to 90%.

Titling

We'll now place a text sequence that will sit on the TITLING layer. The text that will zoom towards the user here is, "EVER DREAMED OF EXTREME TOURISM?". Once again, we'll be using fast paced animation and sound to create the effect.

At frame 259 of the TITLING layer, drag the TITLING movie clip from the Library onto the timeline. Place it at x=202.5, y=217.5. Take a look in the movie clip and examine what's going on. We're not going to build this clip from scratch as it's repeating techniques we're using throughout the chapter. Look at each layer at a time and see what's going on – once you've got the gist of it, you may fancy making your own titling sequence. This one has quite a lot of elements to it, but they're all basically static images, text, and motion tweens. Take a look at Sham Bhangal's Text Effect's chapter for ideas on how you could alter this titling clip.

Vertical clouds

Our next step is to create some vertical clouds. You'll see that we've got four of our masked layers set aside for this, all named VERTCLOUDS. We can create this effect very easily, as we've already created a cloud animation earlier: cloudsanim. With a bit of rotation of this animation, we're sorted.

1. Drag a copy of cloudsanim from the Library onto frame 269 of the bottom VERTCLOUDS layer. Rotate this symbol 90 degrees counterclockwise (CTRL+SHIFT+7). Reposition and tint this clip, as shown in the screenshot:

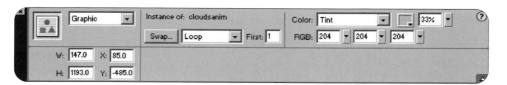

2. On the next layer up, drop an instance of `cloudsanim` onto frame 275. Rotate the symbol 90 degrees counterclockwise again, and tint it in the same manner as the last step. We'll position this copy further across the stage, and make it smaller.

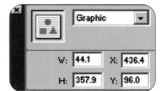

3. On the next VERTCLOUDS layer, drop an instance of the animated clouds onto frame 277, rotating and tinting the clip in the same way as in the last two steps. We'll rescale and position the clip again.

4. On frame 280 of the final VERTCLOUDS layer, drop an instance onto the stage, and rotate it 90 degrees counterclockwise. This time leave the scaling as it is, but apply the same tint again. Position the symbol as shown in the screenshot:

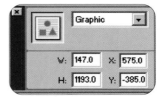

That's all our vertical cloud movement finished! Easy, eh! These clouds help to create the impression that the plane is traveling upwards, towards space. By applying scaling on the symbols, we've created more realism, as not all clouds in the sky are exactly the same distance away.

Horizontal bar

Our next masked layer is HORIZONTALBAR. In this layer, we'll have a horizontal bar that quickly moves downward, and reinforces the impression of upward movement.

1. On frame 324 of the HORIZONTALBAR layer, draw a rectangle (#CCCCCC gray fill, no stroke) measuring 685x379. Align the rectangle so that it's centered horizontally, but has its top edge at the top line of the viewing window. Make sure you have the MASK layer hidden, so you can see this correctly.

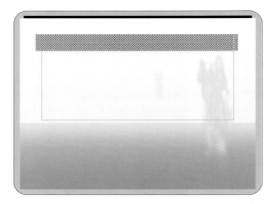

2. With the rectangle selected, press F8 to convert it into a graphic symbol named bar. Double-click into the new symbol. Create a keyframe at frame 4 of the default layer, and move the y position of the bar down to 290.5. This new position is below the bottom of the viewing window. Make a blank keyframe at frame 5, which will help us copy the frames quickly in a minute. Create a shape tween between the frames 1 and 4, setting the easing value to 100. There's no need to create a symbol to animate here, because, being a vector rectangle, the shape tweening can animate this shape vertically from top to bottom itself.

3. Copy the frames on Layer 1, create a new layer, and then paste the frames at frame 5 of the new layer. Insert an extra frame at the end of the timeline so it's 11 frames long.

4. Back on the root timeline, select the bar symbol, and set its Brightness to 72% in the Property inspector.

5. Insert a keyframe at frame 347 of the HORIZONTALBAR layer, and reposition and tint the bar symbol as shown in the screenshot. Note that the first frame is set to 4 rather than 1, and the tint color is black.

Into the dark

The next masked layer has the purpose of turning the sky dark as we leave the earth's atmosphere. This is a simple symbol containing a black rectangle that is shape-tweened into the viewing window.

1. At frame 368 of the BLACK layer, draw a 714x651 rectangle (black fill, no stroke), and center this on the stage. The rectangle covers the viewing window. With the rectangle selected, press F8 to convert it into a graphic symbol called black. Still on the main timeline, set the black symbol to Play Once in the Property inspector.

2. Double-click into the symbol's edit mode. Create a new keyframe at frame 7 of the default layer. On frame 1, change the y position of the rectangle to −485.6. This moves the rectangle so that its bottom is just above the top edge of the viewing window. Create a shape tween between frames 1 and 7, setting the easing to 100. When the movie is run, the rectangle will now move down over the viewing window to make things black as we leave the atmosphere.

Comets

Our final four masked layers are all called COMETS, and that's what will live on them. This emphasizes the fact that we've now left the earth's atmosphere and are in space. The movement of the comets will once again highlight the vertical motion, and we can indicate speed through their movement as well.

We created the comet images in Photoshop, and you'll find them in the Library as cometpart1 and cometpart2.

1. Create a new graphic clip symbol called asteroidsdown (CTRL+F8). Into this symbol, drag a copy of each of the two comet parts onto the stage. Position the two images as shown in the screenshots:

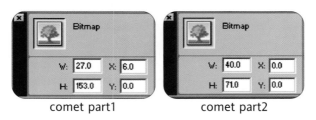

comet part1   comet part2

2. With both images selected on the stage, press F8, and convert them into a movie clip symbol called comet. With the new comet symbol selected on the default layer of the asteroidsdown symbol, flip it vertically (Modify>Transform>Flip Vertical). Position the clip at x=−17.9, y=−177.3.

3. Create a new keyframe at frame 5 of the default layer, and change the y position of the clip to 232.7 at this frame. Now set a motion tween between frames 1 and 5, and set the easing of this tween to 100. The comet will now fly downwards as you go through the tween. Create a blank keyframe at frame 6 – again this will be useful for copying the frames, which we'll do in the next step.

4. Select all the frames on Layer 1, and copy them (CTRL+ALT+C). Now insert a new layer (Insert>Layer), and paste the frames at frame 6 of the new layer (CTRL+ALT+V).

5. Finish off the asteroidsdown symbol by changing the clip positioning at the start and end keyframes of the Layer 2 tween. For keyframe 6, x=42.1 and y=-277.3, and for keyframe 10, x=42.1 and y=-132.7. If you now go back to the root timeline, we can position the animation we've just made onto the COMET layers.

6. On the bottom COMET layer, drop a copy of asteroidsdown onto the stage from the Library at frame 373. Position this instance at x=123.6, y=-198.8. Use the table opposite to position and scale the asteroidsdown instances for the other 3 comet layers – with one instance on each layer, placed at the pre-existing keyframes.

Frame	X	Y	W	H
377	443.1	-198.8	default	default
384	591	-171.1	86.8	634.1
379	268.8	-143.3	77.1	563.7

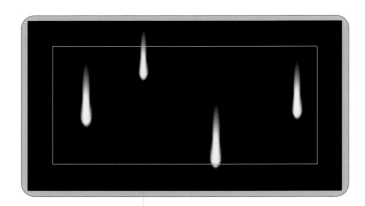

Congratulations! You've just completed the final masked layer, and consequently everything that will be seen while the viewing window and mask exist on the stage. Our next part of the movie is the animation of the MirCorp logo, but before we get to this, drop a copy of whiteanim from the Library onto the WHITEANIM layer at frame 430, centering it to the stage. If you remember back, this graphic acts as a divider to the sections of our movie.

Branding

Now, while you may want to create your own space flights in the future, I doubt that you'll need to create the MirCorp logo in your own work! Consequently, we won't guide you through how to create this logo step-by-step, as it's of limited use to you. However, you'll find a copy of the logo in the Library as logoanim. Take a look in this symbol; you'll see that it's constructed of a number of motion tweens and various symbols. The good thing to know is that we've already used the techniques that created this logo previously in the chapter.

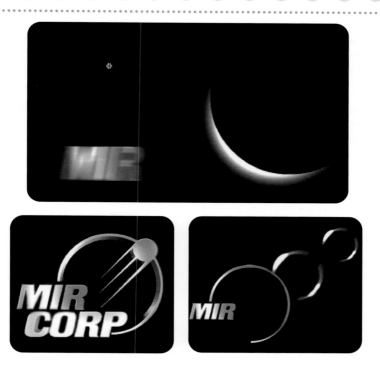

1. Drop a copy of logoanim onto the stage at frame 467 on the BRANDING layer. Position this clip at x=-222, y=-31.2, and set the logo to Play Once.

2. On frame 628 of the MIRCORPBLUR layer, we'll drop a copy of mirbluranim onto the stage at x=96.5, y=7.8. This clip carries on where the main logo clip left off, by zooming in, and then reverting to a black screen.

3. At frame 634 of the STRONGAMBIENT layer, draw a white rectangle (no stoke) that covers the entire stage (701x431). This rectangle acts as a flash of white dividing up the blur logo and the black screen that follows.

Out in space

Our movie is coming near to the end now, so things start to slow down a bit after the hectic action of the flight and the comets. Phew!

1. At frame 655 of the AMBIENTFLYING layer, draw a rectangle (with no stroke) just smaller than the stage (768x428). Position this at x=1.5, y=1.5. With the fill of this rectangle selected, open the Color Mixer (SHIFT+F9), and select Bitmap from the Fill style drop-down menu. Choose the icon that represents the spacebg.jpg image. This rectangle will act as our static space background.

2. We want the space image to fade in, so make another rectangle, this time at frame 655 of the STRONGAMBIENT layer. Make the rectangle cover the stage in the same fashion as the rectangle in the previous step, but this time give it a black fill (once again with no stroke). With the rectangle selected, press F8 and convert it into a graphic symbol named BLACK3.

3. Create another keyframe at frame 700 of the STRONGAMBIENT layer, and, from the Color drop-down menu in the Property inspector, set the Alpha to 0%. Finally, create a motion tween between the two keyframes. The background space scene will now seamlessly fade in.

4. Copy the rectangle at frame 655 of the AMBIENTFLYING layer (with the space image), and paste it in place onto the keyframe at frame 715 of the MOVE layer. Convert the rectangle into a movie clip named bg1 (F8). Convert this clip into another clip, called cometsfinal. The bg1 clip should be nested inside cometsfinal.

5. Go into the cometsfinal timeline, and insert a new keyframe at frame 15 (F6), followed by a blank keyframe at frame 16 (F7), and a normal frame at frame 67 (F5). The timeline will now be 67 frames long. At frame 15, move the bg1 clip to the right, so that its x position is now −237.5. Create a motion tween between frames 1 and 15, with the easing set to −100.

6. Create two new layers within the cometsfinal clip. On the middle layer, create a keyframe at frame 2, and attach the sound moverealfast.wav to this frame through the Property inspector. Once again, use a custom effect on the sound:

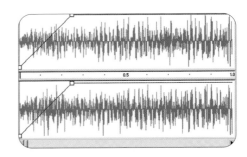

7. Create a new keyframe at frame 12 of the middle layer, and drag a copy of asteroiddown onto this frame from the Library. Select this clip on the stage, and press F8 to convert it to a graphic symbol called moveit.

8. Double-click into the edit mode for the moveit symbol. Select the asteroid symbol on frame 1, and rotate it 90 degrees counterclockwise (Ctrl+Shift+7). Resize and position the symbol as shown in the screenshot:

9. Press F5 at frame 89 to extend the timeline, and the duration of the symbol. Next, insert three new layers. We'll place instances of asteroiddown on each of these layers, rotating each by 90 degrees counterclockwise, so that they all travel from left to right. Use the following table to note where to create the keyframe for the symbol on each layer, and how to scale and position each symbol.

Layer	Keyframe	W	H	X	Y
Layer 2	5	704.6	37.1	-574.8	130.3
Layer 3	7	771.7	28.3	-432.8	-71.8
Layer 4	10	771.7	28.3	-512.8	68.2

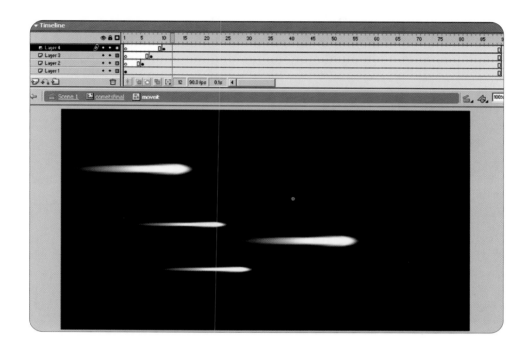

10. Back on the `cometsfinal` timeline, insert a blank keyframe at frame 56 of the middle layer. Also create a keyframe at frame 56 of the top layer. Onto this keyframe, draw a white rectangle covering the stage – this will act as a flash screen like we used earlier. Insert a blank keyframe at frame 57, and add the following to the Actions panel for this frame:

```
_root.play();
stop();
```

This code restarts the root timeline, which is stopped at the moment, and also stops the `cometsfinal` symbol's own timeline to prevent it from looping.

11. Return to the movie's root timeline, and add a `stop();` action at frame 715 of the SKIP layer. The code we used in the previous step restarts the timeline after this stop action.

The end of the journey

We've finished our journey now, and we'll finish the movie with one final piece of animation. A view of the earth from outer space is going to move onto our screen.

61

1. At frame 717 of the BORDER layer, draw a rectangle (with no stroke) that measures 312 pixels wide and 433 pixels tall. Select the rectangle, and using the Color Mixer's Bitmap option once more, select the icon that represents EARTHHALFFINAL.png as the fill. Convert the rectangle into a graphic symbol called BGPLANET. Position the symbol off the left side of the stage.

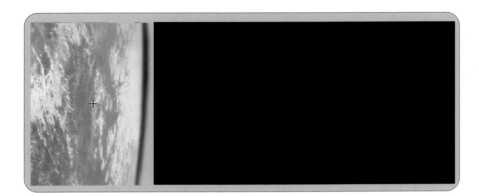

2. Create a keyframe at frame 763 of the BORDER layer, and move the symbol across the stage horizontally, so that the x position is now −38.5.

3. Create a motion tween between the two keyframes. At frame 1 set the easing value to 100, and set the Brightness of the symbol to 74%. At frame 727, create another keyframe, which will turn one tween into two. On this keyframe, change the x position of the symbol to −22.5, the easing of the tween to 0, and the Brightness of the symbol to 34%.

Tying up the loose ends

Our movie is now complete, apart from the tidying up of a few loose ends.

The RADIO layer

1. At frames 259, 260 and 769, add stop(); actions to the keyframes. At frame 261, add the following code:

```
stop();
_level0.go = "yes";
```

This code sets our go variable to "yes". Remember earlier in our horizon clip when we had a statement checking whether go was set to "yes"?

2. We set the go variable to no initially at frame 5:

```
_level0.go = "no";
```

3. At frame 262, add the frame label GO in the Property inspector.

4. Attach chemicalexplode1.wav to the timeline at frame 405, setting the custom sound as follows:

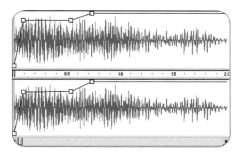

5. At frame 430, attach the ambientflying.wav file again. Have no effects on the sound this time. At frame 467, use the chaf.wav sound and adjust its custom settings as shown:

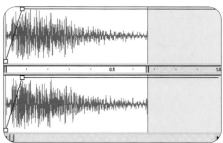

6. Finally, at frame 628 attach the appeartitling sound. Once again, this is a custom sound:

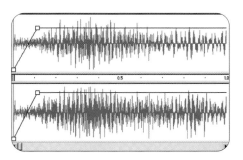

The STRONGAMBIENT layer

1. Attach `pororo.wav` at frame 702. Set the volume levels as shown in the screenshot:

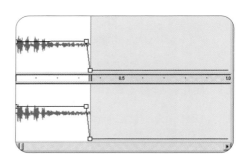

2. At frame 713, attach radioconv1 to the timeline. If you remember, we've already used this sound in the horizon symbol.

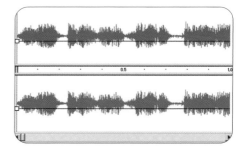

And finally...

As with all good Flash intros, we have a skip button. Why anyone would want to skip this intro without watching seems a mystery, unless they've already watched it hundreds of times before! However, we best include one as good usability practice.

Create your own skip button and drop it on frame 1 of the SKIP layer. Remember not to make it too good looking, as we don't want anyone to press it!

One final point about the production...

When we create an intro, the fact of viewing it quickly while we enjoy it in the browser doesn't mean that the intro's "production" must be linear. You'll have seen that throughout this movie we've had `stop();` actions on the main timeline. This allows us to have a placeholder for something we are going to create later, such as a logo. As you've seen, we can simply insert such a symbol into the movie on one frame, and restart the main timeline from within the symbol when it's finished playing! Ingenious. This helps us improve the quality of what we are trying to show, and achieve more complex and concrete presentations.

The future

To get inspired and start creating the experience you've just seen in this intro, we decided to travel to the land where we are currently negotiating with the local governments to build a new state of the art development center and Studio. This is a very small yet very inspiring place in Argentina called San Luis. This could be the place to watch for more groundbreaking Flash coming in the future!

In the near future, the digital world as it is known today, will change. It has been mandated by the FCC (Federal Communications Commission) that by the year 2006 all new television sets must be HDTV capable. Additionally, more and more devices and household appliances are becoming "smart." This opens up a tremendously large market for WideGroup's high impact services, since digital design will become a mandatory feature of these new products and services. Furthermore, with the emergence of digital film, the nature of filming and production in the entertainment industry will become increasingly dependant on digital design and PC-based solutions. As a result, Widegroup is at the forefront of a "digital tidal wave" that will materialize over the next 3-5 years. From now on, you should get ready to see some of the most unbelievable online and offline productions, interfaces and intros/transitions around coming from the WideGroup team.

With what you've learnt here, you could well be in a position to take advantage yourself!

About the Author
Jordan Stone

www.sofake.com
www.walkingincircles.com

"Anyone who thinks web designers are rock stars is a web designer," Jordan Stone said in a recent interview. "With lots of web designer friends to grease them," he added.

He grew up on the hard streets of Katy, Texas, with his sister Josh. After leading his high school to an unbelievable seven state football championships, Jordan set out to conquer the secret rodeo circuit. Sometime during this period, he met his wife Melanie, who married him based solely on the fact that he was, and continues to be, to a lesser extent after the long periods devoid of human interaction, a handsome cowboy.

After spending 15 years on the circuit, a dazzlingly brutal injury convinced him to divide his time between secret rodeos and web design.

"Let's get one thing straight," he said, "I am proud of my design work, but this is by no means a healthy way to spend one's life."

Recently, he has become increasingly interested in navigational structures that encourage user interaction. Also, Jordan has been assigned to a top-secret government project codenamed SNOWMAN, in a dream he had.

After sofake.com launched, the reasonably happy couple celebrated by having their first child, a dog named Sally, much to the dismay of the fish that now remains largely neglected.

"Remember, anything printed in a book is true," Jordan said, scuttling off to check his Hotmail mid-interview, "and don't take yourself too seriously. It's only web design, nobody lives or dies."

Keeping it Real: the skin and the bones behind Sofake.com

Jordan Stone

About the Effect

Every site on the web, except those consisting of one static page, needs a navigation system. The secret to success with your navigation is novelty plus usability. There's no point in having a cool navigation that does work, or doesn't work unless you're in on the creator's secret.

This chapter will provide you with a novel navigation that uses both imagery and sound to convey a feeling of depth to a site. It's not just a computer screen in front of you; it's a whole virtual world. Once the novelty of this effect wears off, you'll still find the navigation extremely usable, and this is the key to success.

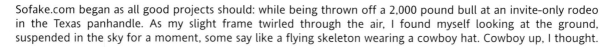

Sofake.com began as all good projects should: while being thrown off a 2,000 pound bull at an invite-only rodeo in the Texas panhandle. As my slight frame twirled through the air, I found myself looking at the ground, suspended in the sky for a moment, some say like a flying skeleton wearing a cowboy hat. Cowboy up, I thought.

Then, eyes wide open, I came down. There was a sensation that occurred though, I mean before the multiple-level concussion, of the textured dirt and grit 'zooming' into my face, gaining detail and intricacy. As I was being carried away, in a fair to middling state of consciousness, I decided to cut back on secret rodeos and get back to dabbling in web design. And so, here we are, with a bit of physical therapy and ActionScripting gone by, I have come to understand that the mechanics behind Sofake.com are more than just a gimmick. Oh, they are a gimmick, and a good gimmick for sure, but beyond that gimmick is a method of navigation that engages the user.

In this chapter, we'll create a site navigation system that puts contents at the fingertips of the user. They can flip and fan through the contents with the ease of a magazine, while being engaged by an effective visual metaphor that takes them out of a 'web page' and into a 'web place'.

We'll then increase the experience by adding a sound engine that reacts to the depth of the user, further strengthening their sense of place. We'll also take a moment to rough up some images in Photoshop and then discuss how to keep these bitmap images scaling smoothly in Flash. So, if everyone has gone to the bathroom, let's get moving!

A quick vivisection of Sofake.com

Let's first take a look at Sofake.com and explain exactly what the user is seeing.

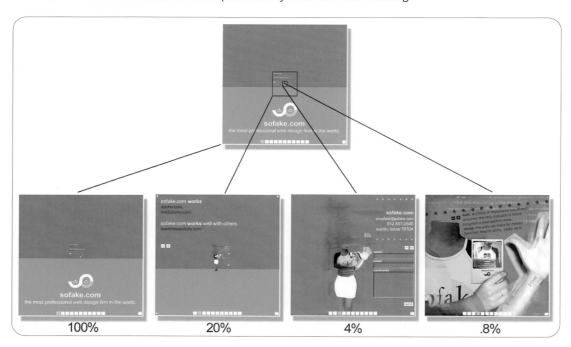

As shown, at any one time you can see up to four images laid on top of each other. What appears to be the topmost 'panel' is in fact located all the way at the 'back' of the site. So, with a few lines of ActionScript, we'll build an engine to scale these panels up and down as appropriate. The aim of this particular engine is not to impose forced 3D visual trickery with panels moving at different speeds, but rather to create the illusion of one giant panel that we zoom into. Fake 3D is certainly something you can toy with later by changing variables and coordinates around. In my opinion, fake 3D is better than real 3D because it is fake. Of course! We'll also need to write a condition that affects the visibility of the panels according to their scale. This will reduce the ridiculous strain we put upon the shoulders of our computers. It will also keep the panels in the back from being visible when inappropriate.

So, with trembling hands, let us open this beast once more that is Macromedia Flash MX.

Sofake setup

In this first section, we'll set up all the necessary timelines and symbols for the engine that controls the Sofake scaling effect.

1. Open a new movie (CTRL+N) and bump up the frames per second to 24 fps (Modify>Document). It's good enough for the movies so it's good enough for you. Stick to the default stage size of 550 pixels wide by 400 pixels high.

2. Now let's create the symbols we're going to need. First, draw a rectangle with no stroke and make it the same size as the stage (550x400 pixels). I filled mine with the color #76A4D1, entering this code directly into the Color Mixer panel (SHIFT+F9). Try something in the #72000's. The physics engine will work with almost any color except for lime green (honest!).

3. Convert your rectangle into a movie clip (F8), name it `panel`, and give it a **central** registration point. Set its coordinates in the Property inspector to (275,200) so that it completely covers the stage.

4. Now make another movie clip (Insert>New Symbol.../Ctrl+F8) and call it button. In this button movie clip rename the default layer graphics and draw a white rectangle with no stroke that measures 33x15 pixels (you might need to change the background color to see the white shape).

5. Add a keyframe at frame 2 of the graphics layer (F6). Use the Paint Bucket tool to fill it with a gray color. This will be the rollover state of our button.

6. Add a new layer to the button movie clip (Insert>Layer) and call it actions. Place another keyframe in frame 2 (F6) and add a stop(); action to both frames in this layer. Your button timeline should now look like this:

7. Go back to the root timeline. Select the panel movie clip and convert it to a movie clip called main with a central registration point (F8). Use the Align panel (Ctrl+K) to center this new movie clip on the stage. Double-click on main to go into its timeline and let's do a little work. Rename the existing layer main1 and insert six new layers (Insert>Layer) so that there are seven in total, arranging the timeline like so:

8. Select frame 1 of the buttons layer and drag six copies of your button symbol out of the Library. Arrange them at the lower center of the stage using the Align panel (Ctrl+K). Working from left to right, give each button an instance name in the Property inspector of button1, button2, and so on, all the way through to button6.

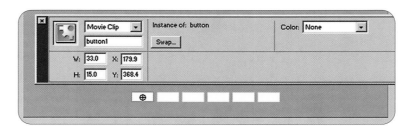

9. Select all of the buttons and convert them into another movie clip with an instance name of button_nest. In button_nest's timeline, add a new layer called actions (Insert>Layer) and rename the existing layer buttons. Add keyframes to each of frames 2 through 6 on both layers (F6).

10. Next, place a stop(); action in each of the keyframes on the actions layer. Then, select the button in frame 1 of the buttons layer and use the Property inspector to give it a 100% gray tint.

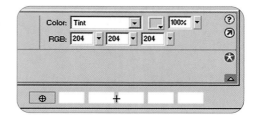

11. Working from left to right, repeat this tinting process for each of the button instances. So, in frame 2 apply the tint to button2 and so on, through to button6 in frame 6. When finished, you'll have the correlating button in each frame grayed out. Now, as the user navigates through the site, they will be cued into where they sit in relation to the remainder of the site. This will strengthen their sense of place while visiting your site and make them a generally happier person!

12. Now go back into the main movie clip's timeline. Your panel movie clip should be on the main1 layer. Let's identify it with the instance name main1. Now duplicate the panel clip in the Library and drag the duplicate onto the main2 layer below, this time giving it the instance name of main2. With the main2 instance selected (you'll need to lock the layer containing main1 above it), use the Color drop-down menu in the Property inspector to set its brightness to −5%.

13. Repeat this process until you have filled your remaining layers with extra panel instances named main3 through to main6, as dictated by their respective layer names. Each time reduce the brightness value by 5% (you should finish with a brightness value of -25% for main6). We are only doing this so as to be able to tell our panels apart when testing the engine. You could, if you want to, use the same Library symbol for each main instance, but this would mean you have the same stuff on each panel when you come to add content later – this is why I've created duplicates that look identical. They are identical at the moment, but will not be if and when content is added to the engine.

14. Lastly, head back out to the root timeline and give the main movie clip the instance name main. You should now have the main movie clip sitting in frame 1 of the default layer of the root timeline:

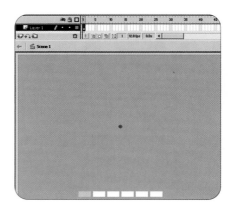

Okay, you can take a breather now. In the next section, we're going to write the ActionScript that'll make this movie come to life. Woohoo!

Scripting Sofake

We're going to house all our code on frame 1 of the main movie clip, rather than the root timeline. This will enable us to have our entire navigation as a modular movie clip that can be dragged and used in any movie you make.

1. On the timeline of the main movie clip, add a new layer called actions (Insert>Layer). Open up the Actions panel on frame 1 (F9). We'll start the code by setting the initial target scaling value for each panel we have created. We'll also store this value as an appropriately named variable with a set prefix. Type the following code:

    ```
    set1 = main1._xscale=0;
    set2 = main2._xscale=0;
    set3 = main3._xscale=.8;
    set4 = main4._xscale=4;
    set5 = main5._xscale=20;
    set6 = main6._xscale=100;
    ```

    If all these = operators look confusing, don't worry. What we've used is just a shorthand way of saying:

    ```
    set1 = 0;
    main1._xscale = 0;
    set2 = 0;
    main2._xscale = 0;
    set3 = .8;
    main3._xscale = .8;
    set4 = 4;
    main4._xscale = 4;
    set5 = 20;
    main5._xscale = 20;
    set6 = 100;
    main6._xscale = 100;
    ```

    If we take the first panel (main1) as an example, you can see that we simply set the scale of main1 to 0. Then, we actually set the initial _xscale factor to match this value. Since our engine keeps _xscale and _yscale in direct proportion to each other, we need only set _xscale. Of course, you could set the panel movie clips' correct scale properties manually on the stage, but this would make any future editing of the movie clips much more difficult than is necessary.

2. Next, type in the following function beginning:

    ```
    function SCALE(CLIP, SET) {
        //scale
        start = CLIP._xscale;
        end = SET-start;
        CLIP._xscale = start+(end/5);
        CLIP._yscale = start+(end/5);
    ```

The purpose of this function is to scale each of the panels. Two parameters are passed into the function, one being the instance name of the `panel` movie clip, and the other being a target value to set the scaling to. There are two variables in the function. The first one, `start`, is the scaling of the panel when the function is called; the second, `end`, is the target scaling value minus the `start` value. Dividing `end` by 5 determines the amount of inertia, or easing, that occurs when the panels rescale (you could call it deceleration). Go with higher numbers for slower transitions from panel to panel, or lower numbers for speedier transitions.

3. Underneath the previous lines, type in the following code to add the next part of the function:

```
//visible
if (CLIP._xscale<850 && CLIP._xscale>=.1) {
    CLIP._visible = 1;
} else {
    CLIP._visible = 0;
}
}
```

Here, a simple `if` statement evaluates whether the panel's scale is less than 850% *and* greater than 0.1%. If this is `true`, then the panel is visible (1). If either of these conditions is found to be false, then the panel is made invisible (0).

4. Now we need to call the function and target our six panels using an `onEnterFrame` event handler like this:

```
this.onEnterFrame = function() {
    SCALE(main6, set6);
    SCALE(main5, set5);
    SCALE(main4, set4);
    SCALE(main3, set3);
    SCALE(main2, set2);
    SCALE(main1, set1);
};
```

Here, we call the function for each of our six panels (using the instance names we gave them earlier). The first parameter identifies the clip to apply the scaling to, and we pass the appropriate target scaling value into the function as the second parameter. Each time the function is called, our panels get closer to their desired scaling level. We put these function calls in an `onEnterFrame` handler so that the function is repeatedly run through on every frame, and the target scaling values are reached. With every frame, our `start` value and target value (`SET`) become closer, until they are the same.

5. Okay, it's time to get our buttons talking! First off, underneath all the previous code, add this ActionScript to make `button1` function:

```
button_nest.button1.onPress = function() {
    set1 = 0;
    set2 = 0;
    set3 = 0.8;
    set4 = 4;
    set5 = 20;
    set6 = 100;
};
```

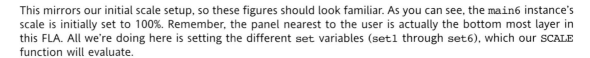

This mirrors our initial scale setup, so these figures should look familiar. As you can see, the `main6` instance's scale is initially set to 100%. Remember, the panel nearest to the user is actually the bottom most layer in this FLA. All we're doing here is setting the different `set` variables (`set1` through `set6`), which our SCALE function will evaluate.

6.   Now type in the code to set up `button2`:

```
button_nest.button2.onPress = function() {
     set1 = 0;
     set2 = 0.8;
     set3 = 4;
     set4 = 20;
     set5 = 100;
     set6 = 500;
};
```

Basically, all the `set` variables are multiplied by five. 'But zero times five is zero!' you cry. The reason why our panels at the back, beyond the 0.8% scale level, are set to zero is because the human eye will never know the difference. Now, don't get me wrong, the human eye is an amazing and incredible thing! So, the only thing you really need to calculate is the new value of `set6` and then push all the other values 'up' a level (the value for `set6` becomes the value for `set5`, the value for `set5` becomes the value for `set4`, and so on).

7.   Alright, go ahead and finish off the rest of the buttons with this code:

```
button_nest.button3.onPress = function() {
     set1 = 0.8;
     set2 = 4;
     set3 = 20;
     set4 = 100;
     set5 = 500;
     set6 = 2500;
};
button_nest.button4.onPress = function() {
     set1 = 4;
     set2 = 20;
     set3 = 100;
     set4 = 500;
     set5 = 2500;
     set6 = 12500;
};
button_nest.button5.onPress = function() {
     set1 = 20;
     set2 = 100;
     set3 = 500;
     set4 = 2500;
     set5 = 12500;
     set6 = 62500;
};
button_nest.button6.onPress = function() {
     set1 = 100;
```

```
set2 = 500;
set3 = 2500;
set4 = 12500;
set5 = 62500;
set6 = 312500;
};
```

There's a little bit more scripting left to do on these buttons. Remember how we made a separate keyframe and colored the button gray (we also tinted the instances of each button in the button_nest movie clip)? We need to add the necessary code to make the buttons 'listen' for the mouse over them, and then display the appropriate color: gray or white. We'll use the gray button states as simple visual cues to increase the user's awareness of where they are in relation to the rest of the site.

8. Add this function at the bottom of your code:

```
function buttonActive(buttonPath, frame) {
    buttonPath.onRollOver = function() {
        buttonPath.gotoAndStop(2);
    };
    buttonPath.onRollOut = function() {
        buttonPath.gotoAndStop(1);
    };
    buttonPath.onRelease = function() {
        button_nest.gotoAndStop(frame);
    };
}
```

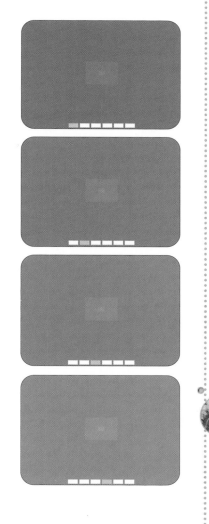

This is a fairly simple function that does two things: it detects when the user's mouse is over the button, and when the button has been pressed. If the mouse is over the button, then Flash goes to frame 2 of buttonPath's timeline (a button instance), where the button is gray. When the mouse exits the button area, the onRollOut event handler sends the playhead back to frame 1, in order to display the default white button. When the button is pressed, Flash sends the button_nest timeline to the specified frame number, in order to retain the gray color until another button is selected.

9. To make this function work, we add this code:

```
for (i=1; i<=6; i++) {
    buttonActive(button_nest["button"+i], i);
}
```

This is exactly the same as:

```
buttonActive(button_nest.button1, 1);
buttonActive(button_nest.button2, 2);
buttonActive(button_nest.button3, 3);
buttonActive(button_nest.button4, 4);
buttonActive(button_nest.button5, 5);
buttonActive(button_nest.button6, 6);
```

However we've used a `for` loop to make the code more efficient. This simply calls the `buttonActive` function for each of the six navigation buttons, so that they all respond to mouse rollovers and presses.

And there you go – all that remains is to save the file and test the movie! You've got a fully functioning scaling navigation engine. If you picked a particularly exciting color for your panels, or used circular buttons, you could go ahead and publish it straight to the World Wide Web. Everyone will be amazed!

Sofake sound engine

When it came to web sites, I was a fully paid-up member of the anti-sound league for a long time. My reasons were simple and egocentrically driven: at the time of development I was constantly listening to MP3s and thus always irritated by web sites that barked at me. However, I also realized that each time I had added sound to a project it seemed to lift it up to an entire new level. So, in short, I've turned around in my thinking when it comes to sound. If it's done well, sound can be an engaging layer of media that adds an extra dimension to your interactive multimedia web site. Ouch, that's cheesy, enough of the ad lines.

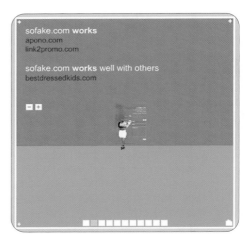

Take a look at Sofake.com once more. There are a few subtle dynamics going on, some of which are aided by the extra soundtrack elements. At first, there is completely impersonal music, dimly generated from the 'professional' section of the web site.

As the user delves deeper, this takes a turn towards the more personal until, at the back of the web site, I'm using blue words and the entire concept of 'professional' has completely gone out the window. All loose metaphors aside, the music fading in and out and meshing together awkwardly is pretty neat too.

To achieve this we are going to create two separate Sound objects and control the volume of each object independently.

Creating the sound engine

For this example, we are going to need two sound loops. These loops can be whatever you wish, but if you really want to set your site apart may I suggest using futuristic techno music. We are going to make these loops indicate the front and the back of our engine, or 'web space', with a little bit of blending in the midsection of the engine. In the download files for this chapter, there are two WAV files that have been specially edited in an expensive London studio to loop super-smoothly.

1. Open up the navigation movie you were working on at the end of the last section. Go to File>Import to Library... and import two sound files.

2. Open up your Library (F11) and select Linkage... from the context menu at the top-right of the Library window. In the following Linkage Properties dialog box check Export for ActionScript and type in a suitable identifier name for your sound file. Do this again to give your second sound file a linkage identifier.

Now, onto the part you all love the most: the code! This code will live in the same frame as the navigation code, so go to frame 1 of the main movie clip and open the Actions panel (F9).

3. We'll start by creating some variables for the sound engine. Add the following variables to the start of the code, after the set variables. It's often a good idea to have all your variables defined in one place – so that you know where to look for them!

    ```
    muted = false;
    target1 = 40;
    target2 = 0;
    ```

    The first variable here is whether the sound is muted or not. This will be linked to a mute button we'll create later. target1 is the target volume for the first sound, and target2 is the target volume for the second sound.

4. Now scroll down to the end of the onEnterFrame handler, just before the button code; we're going to add the rest of the sound engine after the onEnterFrame handler. We need to create an empty holder clip for each of our sounds, so that we can control their volumes independently. Add the following code:

    ```
    this.createEmptyMovieClip("sound1holder", 1);
    this.createEmptyMovieClip("sound2holder", 2);
    ```

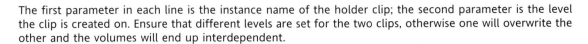

The first parameter in each line is the instance name of the holder clip; the second parameter is the level the clip is created on. Ensure that different levels are set for the two clips, otherwise one will overwrite the other and the volumes will end up interdependent.

5. The next step is to create our first Sound object. This is for the first of our sound loops. Add the following code:

```
loop1 = new Sound(sound1holder);
loop1.attachSound("strings");
loop1.setVolume(40);
loop1.start();
```

The first line of our code creates a Sound object called `loop1`, and targets the sound at our first holder movie clip. The second line attaches our first sound from the Library, using the identifier we set earlier (use whatever name you set). The next line sets the initial volume of the sound (which is the same as the initial `target1` variable that we defined), and the final line starts the sound playing.

6. Now add the code for the second sound, using the same format, but changing the values as appropriate:

```
loop2 = new Sound(sound2holder);
loop2.attachSound("buritto");
loop2.setVolume(0);
loop2.start();
```

7. As things stand, each of our sounds will play once and then stop, but we want them to loop. Add the next block of code to the end of your existing script:

```
loop1.onSoundComplete = function() {
    loop1.start();
};
loop2.onSoundComplete = function() {
    loop2.start();
};
```

Using an `onSoundComplete` handler, we can define what happens when a sound has finished playing. We want a loop, so we just tell it to start playing again. Now, whenever either of the sounds finishes playing, it will always look at these handlers and loop.

8. The next job is to define variables for the volume of each sound. This is what the volume level actually is, and not always what we want it to be (`target1`, `target2`). Add the code now:

```
volume1 = loop1.getVolume();
volume2 = loop2.getVolume();
```

We've used the `getVolume` method of the Sound object to retrieve the information. We've defined these variables here, rather than with the other variables, because they are related to the loops that haven't yet been defined at the start of the code.

Now it's time to build the function that will actually alter the volume of our loops.

9. We start by typing in the function opening and the first `if` statement:

```
function VOLUME(value1, value2) {
    if (volume1 == value1 && volume2 == value2) {
        for (i=1; i<=6; i++) {
            // clear the onEnterFrame for each of the buttons
            button_nest["button"+i].onEnterFrame = undefined;
        }
    }
}
```

Two parameters are passed into the VOLUME function. When we call the function later, the values that we will be passing in as the parameters are the target volumes, `target1` and `target2`. This `if` statement checks whether both the target volumes are equal to the actual volumes. As you'll see shortly, the VOLUME function will be called when one of our six navigation buttons is pressed, and it will be called for every subsequent frame through an `onEnterFrame` handler. When our volume has reached the target levels, we don't need the function to run anymore – to do so is wasting processor resources. So, this `if` statement is 'clearing' the `onEnterFrame` handler for each of the buttons, so that the function is no longer being needlessly called, thus giving our processors a breather. As the function can be called from any of the buttons, we have to clear them all to ensure we've caught the guilty culprit.

10. The next section of the VOLUME function deals with the volume of the first sound loop. If the actual volume is greater than the target volume, then the volume needs reducing. We've set the volume to decrease by 2 every time the function is called, until it is equal to the target volume. If the actual volume is lower than the target volume, then we increase it by 2 every time the function is called. In both cases, once we've modified the `volume1` value, we then set the volume of the loop to the new value. Add this code to the function to achieve the desired fading:

```
if (volume1>value1) {
    volume1 -= 2;
    loop1.setVolume(volume1);
} else if (volume1<value1) {
    volume1 += 2;
    loop1.setVolume(volume1);
}
```

11. The function is finished by using the same code to fade the second loop's volume to the desired level. The only changes we make here are to reference the `volume2` and `value2` values, rather than those for the first loop. Don't forget to include the brace to close the function when typing it in.

```
if (volume2>value2) {
    volume2 -= 2;
    loop2.setVolume(volume2);
} else if (volume2<value2) {
    volume2 += 2;
    loop2.setVolume(volume2);
}
}
```

There you go then! We've got our volume fading function finished.

Turn it down – the mute button

Great, we've got two sound loops that we can control. Alas, the sad truth of the matter is that not everyone wants to hear your futuristic techno music. So, in the spirit of kindness, we'll add a mute button that can be toggled to fade out both of the sound loops completely or bring them back up to their original levels. Brilliant!

1. In the `main` movie clip's timeline, lock all of the layers except for `buttons`. Select frame 1 of the `buttons` layer and drag out a copy of `button` from the Library, placing it at the bottom right of the stage. Give it the instance name `mute`.

2. Double-click on this mute button to go into its timeline. Rename the default layer `button` and insert two new layers (Insert>Layer) above it, called `actions` and `graphics`. Add a keyframe to frame 2 of both the `actions` and `graphics` layers (F6). Add a blank frame to frame 2 of the `button` layer (F5).

3. Select frame 1 of the `graphics` layer and draw a graphic signifying that sound is playing. I've used a speaker icon, but you could just as effectively use a piece of text. I've decided to have 'on' stand for 'music is currently on', and 'off' stand for 'music is currently off' but if it makes more sense to you, you could easily switch the button graphics around making 'off' stand for '*turn* music off' and 'on' stand for '*turn* music on'.

4. Next, select frame 2 of the `graphics` layer and alter the graphics (or the text if you've used any) too signify a 'mute' sound status.

5. Finally, to stop things getting too mad, add a `stop();` action to both of the keyframes in the `actions` layer. That's the mute button built. Grand!

6. Now, let's add some code to make our mute button actually work. Go back to the Actions panel for frame 1 of the `main` movie clip timeline. We want to mute all the sound in the movie, so we'll create a new Sound object that will control all of the `main` clip, overriding the two sound loops. Add the following code at the end of your existing mass of code:

```
master = new Sound(this);
master.setVolume(100);
mastervol = master.getVolume();
```

This creates a new Sound object called `master`, which is attached to the current timeline (`this`). We set the initial volume to 100%, and create a variable to store the volume.

7. Now is when the mute variable we defined earlier comes into play. Add the following code, which will mute the volume of the movie by fading out the sound.

```
mute.onPress = function() {
    if (!muted) {
        muted = true;
        // set mute symbol
```

```
mute.gotoAndStop(2);
// fade volume out
this.onEnterFrame = function() {
    mastervol -= 2;
    master.setVolume(mastervol);
    if (mastervol == 0) {
        this.onEnterFrame = undefined;
    }
};
```

When the button is pressed, the code looks to see if the movie is already muted (muted=true). If it isn't, (!muted/muted=false) then the music is faded out. The muted variable is set to true, and the mute button is sent to frame 2 to show its muted symbol. The volume fade occurs in an onEnterFrame handler, decreasing the volume by 2% every frame until the volume is at 0%. When 0% is reached, the onEnterFrame handler is cleared to stop mastervol going into negative values.

8.   If the sound is already muted when the mute button is pressed, we want to fade the music in again. We can do this through an else statement. Add this code to complete the if/else pair:

```
} else {
    muted = false;
    // set mute symbol
    mute.gotoAndStop(1);
    // fade volume in
    this.onEnterFrame = function() {
        mastervol += 2;
        master.setVolume(mastervol);
        if (mastervol == 100) {
            this.onEnterFrame = undefined;
        }
    };
}
};
```

This code works in an identical way to the if part of the statement, except that the volume is increased by 2% with every frame until it reaches 100%. The muted variable is switched back to false, as the sound will be on again, and the mute button is sent back to its sound playing graphic.

Talk to the buttons

1.   Now we've got the mute button covered, we can put the sound engine into action by attaching the code to the buttons to call the VOLUME function and fade our sounds to the desired levels. Find the code for button1 in your script. Add in the highlighted code:

```
button_nest.button1.onPress = function() {
    set1 = 0;
    set2 = 0;
    set3 = 0.8;
    set4 = 4;
    set5 = 20;
    set6 = 100;
    target1 = 40;
    target2 = 0;
```

```
        this.onEnterFrame = function() {
            VOLUME(target1, target2);
        };
    };
```

Here, we're adding the target values for our two loop volumes. We then use an onEnterFrame for the button, which will call the VOLUME function every frame and fade the volume to our required levels. The onEnterFrame is important here, as this is what keeps the VOLUME function running until the right level is reached, as opposed to running once, getting 2% closer to the target volumes, and then stopping.

When choosing target volumes, it's important to keep even numbers. As all our volume changes are in 2% values, we don't want the situation to arise where certain values can never be reached. For example, 0% could never be reached if coming from an odd volume, as our code would constantly alternate between plus and minus one.

2. The code alterations for our other buttons are the same, except that we set different target volumes. Here's the rest of the code for you to modify:

```
button_nest.button2.onPress = function() {
    set1 = 0;
    set2 = 0.8;
    set3 = 4;
    set4 = 20;
    set5 = 100;
    set6 = 500;
    target1 = 100;
    target2 = 0;
    this.onEnterFrame = function() {
        VOLUME(target1, target2);
    };
};
button_nest.button3.onPress = function() {
    set1 = 0.8;
    set2 = 4;
    set3 = 20;
    set4 = 100;
    set5 = 500;
    set6 = 2500;
    target1 = 70;
    target2 = 30;
    this.onEnterFrame = function() {
        VOLUME(target1, target2);
    };
};
button_nest.button4.onPress = function() {
    set1 = 4;
    set2 = 20;
    set3 = 100;
    set4 = 500;
    set5 = 2500;
    set6 = 12500;
```

```
                target1 = 30;
                target2 = 70;
                this.onEnterFrame = function() {
                    VOLUME(target1, target2);
                };
        };
        button_nest.button5.onPress = function() {
                set1 = 20;
                set2 = 100;
                set3 = 500;
                set4 = 2500;
                set5 = 12500;
                set6 = 62500;
                target1 = 0;
                target2 = 100;
                this.onEnterFrame = function() {
                    VOLUME(target1, target2);
                };
        };
        button_nest.button6.onPress = function() {
                set1 = 100;
                set2 = 500;
                set3 = 2500;
                set4 = 12500;
                set5 = 62500;
                set6 = 312500;
                target1 = 0;
                target2 = 100;
                this.onEnterFrame = function() {
                    VOLUME(target1, target2);
                };
        };
```

All right. How absolutely fanciful! Give the movie a run, and watch with marvel as the sound and panels zoom around as you press the buttons. This is only a conceptual example to give you an idea of how to construct such a thing. Extrapolated and fleshed out, you could achieve some very impressive effects.

Roughing it up

Well, that's the navigation complete, but as a special bonus I'll give you a few pictures showing how the scratched up imagery at Sofake.com was created. It only takes a few moments and is completely artless, I assure you. Photoshop is the tool I use, and if you've never delved in Photoshop before, you can download a tryout of version 7.0 from www.adobe.com/products/tryadobe.

I'm going to use a picture of a distant ancestor of which I am particularly fond. An unflattened version of the final file (called `mummy.psd`) is included in the download files for this chapter, so if you're interested, take a look at this file and see what effects have been applied to each layer. If you want to have a play with the original file and create your own, take a look at `base_photo.tif` in the download files.

Here's the original file which is roughed up to achieve the above effect:

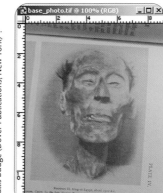

"Plate IV from *The Dwellers on the Nile* by EA Wallis Budge (Dover Publications, New York)".

Here's a look at the transition from the original image to the end Sofake product:

Always add some propaganda when you can, whatever that may mean to you. Remember to be careful when you spell your name though, as you could otherwise find yourself embarrassed and ashamed.

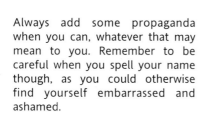

Optimizing the image for Flash

Before we forget about Photoshop totally and return to Flash, let's quickly look at the options for exporting an image from Photoshop to Flash. Open the `mummy.psd` file, assuming I've intrigued you enough to use Photoshop. We export the image using the **Save For Web** function (File>Save for Web). We are immediately confronted with several image format options. We're going to be using the PNG-24 format, but before we do, let's take a quick peek at the options available and how they each affect image optimization for Flash.

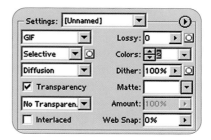

The first option in the Optimized file format drop-down menu (on the right-hand side of the Save For Web window) is the GIF. We're not going to be using the GIF as it's more appropriate for images containing lots of nice flat areas of flat untextured color. A quick tip though is that you can get some fairly neat effects by exporting your image as a GIF with very few colors (usually somewhere between 2 and 16). Try it out on your mummy image.

The JPEG format is the second option in the menu. This would be a fine choice indeed for our image, with its texture and photographic qualities. We won't be using it, but let's add a quick helpful tip here. You should ideally compress your JPEGs with a Quality setting around 50, maybe 60 if you want to push it.

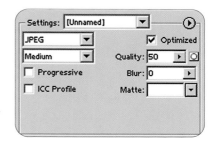

Some people may tell you that you should export your JPEGs with the Quality set at 80 or higher. You should consider disassociating yourself with these people. I can most definitely tell a greater difference between the 48k file size that a Quality of 80 costs me, and the 21k that a Quality of 50 costs, rather than the actual loss in image quality between the two.

Moving on to the third selection, there is the shifty and clever PNG. We're talking about PNG-24 here, though PNG-8 is a viable choice for low color depth images. Our PNG-24 weighs about 180k!

Be ye not afraid, reader; for a long time this factor has kept me far away from the PNG, but the mighty Macromedia Flash MX will easily crush this file size down to a comparable or lower size than the JPEG. Another dazzling aspect is that we will have a nice uncompressed image in Flash, which gives us the freedom to experiment with publishing the movie at different quality levels to easily compare image quality versus file size ratios.

Also, have you ever tried using a transparent GIF in Flash? It's quite dreadful, really, but a transparent PNG is really lovely. My other reason for choosing the PNG for this particular project was that I overheard a person I didn't even know say that Flash could push PNGs with greater savvy than JPEGs or GIFs. This is a completely unsubstantiated claim made by a person for whom I cannot vouch for, but it was good enough for me.

Okay then, we'll choose the PNG-24 option with Transparency checked for our mummy. Select these options and click on Save to finally export your image.

Scaling bitmap images smoothly in Flash

Take another look at Sofake.com. Navigate from section to section and notice that the images stay smooth and sweet when they scale up and down. It's not something you would really notice, as this is rather something you would expect, but oh what a feat it was to reach this satisfactory point!

Let's get back into Flash and see what we can do. We'll take a look at the available options of how we can control our bitmap image in Flash, and then choose a final method that avoids the common pitfalls and problems associated with scaling bitmaps in Flash.

1. First of all, open up `base_engine_pop.fla` from the download files. This movie has the `mummy.png` image imported into the Library. The image has been added into its own movie clip called `panel1`, which also contains an instance of the original `panel` movie clip as the background. Finally, `panel1` has been added to the `main1` layer in `main`'s timeline and given the instance name `main1`.

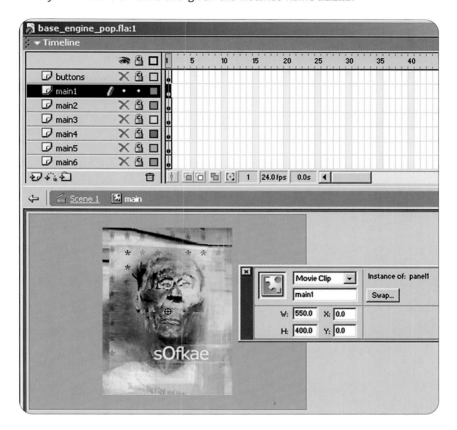

2. Test the movie and navigate through to the last panel (which is our adapted `panel1`).

   Look carefully at the image as it scales up into position and let's discuss what is happening. Upon scaling to the last section, Flash begins to anti-alias the bitmap, which is just fine, but when it reaches the new stopping point, where the bitmap becomes a perfectly scaled 100%, Flash no longer feels the need to anti-alias the image. At this point, the bitmap annoyingly 'pops' out of its anti-aliased state in a four-quadrant method that to this day makes me queasy. So, what can we do?

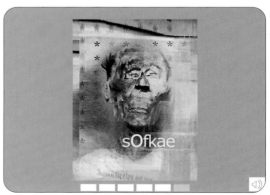

3. Well, we can turn off smoothing in our bitmaps. Right-click on the bitmap in the Library and select Properties. In the following Bitmap Properties window, uncheck Allow smoothing.

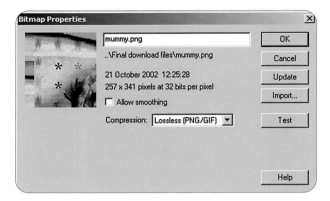

4. Alternatively, to test this doomed method, you can set the quality of your movie to Low on the HTML tab of the Publish Settings window (File>Publish Settings).

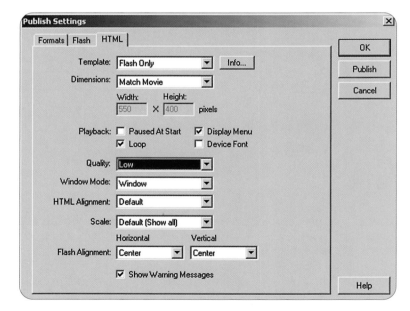

All right, let's check it out (this is `base_engine_ripple.html` in the download files). We now no longer experience the horrid bitmap popping, as discussed above, but what do we get for our troubles? The pond ripple effect! Now each and every transition is accompanied by the heartbreaking pond ripple effect. Terrible!

We're down to our last option. This is where I divulge the methodology behind the smooth bitmaps at Sofake.com.

5. Check Allow smoothing back on in your Bitmap Properties window, if you previously flipped it off. Let's also reset our movie quality back to High in the Publish Settings. Okay, now this is going to hurt, just a little. Go up to the root timeline and using the Transform panel, scale your `main` movie clip (containing all of your individual panels) to 99% of its original size.

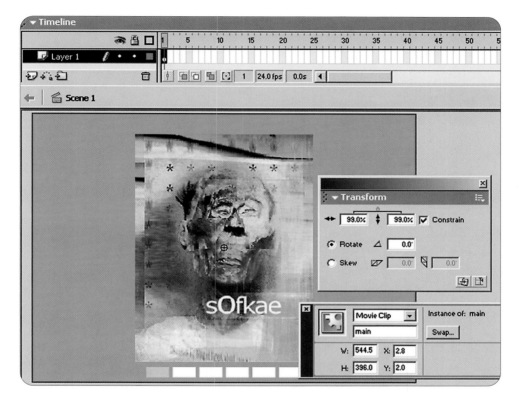

Let's quickly discuss what is now happening. All of our images receive a small dose of anti-aliasing action from Flash. This is akin to, say, a 0.1% Gaussian Blur in Photoshop. Test the movie out to see the smoothly scaling image (this is `base_engine_final.html`).

We'll certainly notice the effect ourselves until we grow used to it, but it's my assertion that no normal and reasonable person will have the slightest idea this is happening to our images; they'll take the smooth scaling for granted. What we stand to gain, though, is nothing short of splendorous. When navigating between any of the sections, we'll now have smoothly scaling bitmaps. No popping, no pond ripples. A simple bit of anti-aliasing that goes a long way. Fantastic.

Thanks

That's it. The skin and bones of Sofake.com revealed. So, as I slip back into infamy on the underground rodeo circuit, I hope that you've taken something away from this. In closing, I would like to take a single sentence, this one here will do: to thank my wife Melanie and our dog Sally for their support, the level and consistency of support not necessarily reflected by the order in which they have been named.

About the Author
Sham Bhangal

Sham found himself working with friends Of ED after being mislead into thinking he was applying for a Flash web design position for an Internet-Startup (remember those?). This misunderstanding was soon forgotten, and this is the 14th book he has contributed to so far. He would like to point out that he has moved on from wearing black leather and looking sullen, but has run out of the cute 'Young Sham' pictures seen in the aforementioned other books.

Sham lives in Somerset, England, with his partner Karen.

Text Effects

About the Effect

Text is the primary method of conveying information over the web. However, there's much more to text than that: it is a major visual tool. Text is traditionally static, but as Flash is such a great animation tool, it would be criminal not to explore the world of animated text.

This chapter will demonstrate how creating great memorable text effects can easily be achieved in Flash. You soon see that the meaning of text is often not as important as the way it is actual displayed.

The world of text

Text is important because it is a primary method of effectively communicating certain kinds of information. Even in these days of sound, animation, 3D virtual worlds, and streaming video, people like to read.

Text has not been immune to the march of progress though. We no longer use boring old plain text, because we understand that there is much more that can be communicated with this medium. Just like the spoken word has an associated non-vocal level of communication that we call body language, written text also has additional non-textual communication channels other than the actual words themselves. The choice of line spacing, text styles (bold, italic, etc.), color, and so on, can add additional levels of emphasis, importance, or simply readability. But that's only the tip of the iceberg, because the overall graphic design and layout of your text can speak volumes...

Modern graphic design arguably took off in the post-1917 Soviet Union with the Constructivist and Modernist movements. In the 1980s, armed with computers and software, designers such as Neville Brody took inspiration from the original styles to create new typographical conventions.

Compare and contrast the Soviet-Modernist typographical style with typography used in modern magazines and books, and you'll soon begin to see how influential the style actually is, and how much we now take it for granted!

For our purposes, the important idea to grasp is the way in which text can be treated as a **graphic entity**. It can form part of the final graphics rather than just exist as something that is meant to be read, and can in many cases (such as logo design) be the *only* graphic in a design.

Text in motion

Macromedia Flash is different from traditional print based graphic design because we are playing with **Motion Graphics**. As well as the rules of graphic and logo design, we can also experiment with movement. Take a look at some previous Flash-texters:

Yugo Nakamura http://surface.yugop.com/

See also http://yugop.com/ver2/ for the archive Flash site seen here:

Another good example is this text effect by the**void** (www.thevoid.co.uk), which we'll take a look at later.

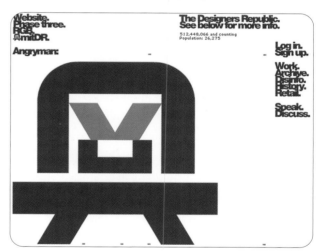

For a more extreme example of the use of text on the web, go to the Designers Republic at www.thedesignersrepublic.com, where the whole design is based around text or icons that seem to be built up from text. This is an interesting crossover (and discussion point) between a print-based design and what we would normally associate with Flash graphics.

As well as what has already been created in the Flash world, one of the richest sources of animated text is **cinema**. The opening titles of many popular films contain memorable text effects, and they are a good source of text effects to use in a program like Flash.

For example, one of the most memorable effects in recent movies is the 'text waterfall' from *The Matrix*. Another instantly recognizable effect is the scrolling opening text at the start of each episode of the *Star Wars* series. We'll recreate both of these effects in this chapter, and the images above are our versions.

Implementing text effects in Flash

We will be looking at a number of different ways to create text effects in Flash.

Tween based effects

Text effects are one of the easiest animations to set up if you are only using tween-based transitions. This is because the graphics are already there for you; all you have to do is select a font and prepare it for your tween. More compelling effects can be created if you mix your text animations with other effects to generate an overall mood. For example, the opening titles to David Fincher's film *Seven* combine distressed text, hard gritty graphics, and an appropriate soundtrack to create an overall dark, foreboding atmosphere.

Scripted text transitions

Sometimes you simply want to liven up a block of text by making it appear in a novel way. Everything from ticker tape or typewriter effects, to the perspective scroll seen at the beginning of *Star Wars* can be used to liven up text that may otherwise remain unread. Such transitions are widely used in banner adverts.

Stand alone text effects

There are occasions where the text effect itself is the star of the piece. Flash toys such as text mouse followers are created for their own sake. Although such effects are sometimes ridiculed as nothing more than Flash eye-candy, they have useful applications in areas such as preloaders, where you want to maintain the user's attention for 30 seconds while your main site loads up.

A point worth emphasizing is that the graphic components of text effects (the individual text characters that you will be animating) are very easy to create. This means that you can quickly set them up and concentrate on the mechanics of the underlying effect itself. This makes text-based animated effects a good starting point for many animations you have in mind, irrespective of whether the finished effect will involve text. Many animated effects will use text as placeholders for the real graphic elements, which you may not want to create until you have got the animation itself working.

Okay, let's get cracking! We will start gently with some general information on how Flash handles text, and then move quickly onto some typical effects themselves.

Flash and text

Flash handles fonts in three different ways and it's not always obvious which one you're forcing Flash to adopt. An appreciation of this issue is therefore crucial when creating text effects.

The following information is not directly associated with any of the text effects we will be looking at later in this chapter. However, you'll need this information to integrate them into your SWFs without adding massive font download times, or to avoid you trying to work out why your fonts aren't visible as they should be on certain machines.

The different ways of handling fonts is split into three groups: **System fonts**, **Device fonts,** and **Embedded fonts**.

System fonts

System fonts are taken from the user's machine (they are not included as part of the SWF download). There are three system fonts, called **_sans**, **_serif**, and **_typewriter**, corresponding to Times New Roman/Times (for PC/Mac systems), Arial/Helvetica, or Courier New/Courier. Flash doesn't treat system fonts in the same way as it treats vector shapes. In particular, it doesn't have access to the point and line information of each font shape, and cannot therefore rotate, resize, or mask the text. System fonts also don't appear with anti-aliased edges due to this same reason. The upside of this is that Flash can render them very quickly and, as mentioned, they don't increase the size of your SWF.

To use a system font you would do the following:

1. Using the Property inspector, select either _sans, _serif, or _typewriter in the Font drop-down menu:

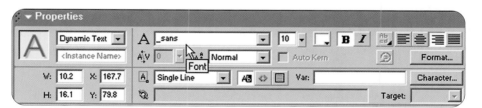

2. Still in the Property inspector, hit the Character... button to bring up the **Character Options** window. Select No Characters.

    Now, here's the rub. Because you cannot treat system fonts as graphics, some text effects will not work if they rely on this feature, so be careful when using system fonts.

Device fonts

Device fonts are just like system fonts, except that if the font you have selected is not available on a particular user's machine, Flash will default to _sans, _serif, or _typewriter. The process of selecting a device font is the same as that for system fonts, but you choose any font *except* _sans, _serif, or _typewriter. For example, if I use the left-hand, non-standard font shown below as a device font, there is a very good chance that most users will not have this font installed. Although the text will appear correctly on my development machine, the text will look as shown on the right for the vast majority who don't have my eclectic taste in fonts...

Embedded fonts

Embedded fonts are, as their name suggests, embedded into the final SWF. This has the disadvantage of generating a larger SWF file for the user to download, but has the advantage that the final SWF will look the same for *all* users. It also means that Flash can treat the text as any other vector graphic, because the point and line information for the characters is saved as part of the SWF.

To embed a font, you need to bring up the Character Options window as before, but this time select either All Characters or Only. If you select All Characters, Flash will embed the entire font. For some fonts, this can easily be anything up to an additional 40-50k per font, so don't select this unless you're actually using the entire font!

If you select Only, you can select only part of the font for embedding, and this is recommended because it limits the font download to just the characters you actually need. For example, if you were building a LCD display for a simple Flash calculator, you would only need to embed the number characters, minus and decimal point symbols (so that you can show floating point and negative numbers), and the letters to write the word 'error'.

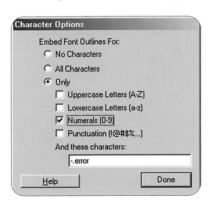

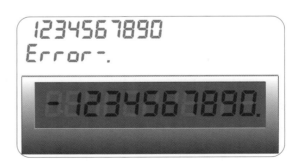

Okay, on with the effects...

Timeline effects

Fonts are essentially nothing more than filled shapes with no outline strokes, and this makes them very easy to animate. In many cases, you don't even have to use ActionScript, and can stick with nothing more complex than a few tweens, and perhaps some masking. The following examples illustrate a number of possibilities for quick no-brainer text effects.

Perspective scroll

This effect shows that motion tweens are about more than just animating motion. As well as movement, you can also add scaling and color/transparency changes, and for this effect we'll be using three out of the four (motion, color change, scaling) in a single effect.

The titles to the *Star Wars* films include a perspective scroll effect. The images below are the same effect, but this time created as a very simple single Flash tween, plus some easy experimentation with the new Flash MX distort option in the Free Transform tool.

To see how we built this animation, have a look at `text01.fla`, and our version of the final SWF `starwars.swf`.

The timeline consists of three layers:

- An `actions` layer. Although this layer contains a script, it is there simply to draw our star field; it has little to do with our text effect.

- A `text` layer, which contains the perspective text tween, extending from frame 1 to 180.

- A guide layer called `guide` that contains some construction lines used in creating our effect.

Here's how it was put together, starting from scratch.

1. Create a new movie with the frame rate and stage size at the normal defaults (12 fps, 550x400 pixels – CTRL+J will open the Document Properties). Change the background color to black and add two new layers (Insert>Layer), arranging them as in

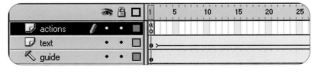

the above image. (Change the bottom layer to a guide layer from the Layer Properties dialog, which is opened from Modify>Layer..., or by choosing Guide from the drop-down menu that appears when you right-click on a layer name.)

2. In the `guide` layer, add a couple of perspective lines with the Line tool (N) as shown here, starting from the two lower corner points and meeting at the top center of the stage.

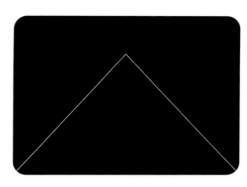

3. Next, create your text within a static text field on frame 1 of `text` layer, placing it around the middle of the pyramid formed by the perspective lines. Use a system font (make sure you don't use embedded fonts, which should be the default in any case). Because the perspective distortion we will be creating may make some thinner text fonts difficult to read, you are advised to go for a bold font (we used Arial Black, a thick bold version of Arial).

4. We will be breaking this text apart in a moment, so it would be a good idea to keep a version of this text in a safe place if we need to edit the text later. Select the text field, copy it using CTRL+C, and place the copy at the top left-hand corner of the `guide` layer.

    This is what you should see so far:

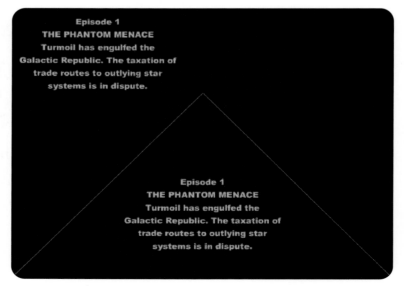

5. Lock the guide layer, and select the text field between the perspective lines. Move the text so that both the top corners of the field touch the perspective lines (in the next few diagrams we've removed the text at the top left to keep things simple):

6. With the text still selected, hit CTRL+B once to break it into individual letters, and then again to break it into vector shapes. Now select the **Free Transform** tool (Q) from the toolbar. You'll see a bounding box appear. The two top corner points may no longer be touching the perspective lines, so use the arrow keys to nudge the text up slightly until they are.

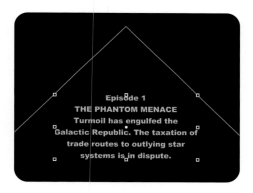

7. Now, here's the important bit. In the Options part of the toolbar, select the **Distort modifier**. Hold down the SHIFT key, and select either of the two bottom corner points of the text bounding box. Drag it onto the corresponding perspective line. The opposite corner will also move towards its perspective line, as long as the SHIFT key is pressed down.

When you release the mouse, you'll end up with the perspective-distorted text shown above.

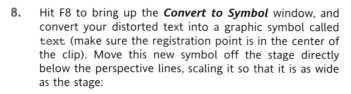

8. Hit F8 to bring up the **Convert to Symbol** window, and convert your distorted text into a graphic symbol called text (make sure the registration point is in the center of the clip). Move this new symbol off the stage directly below the perspective lines, scaling it so that it is as wide as the stage:

9. Extend the text and guide layers to frame 180 (F5), and add a keyframe at frame 180 on the text layer (F6). This will be the target frame for our tween. In this new keyframe, move the text field to the tip of the pyramid, and change both its height and width to 10 pixels. This will make the text get smaller as it scrolls up, getting smaller at the same rate as our two perspective lines get closer.

10. Finally, set the Brightness to -50% via the Color drop-down menu in the Property inspector. This will make the text fade as it moves towards our vanishing point.

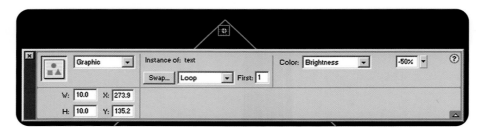

11. All we have to do now is add the tween. Select frame 1 of the text layer and, using the Property inspector, select Motion from the Tween drop-down menu. We want the text to slow down as it moves away, so set the Ease value to 75:

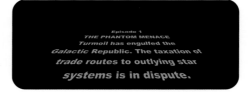

    Done! Test the movie (CTRL+ENTER) to see your effect.

    If you want to add more blocks of text, simply add a new text layer that will cause the new block of text to start moving as soon as the first one is fully on the stage. See text01b.fla for an example of this.

first text block
second text block

It is preferable to do this rather than make one large block of text because:

- the final movie will stream better.

- you force Flash to move fewer graphics at any one time, thereby making the animation faster.

As long as you are happy with the fact that you cannot change your text dynamically, or that the text effect cannot react too much in the way of user interaction (other than start and stop on demand), motion tween effects are easy to implement.

Sometimes, a tween-based text example requires nothing more than experimentation and a lot of simple animations. Have a look at `passages.fla` in the download files for a text-based intro that is nothing more than a few tweens with color and position transitions...

figure 1a
the wonder of existence

Shape tweening text

Although shape tweening of text is possible, and used widely by beginners for text transitions, it is actually very difficult to do well. This shape tween, which changes from a square to the letter 'e', shows how most shape tweens end up:

There are a few problems here.

Firstly, shape tweening doesn't like enclosed areas such as the eye of the 'e' here. This confuses the tween at the start, and it makes the square disappear at frame 2, creating a large initial transition.

Secondly, many fonts (especially free public domain fonts) may look cool, but are created without well-spaced curve points. You'll usually find lots of odd points that don't really need to be there. This occurs because the application usually used to create such fonts (Macromedia Fontographer) has a cool feature that allows you to mix two fonts to get a third. This is a fast way to get a font like the one you are aiming for (if you want to do it quickly or cheaply), but doesn't usually result in a pretty distribution of points around the character outline.

Looking at our 'e' (break a character apart and select the shape outline with the Sub-selection tool to get the same picture), we see that there are lots of bunched-up points at the two corners of the 'e' and the right-most outer corner point:

This has the unfortunate effect of giving these three corner points more weighting in the tween than they should have, and this throws the tween.

You *can* fix some of these problems by using shape hints, but you usually still end up with a mess of a tween that only starts to look like the target shape a few frames from the end (or means hours of painstaking work getting the tween right). Unfortunately, there aren't many ways around this and we wouldn't recommend using shape tweens with most text unless you are happy with the 'messy jumble that doesn't look like anything for ages' type of tween shown above.

However, here are a few tips for the brave who want to go up against us and give it a go:

- Don't use serif fonts (such as Times).

- Use simple fonts with few curves, and check that the font is well built with no bunching of points before using it.

- Don't use fonts that include enclosed spaces (which is a pretty big constraint!).

- Don't use characters that are not one continuous shape, such as i and j, unless the start of the tween is also two shapes (otherwise this throws the tween almost as much as the enclosed space problem noted above).

Timeline masking

One of the simplest masking tricks is emulating handwritten text, which we'll learn how to do in a moment. Before we do so, take a look at text02b.swf to see the effect in action.

Notice here how the finished effect is in a context; the opening book animation makes the handwriting effect seem more realistic. This often occurs, and many effects only really start to look cool when they have supporting animated effects around them that add realism and/or a context.

The basic animation effect is actually very easy (this exercise is `text02a.fla` in the download files).

1. Start a new movie, rename the default layer `text`, and create some text on it. In the example file, we broke the text up to make sure that even those without the font installed will see it, but to keep the bandwidth down (and retain the ability to change the text by using a dynamic text field), you may consider using embedded fonts. Our font is called Edwardian Script Italic if you want to look for it on the web.

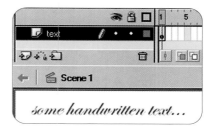

2. Lock the current layer. Add another layer above `text`, naming it `mask`. Create a black rectangle with the Rectangle tool (no stroke) that will completely cover the text, and place it to the left of the text as shown:

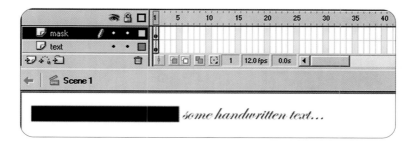

3. If you are using italic text (the effect seems to work better when you do), zoom into the front edge of the rectangle and slant it as shown, so that its taper is just less than the slant of the text:

some handwritten

4. Select the rectangle, and hit F8 to open the Convert to Symbol window. Convert the rectangle to a graphic symbol, and call it `line mask`.

103

5. Add a 60-frame motion tween to the mask layer, with the rectangle moving right to completely cover the text at frame 60. Extend the text layer to frame 60 (F5):

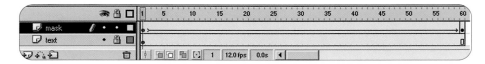

6. Finally, turn the mask layer into a mask layer by right-clicking on the layer title and selecting Mask from the pop-up menu that appears.

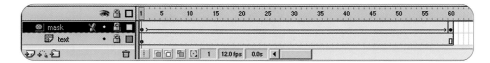

The layers will now change as shown above, and when you test the movie, you'll see the text appear gradually as if it were being handwritten. In the fuller final version (text02b.fla), you can see that this basic effect is taken further by making the mask an animated movie clip.

You can also use this effect to create a typewriter effect, although you would then choose a computer-like font and make the tween much quicker (to hide the fact that it is not really typing a character at a time).

There are better ways to create such effects via scripting though, and we'll illustrate this in the next section.

Simple scripted text effects

You can go a long way with text effects by just adding a little bit of scripting. You can add basic effects such as scrolling or a typewriter with very little code, and in a much more efficient way than tweening. This is due to the fact that these effects rely on a simple but repetitive set of instructions, something that code is very good at implementing.

Scroll and typewriter effects are a little underwhelming, unless you either use them in a novel way or embed them in a larger effect. Have a look at main.swf, which is part of my current site (you can see how the interface was built up in *Foundation ActionScript MX*, or simply just download the source FLA for the interface from the downloads page for this book from the friends of ED site). If you navigate to the home>futuremedia>contact page, you'll see a scrolling map:

Closer inspection reveals that it is actually some ASCII art; a world map built up from text. The map is simply a single large scrolling text field! Here's how the basic effect works.

See the example movie `text03a.fla`. We have two layers called `actions` and `textfield`. The `textfield` layer has a dynamic text field on it called `tape_txt`.

The code on the `actions` layer looks like this:

```
function tickerTape(chars) {
    displaytext = chars;
    displayLength = chars.length;
    this.onEnterFrame = tickerControl;
}
function tickerControl() {
    displayText = displayText.substr(1, displayLength-1)+displayText.sub
    ➥str(0, 1);
    tape_txt.text = displayText;
}
tickerTape("  hello world");
```

The effect will constantly scroll the text you pass to the `tickertape` function. This function stores the value of this text as `displayText`, and its length as `displayLength`. Finally, it sets up an `onEnterFrame` event as the function `tickerControl`, and it is this function that actually performs the animation. All it does is to use the `string.substr` (string substring) function to constantly take the first character in the current display and move it to the end. So, for example, if the text were 'cat dog', we would get the sequence:

```
cat dog
at dog c
t dog ca
dog cat
```

> *Tip: This effect works best with a proportional font, such as _typewriter.*

The map effect we looked at initially actually scrolls in the other direction, and text03b.fla shows how to alter the code to achieve this. All that changes is our substring splicing in the first line of tickercontrol, which is now:

```
displayText = displayText.substr(-1, 1)+displayText.substr(0, displayLength-
➥1);
```

The only difference between this effect and the final map is that we are doing this to a text field that contains many text strings. In fact, we are using an array of strings that are fed into a loop. You can see the ASCII map if you look at the definition of this array from a distance (or, as below, view the code with a small font):

```
// define map array...
map = new Array();
map[0] =
map[1] =
map[2] =
map[3] =
map[4] =
map[5] =
map[6] =
map[7] =
map[8] =
map[9] =
map[10] =
map[11] =
map[12] =
map[13] =
map[14] =
map[15] =
map[16] =
map[17] =
map[18] =
map[19] =
map[20] =
map[21] =
map[22] =
map[23] =
map[24] =
map[25] =
map[26] =
map[27] =
map[28] =
map[29] =
map[30] =
map[31] =
map[32] =
map[33] =
map[34] =
map[35] =
map[36] =
map[37] =
map[38] =
map[39] =
map[40] =
map[41] =
map[42] = "ISN'T THE WORLD WIDE WEB WONDERFUL? ...";
```

Time for another one...

If you also look at the **home>future work>print>public** page in main.swf, you'll see a typewriter effect at work. The barcode data and title will slowly appear, as shown below right, after you select an option form the drop-down menu.

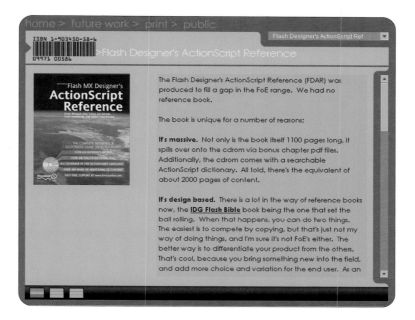

The effect works by using four separate typewriter effects running in four text fields, one each for the ISBN number, barcode (which is actually using a font that creates barcodes called *3 of 9 barcode*), barcode number, and book title. To see how the basic effect works, have a look at text04.fla.

We have the same timeline setup as the last example, (text03a.fla and text03b.fla). The textfield layer consists of a dynamic text field called typewriter_txt, and this is set to show multiline text.

The script on the actions layer looks like this:

```
function typewriter(chars) {
    this.onEnterFrame = writeText;
    this.count = 1;
    this.message = chars;
    this.maxLength = this.message.length;
}
function writeText() {
    this.typewriter_txt.text = this.message.substr(0, this.count);
    this.count++;
    if (this.count>this.maxlength) {
        this.onEnterFrame = undefined;
    }
}
typewriter("hello everybody!  \nHow are you?");
```

The \n is a control code that represents 'new line'.

The typewriter will type any string you set as the argument for the `typewriter` function. This does the following:

- Creates an `onEnterFrame` event handler, and equates it to the function `writeText`.

- Sets up a variable `count`, which is used to specify how many characters have been typed so far.

- Sets up a variable `message`, which is the text you want to type.

- Sets up a variable `maxLength`, which is the length of `message`.

The `writeText` function acts as the `onEnterFrame` event handler, and this will type one character per frame until all the characters are typed. It works like this:

- Line 1 sets the text to be displayed as what is already there as the first `count` characters. Since `count` goes up by 1 every frame (via line 2), this will look like an extra character has been added to the end of the text every frame.

- The `if` statement compares the current `count` value with the length of the text to be printed. If it is greater, then all of the text has now been printed, and the event handler undefines itself (which stops it from running again).

Notice that you cannot attach event handlers to text fields. Although the text field is a lot more like a movie clip in Flash MX, it is still not as flexible because of this, and the event handler is actually attached to the current timeline (in this case, it is the timeline pointed to be `this`, which is `_root`).

If you want to see the effect as per the *Futuremedia* web site, have a look at `typewriter.fla` in the Main folder of the download files. (Note that the movie will not render properly if you do not have the 3 of 9 barcode, OCR Extended, and Century Gothic fonts installed.) Also notice that because I have a number of different typewriters running at the same time (all of which will finish typing at different times), I have had to attach several dummy movie clips to the current timeline. I am hanging the event handlers on these for the four individual typewriter effects driving the four text fields.

```
// create four clips to hang the onEnterFrame scripts
// onto
this.createEmptyMovieClip("isbn", 1);
this.createEmptyMovieClip("barcode", 2);
this.createEmptyMovieClip("barcodeNumber", 3);
this.createEmptyMovieClip("book", 4);
```

Advanced scripted text effects

You can start to create much more advanced effects once you start to use the ability to create text fields dynamically, and combine this with event driven animation. These effects can be very eye-catching, making an otherwise boring block of text move on screen in a funky way that screams "read me!" When overused though, such effects may start to look a little too much like overkill, so go easy.

Here's a smorgasbord of effects to finish with...

The Matrix waterfall effect

Have a look at `waterfall.swf`. It's the Matrix text effect. To reproduce it, you first need to know how the actual movie effect is put together. It consists of **katakana** (a Japanese text) but with a twist; the characters are all displayed backwards. A few light colored characters (which we will call the **heads**) start at the top of the screen and drop down, leaving behind a trail of green characters. These trails disappear after a while.

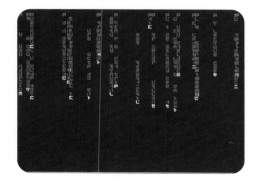

Okay, let's have a look at how we've done this in Flash.

To do the 'how the hell do we display katakana backwards?' is easy in Flash; simply display katakana in a text field that has been scaled by -100% in the x direction. You can find several katakana text fonts on the web (searching Google with 'katakana ttf' is a good start).

The 'how do we make the characters drop and leave trails' deal is quite a bit harder:

- We need to make the heads drop by property-based animation, controlled by an event attached to each head.

- As they drop, we need to duplicate a series of green copies of the heads, and these will form a trail. They need to have a different event script attached to them that makes them disappear after a short time.

The text fields used in the example file (`text05.fla`) are inside a movie clip called `mc.katakana` (it's the only symbol in the Library).

Why embed it in a movie clip? Well, remember that you can't attach event scripts to text fields, and this is something we will need to do per character in our waterfall. Although there are several ways round this problem, the easiest for the busy designer who doesn't want to get bogged down with ActionScript for its own sake is the way we have chosen.

Here's the script in its entirety, from frame 1 on the main timeline:

```
function dropStart() {
    if (Math.random()>0.9) {
        this._visible = true;
        this.onEnterFrame = drop;
    }
}
function drop() {
    // create a trail character at the current position
    trailName = "trail"+trail;
    trail++;
    attachMovie("katakana", trailName, trail);
    _root[trailName]._x = this._x;
    _root[trailName]._y = this._y;
    _root[trailName].kata_txt.text = this.kata_txt.text;
    _root[trailName].fader_color = new Color(_root[trailName]);
    _root[trailName].fader_color.setRGB(0x008000);
    _root[trailName].onEnterFrame = fadeTrail;
    //
    //Move the head character of the trail down by one
    //character
    this.kata_txt.text = String.fromCharCode(Math.floor(Math.ran
    ➥dom()*26)+97);
    this._y += 10;
    // If the head character has reached the bottom, restart
    //it at the top
    if (this._y>400) {
        this._x = Math.round(Math.random()*550);
        this._y = 0;
    }
}
function fadeTrail() {
    if (Math.random()>0.95) {
        this.removeMovieClip();
    }
    if (trail>1000) {
        trail = 100;
    }
}
/*
MAIN PROGRAM INITIALIZATION
*/
trail = 100;
for (i=0; i<30; i++) {
    newName = "char"+i;
    attachMovie("katakana", newName, i);
    _root[newName]._x = Math.round(Math.random()*550);
    _root[newName]._visible = false;
    _root[newName].onEnterFrame = dropStart;
}
```

This may look a bit complicated, but it makes a lot more sense if you follow it through while looking at what waterfall.swf does when you run it.

The first thing that happens is that the section marked MAIN PROGRAM INITIALIZATION runs. This copies 30 of our movie clips to the top line of the screen, and makes them disappear by setting their _visible property to false. It also attaches the dropStart function to each as an onEnterFrame script. If you could see everything on the screen at this point, you would see something like this, with all the text sitting at the top of the screen.

dropStart doesn't actually do much. It just keeps generating a random number between 0 and 1 every frame, until it sees one that is over 0.9. As soon as that happens, the if statement in dropStart does two things:

- It makes the text character visible by changing _visible to true.

- The onEnterFrame for the movie clip is changed to one that starts the animation process, drop.

This raw description does hide the purpose of dropStart somewhat, which is actually very simple: to make each trail start at a slightly different time from all the others. Think of all the characters sitting at the top rolling dice. If they hit a six, they can leave home and start on the board.

Anyway, once drop is called by the onEnterFrame, the head character starts to move down with the following lines:

```
//Move the head character of the trail down by one
//character
this.kata_txt.text = String.fromCharCode(Math.floor(Math.random()*26)+97);
this._y += 10;
// If the head character has reached the bottom, restart
//it at the top
if (this._y>400) {
    this._x = Math.round(Math.random()*550);
    this._y = 0;
}
```

This simply changes the character being displayed every frame, and also moves it down the screen. If it actually hits the bottom of the screen (_y>400), it is simply moved back up to the top of the screen and starts again.

The other thing that the head does is to create trails, the darker green characters. These are created via the following code chunk:

```
// create a trail character at the current position
trailName = "trail"+trail;
trail++;
attachMovie("katakana", trailName, trail);
_root[trailName]._x = this._x;
_root[trailName]._y = this._y;
_root[trailName].kata_txt.text = this.kata_txt.text;
_root[trailName].fader_color = new Color(_root[trailName]);
_root[trailName].fader_color.setRGB(0x008000);
_root[trailName].onEnterFrame = fadeTrail;
```

This simply attaches a new trail movie clip at the current position, and colors it a darker green than the head, using a `Color` object. The trails don't actually move, but they have an `onEnterFrame` event handler called `fadeTrail` attached to them. This is actually very similar to `dropStart`, in that it waits a random amount of time (based on how long it takes to generate a random number greater than 0.95) before making the trail disappear:

```
function fadeTrail() {
    if (Math.random()>0.95) {
        this.removeMovieClip();
    }
    if (trail>1000) {
        trail = 100;
    }
}
```

Although this function is called `fadeTrail`, it's obvious that the trail isn't really faded, it's just that pieces of it disappear over time, and this is the basis of the effect.

If the effect runs too slow for your machine, change the 30 in the for loop in the main program initialization (the code at the end of the listing).

If you've seen the film, you might be thinking 'wow, I thought the effect was more complicated than that!' Well, so did I until I actually looked at it carefully. The difference is that the film uses very small text and, from a distance, it looks as if the trail characters are fading rather than bits of the trail just simply disappearing. I was so disappointed with this revelation that I decided to change it so that the text really did fade, and you can see this in the file `waterfall2.swf`. You can also look at the code that creates this in `text05b.fla`.

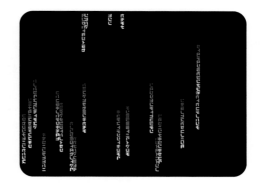

Transition effects

There are a few Flash text effect generation programs out there that remove all the stress of coding up these funky text effects. Some of you may have entered this chapter with this thought at the back of your mind: 'why bother when I can just use one of those?' Well, sure, you can do that, but there is something else to bear in mind. The code to make any of them is very similar. Once you've cracked the general method, you can change it to make any number of effects, simply by playing about with the code. The beauty of this, of course, is that:

- If you write your own code you can optimize it.

- If you write your own code, it's much harder for anyone else to replicate it and make it 'So Yesterday' before today has even finished.

- If you do it yourself, you can say that 'I did it myself'.

The killer is that you already know the general code to do these effects. We used it in the Matrix waterfall. Although you might have been thinking 'well, that's nice Sham, but does it have an application?' When we talked about the waterfall, the thing is that playing around with it gave us the code-based insight to crack other problems. We learnt:

- To split the text effect into a number of text fields.

- To control each text field via a separate event handler, using an intermediate 'starter' event handler if you want to stagger the animation starting points.

- If you want to stop an animation, simply delete the event handler by making it `undefined`.

Text without hassle

Okay. Let's go with that and try to replicate one of the most famous text effects of the Golden Age of Flash, the ContentWithoutClutter text transition from thevoid's site (www.thevoid.co.uk).

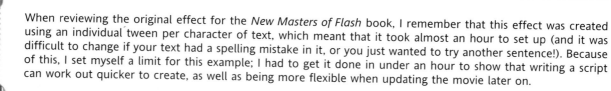

When reviewing the original effect for the *New Masters of Flash* book, I remember that this effect was created using an individual tween per character of text, which meant that it took almost an hour to set up (and it was difficult to change if your text had a spelling mistake in it, or you just wanted to try another sentence!). Because of this, I set myself a limit for this example; I had to get it done in under an hour to show that writing a script can work out quicker to create, as well as being more flexible when updating the movie later on.

Have a look at the finished ActionScript-based effect voidEffect.swf.

Let's look at how the effect is constructed. Open up the source file text06.fla and open the Actions panel for frame 1 of the main timeline. The first job is placing the movie clips on the stage. This is done via the transition function:

```
function transition(chars, startX, startY) {
    // initialize the text format object
    mFormat = new TextFormat();
    mFormat.font = "Arial Black";
    mFormat.size = "32";
    // Assign the initial value of startX to a
    // new variable
    startText = startX;
    // Create a text field per character
    for (i=0; i<chars.length; i++) {
        // create an empty clip
        name = "char"+i;
        this.attachMovie("character", name, depthCount);
        // put it at the appropriate place
        this[name]._x = startX+startText;
        this[name]._y = startY;
        // write the character into the clip text field
        this[name].field.text = chars.substr(i, 1);
        // get this text's width and update the spacing
        mSize = mFormat.getTextExtent(this[name].field.text);
        startX += mSize.width;
        // update depth
        depthCount++;
        // set alpha to zero and resize in preparation
        // for the effect, and then add the event handler
        // to trigger the start of the animation
        this[name]._alpha = 0;
        this[name]._xscale = this[name]._yscale=1000;
        this[name].timing = (startX-startText)/10;
        this[name].onEnterFrame = starter;
    }
}
```

A subtle point to note here is that the text font used (Arial Black) is non-proportional. If I tried to space the characters using fixed character spacing, I would end up with something like this:

The i and l are much narrower than the w, and this causes problems. Instead, we have to space the text fields depending on what character we are displaying in it. The thing that comes to our rescue is the `TextFormat` object. This has a method called `getTextExtent()` that tells us how big the text field has to be in order to fully display a given text string. We can use this to give us our variable spacing depending on whether we are displaying an i or w, or any other character. This is why I have to define a `TextFormat` object at the beginning of the function, even though the text fields themselves have already been set up to display 32 point Arial Black text manually.

At the end of this `transition` function, the text scales up to 1000% and the _alpha property of all the text is set to 0%, making all the text invisible. If you could see it, the text would look like this at the end of the `transition` function:

What we have to do is make each of these oversized but invisible characters scale back to 100%, and get back to 100% _alpha. We also want the transition to be staggered, depending on the how far along the character is within the text, with the left-most character starting its transition first.

This is what the `starter` function does. It looks at the distance of the current character from the beginning of the sentence, and waits a short period before setting off the animation script (the `animate` function). This gives us the cool ripple effect in the final piece, where the transition moves down the text.

```
function starter() {
    // Stagger the start of the effect depending
    // on the position of this character in the text
    this.timing--;
    if (this.timing<0) {
        this.onEnterFrame = animate;
    }
}
```

Finally, the actual animation is handled by `animate`, which comes above the above function. This has to increase the _alpha from 0 to 100%, while at the same time decreasing the scale from 1000% to 100%. So, we have to go from 0 to 100 _alpha at the same time as moving down by 900 in scale. To keep things simple (and because of the fact that I had just exceeded my one hour limit when I stated writing this function) I increased the _alpha by 10 at the same time as decreasing the scale by 90 per frame. This means that _alpha, _xscale, and _yscale will get to their respective target points at the same frame, so I only have to check for any one of them.

```
function animate() {
    // Scale and fade in until the text is
    //back to its original alpha
    this._xscale -= 90;
    this._yscale -= 90;
    this._alpha += 10;
    if (this._alpha>90) {
        this.onEnterFrame = undefined;
    }
}
```

Therefore, the function only checks for _alpha being greater than 90 before it stops the animation for this character, by making the onEnterFrame undefined.

Finally, we simply call the transition function with our text string and the position we want it to start at. We also have to set up a variable that handles depth (the movie clips that make up our text start at a depth of 100).

```
depthCount = 100;
transition("text effects without hassle", 10, 200);
```

Looking at the code, you'll see that the function structure is *very* similar to the matrix effect, yet the two effects look completely different and actually do two completely different things. The core code for many advanced text effects is very similar in structure, and knowing this fact makes it easy for you to create your own. What are you waiting for?

Oh, and I was ten minutes out for my self-imposed one hour limit. Never mind...

No-one can hear you scream

As always, there is a reason why I showed you this last effect. There is a very important bit of code here – the ability to take a text string and:

- separate the string into individual characters.

- place each character into a separate text field, with each text field inside its own movie clip 'wrapper', allowing us to add event driven code to each one.

- space the text fields out so that they stick to the original character spacing (or kerning) of the font.

We can use this attribute to change the effect, using our core code engine. For example, we could combine the masked text effect with our core code so that the masking occurs on each individual character:

Each character appears to be behind its own shutter. Have a look at text6b.fla, where you'll see that each of the mc.character movie clips now has its own timeline-based mask added. The final effect looks almost as if each character is behind a slat, and the effect was used on a certain scary sci-fi movie some time ago...

Notice that we can add a timeline here, because I have not gone down the route of creating the movie clip and embedding text fields via createEmptyMovieClip() *and* createTextField(). *Not only does my method make life easier, and allows us to stick to the effect rather than trying to be clever with the code, it also gives me a timeline to add tweens to during author time, something that cannot happen with movie clips created during runtime.*

Interactive effects

Flash is nothing if not interactive, given that its main purpose is to build mouse-controlled web site interfaces and associated content. The step from timeline-based to ActionScript-based animations may have been a big step, but the step from dynamic to interactive effects is actually a very small one.

In the previous section, we created animations that:

- set up an event-driven script (the onEnterFrame) that animates our characters until they reach a target position (or more correctly, a *target state*, because as well as position, we can also control other properties such as size and transparency, as we did with the ContentWithoutClutter effect).

- when the target state is reached, stop animating.

The simplest interactive effects do exactly the same thing, except for two things. Firstly, the target state is based on something the user is controlling and, in many cases, this is nothing more complicated than the mouse position. Secondly, the animation is never stopped.

One of the most well-known Flash interactive text effects is the 'text ribbon' effect. This is where letters follow the mouse position as if they were printed on a ribbon that is attached to the mouse cursor. Have a look at ribbon.swf for the final effect and text07.fla for the source code.

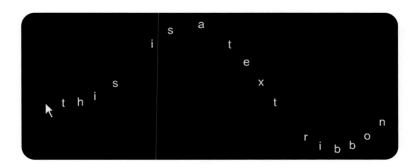

The way this works is actually very easy:

- The first character follows the mouse.

- The second character follows the first character.

- The third character follows the second character.

In essence, each character is following the character preceding it in the sentence, with the first character following the mouse.

This code listing creates the 'one text field embedded in a movie clip' for all characters, which is very similar to the effects we've already looked at. The only thing it does differently is that in the `transition` function, it assigns a different `onEnterFrame` depending on whether the current character is the first letter (i=0) or not:

```
if (i == 0) {
    this[name].onEnterFrame = follower;
} else {
    this[name].onEnterFrame = mover;
    this[name].before = "char"+(i-1);
}
```

If it is the first character, we use the `follower` event script, and this simply follows the mouse:

```
function follower() {
    this._x = _xmouse+20;
    this._y = _ymouse;
}
```

> Tip: You could also just make the first character follow the mouse via `startDrag()`, but this means that it may become hidden. The `follower` function moves the character 20 pixels to the right to make sure this doesn't happen.

If it is not the first character, the event script will use the `mover` function as the animation script. It also sets a variable called `before` for every character, which identifies the character previous to this one (so, for example, `char9` would have `char8` as its `before`).

`mover` is actually a simple inertia effect. It tries to get to the position of the `before` character with a slight bit of inertia to add some subtlety to the effect (set `inertia` to 1 to see it without any inertia).

```
function mover() {
    this.targetX = _root[this.before]._x;
    this.targetY = _root[this.before]._y;
    this._x -= -10+(this._x-this.targetX)/inertia;
    this._y -= (this._y-this.targetY)/inertia;
}
```

This effect is a little overdone and has been ridiculed because of it in some quarters. Surely we can find a use for it so that it becomes a little more than just eye candy? Well...

You could also use it as a Flashy alternative to help text. By changing the text on certain user events (usually rollovers), you can make the ribbon text change contextually. This could finally make useful, as well as pretty, text.

The second file text07b.fla shows this. The effect changes as soon as you click the mouse. All this does is delete all existing text if it has been used before to create a ribbon (i is not undefined). This code occurs at the top of the transition function:

```
if (i != undefined) {
    for (j=0; j<i; j++) {
        _root["char"+j].removeMovieClip();
        }
    }
```

Text effects get a little bit of stick for being just so much eye candy, but as we have seen, it's not the effect but how you use it that makes the difference!

About the Author
Adam Phillips

I was born in farming country in New South Wales, Australia, where I stayed for far too long. It wasn't until the age of 22 that I ran off to the city to join Disney. Here, I concentrated my efforts in the Effects Animation department, where I clawed my way up then decided to step down to spend some time with my new friend Flash 5. Still working for Disney, I live in Sydney with my wife-to-be Jeanette, and our cat Lucy. Here, I use all my free time to maintain *www.oohbitey.com*, animate, draw, to write as much as possible, and play lots of online games.

I'd like to thank a number of people who've helped and encouraged me on my way through Flash.

First, my favorite person ever: Jeanette, for liking me a lot, and for bringing me coffee and chocolate while I work.

The Phillips': mum and dad; for the stories and the years at Brewarra; my brother Brett for competitive hosting prices; my sister Juanita for being sistery; and my daughter Kaela for character inspiration.

My good friends and workmates, who either got me into Flash or helped me out in lots of ways: Bernard Derriman, Kevin Peaty, Stephen Deane, Alexs Stadermann, and Dan Forster.

My Internet friends for the encouragement and feedback: Croc, MishY, Cojack, Xaphan, Phantom, .m0rt, Fusion, and Dan Britton at friends of ED.

Animation: hitchHiker
Adam Phillips

About the effect

When Flash was first released, it was seen primarily as an animation tool, and while the uses of Flash have advanced with every release, animation is still very much at the core. That said, creating a movie style animation is still an art, and there's much more to it that just knowing your way around the Flash interface.

In this chapter, you'll see the creation of an animation progress from the conception through to the post-production, covering the core animation techniques along the way. As the chapter progresses, you'll get the chance to see how the sequel to the successful *hitchHiker* animation was built. Take a look at the original movie at www.chluaid.com/animation.shtml. By the end of this chapter, the ability to make such a movie yourself will be in reach.

In this chapter, I'll be walking you through the steps of making an animated movie with Flash MX. We'll be looking at my latest movie *hitchHiker: part two*, and I'll share my processes and thinking as I plan, design, animate, and polish the movie from start to finish. I'm actually creating *hitchHiker: part two* from scratch as we go along – with me learning along the way, as well as you! You'll have the opportunity to put the skills you learn into practice through a number of parallel projects that cover the main themes and principles of animation.

The download files for this chapter contain a number of FLA files from *hitchHiker*, each with the prefix `hh2_`, e.g. `hh2_Scene18.fla`, which illustrate some scenes, effects, and techniques used in the movie. The files for the project you'll work through all have the prefix `project_`, e.g. `project_Leica.fla`. Miscellaneous exercises and files will not have a prefix, e.g. `backgrounds.swf`.

By the end of this chapter, you'll be well on the way to making your own animated stories, from conception to the post-production stage.

Animation tools: personal choice

You'll see a lot of my artwork in this chapter and I thought it important to let you know how I get my drawings into Flash.

I don't use my scanner at all, and I hardly ever use the Pencil or Line tools in Flash. Every piece of artwork you see in my movies and on the following pages, have been drawn directly into Flash with a graphics tablet. I use a Wacom Intuos 9x12 and sketch everything directly onto the stage with the Brush tool.

I use Flash for *any* illustration work I'm asked to do, and occasionally use Electric Rain's Swift 3D for camera moves, 3D animating props (such as cars), and rough guides for animating backgrounds.

Pre-production

In this first section, we'll look at the initial planning stages of a Flash animation: the inspiration behind a movie and the process of outlining your movie in a **storyboard** form.

hitchHiker inspiration

As a kid, I heard a lot of entertaining stories from my father's side of the family, my dad and grandmother in particular. My mother once told me that she was never scared of anything until she met the Phillips'. From an early age, I was riveted by scary stories of mad people in the country, by tales of burglars, murderers, and ghosts. A lot of those tales shook me, giving me the willies at night, but what I felt then is what I want to communicate to other people by retelling the stories.

When I laid eyes on Flash for the very first time, it was the trial of version 5 and immediately I knew what I wanted to do with it. Around a week into the trial, I bought the program plus a 9x12 graphics tablet. For me, Flash is the ultimate affordable medium for storytelling and the stories I grew up with are an endless source of inspiration. The *hitchHiker* story is one of those and I'm retelling it the way I heard it from my father.

I learned a lot while working on *hitchHiker: part one*: about animation, color, movie-making in Flash, about effects and visual storytelling. These lessons will be put into action as I create *hitchHiker: part two*.

Storytelling

For any storyteller, it's a fact that you'll hold the audience's attention if you make it interesting. The best looking character in the world falls just as hard as the rest if he's boring, or not supported by a story that people want to hear.

I don't mean to say that you need to be a writer to tell an interesting story. It's possible to start with just an idea, or basic plot, and build more of a story around that. I believe that this core idea or plotline is the shiny bit. Take a joke, for example: it's entirely made up of that shiny bit. When you hear a joke, a history behind it or character development isn't always necessary. If you're stuck for ideas, you might try animating your favorite joke. Almost any joke can be made into a short movie; just put some characters into an environment and have them enact the joke.

Speaking of which, the joke is going to be our animation project as we go along in this chapter. I'm going to supply you with a short story (the joke), a storyboard, and some sound files, and you can follow me throughout the chapter in turning it into a complete animated movie.

Project 1: Story

OK, you're going to hear the outcome of the story; I'm about to spoil it for you. The story for our animated project goes like this:

At 3 am a man is woken by a gentle, but persistent, knocking on his front door. He grumbles as he moves along the hallway, annoyed at being woken at this time of night. He opens the door and frowns at a young man who is stamping in the cold and breathing steam on his hands to try and warm up. 'Yes? What is it?'

The young guy replies in a frustrated voice, 'Hey mate, I know what time it is, and I'm really sorry to wake ya, but I've been stopped just around the corner for hours, and I can't get it started again, I've tried everything. I just need someone to come and give us a push to get me started. Could *you* to come over and give me a push?'

Angry, the owner of the door slams it shut without a word and goes back to bed. The young man, dismayed, wanders off into the darkness quietly.

The first man is back in his warm bed and, although tired, suddenly feels sorry for the young guy out in the cold. He lies there for a few minutes but guilt gets the better of him. He gets up, puts on some boots and a jacket, and goes outside. It's a foggy night and he can't see very far, so he calls out, 'Oy! Mate, you still there?'

'Yeah!' comes the excited reply through the fog, 'over here, on the swing!'

Get it? Push, swing...! The part where he says 'on the swing!' won't be needed because we're telling the story with visuals. We can cut out that line of dialog altogether and just have him say '...over here!', after which we pan across to see the young man on a swing.

Keep these visuals in mind and start thinking of how you'd cut it into scenes. As we go through this chapter, I'll show you step by step how to turn this story into an animated movie.

Storyboard

Before we get into the details, this list of storyboard terminology should help:

Board :	Storyboard
Panels :	Storyboard frames
Hard copy :	A real storyboard, on paper
Leica :	A moving storyboard, not on paper
Scratch-track :	A temporary soundtrack

I've had the basic gist for the *hitchHiker* plot in my head for a long time, but before I even opened Flash, I grabbed a blank piece of paper and drew four large squares on it with nothing in them. I photocopied that piece around 20 times and made a little booklet. This was my hard copy storyboard full of fresh, blank panels, and it was here that I planned the movie, scene by scene.

You could try another format to suit your own purposes. This A5 ring-bound system allows you to insert, delete, and shuffle panels, pages or entire sequences as you work through a project, while keeping the whole thing tidy. This allows ease of storyboard editing and updating:

In the film industry, a storyboard is usually where the camera shots and frame composition are worked out, and scene timing and movie flow are established. For me, it's a writing aid too. Much of what you see in *hitchHiker: part one* was written as I boarded, especially the night sequence at the beginning with the car and taillight. Also, when I decided to split the movie into two parts, it was here that I made the changes, figured the flow, and decided a suspense factor would be nice.

I can't stress enough how helpful it is to have a board to follow as you work. However, depending on your project, completing a board can be a very daunting task. Trust me though; once you've done it you'll be grateful when you're a third of the way through and need guidance or inspiration. It doesn't need to be full of lovely, precious drawings, just something raw and rough to jog your memory when you need it for reference.

The good thing about a storyboard hard copy is that it can be taken anywhere, and while working on hitchHiker: part one I often came up with ideas and new scenes on the train to or from work each day. I'd recommend a hard copy for any movie, but especially for long, complicated movies or scenes.

Leica

Since *hitchHiker: part one*, I've completed a few other short movies, and I've also worked on some other projects where deadline pressures made the whole *hard copy* storyboard process a little unrealistic. For projects like that (and for *hitchHiker: part two*), I simply boarded my movie directly into Flash.

In the film industry, a moving board is called the **animatic**. In the animation industry today, the moving board is still called the **leica reel**, which is a term from the old days of traditional animation where the storyboard was shot onto a reel of film, with a scratch-track slotted in. Nowadays, the name is shortened to **leica**, probably more for convenience than the fact that it's no longer shot onto a reel of film. For my *hitchHiker* storyboard, I've made a leica by sketching roughly into blank scenes, and you can find half of it in the download files as hh2_Leica.swf (I've left the second half out, because I don't want to spill the plot before anyone's seen it.)

For short movies, storyboarding directly into Flash streamlines things greatly, not only cutting out the storyboard booklet stage, but also allowing me to get the timing right for each scene.

It's worth noting here, that storyboarding directly into Flash is only feasible for me with my graphics tablet where I have precise control of the cursor. Storyboarding (or drawing any other artwork) with the mouse is very difficult. For example, try writing your name with the mouse.

I highly recommend using a graphics tablet if you need the same level of control over the cursor as a real pencil or brush. If you don't have a graphics tablet, and all your artwork is scanned and imported into Flash, then I recommend that you make a hard copy storyboard, which may then be scanned and imported into scenes, as necessary.

Some Flash animators I know have a tendency to add a scratch-track at the leica stage, and get the dialog or music sync happening. Personally, aside from dialog, I put in all my music and sound effects after the movie is done. It's a personal preference, but if I needed a reason it would be this: if I can make my movie enjoyable without sound or even dialog, then it's bound to be a winner. You'll find that smart sound instantly sends the appeal of a good story through the roof. I often test my movies on a small audience of honest friends before I've added any music or sound effects.

Project 2: Storyboard

As promised, I've provided the leica for our project movie, and it's called project_Leica.fla. However, you may like to board the movie yourself, putting into practice all that we're going to talk about. If that's the way you want to do things, excellent. I suggest you take a quick look through the provided leica though, just to get a feel for what we're about to do.

Storyboarding in Flash

1. Open up a new movie (CTRL+N) and add a whole bunch of blank scenes (Insert>Scene). I've added 14 of them, which is more than enough for our short piece. When you've done that, you can navigate through your scenes by using the PAGE DOWN key to go to the next scene, or the PAGE UP key to go to the previous one. The HOME and END keys take you to the beginning or end of your movie, respectively.

2. Navigate to your first scene by pressing your HOME key, then hold down F5 to add as many frames as you think will be required for your opening shot. You can do this after you've sketched the scene if you like, to help you decide on the scene length.

   Now, we'll probably need a preloader in the first scene, and then titles and credits in the second. The following step is optional but I'm doing it simply to keep the scene numbers starting at Scene 1, onwards.

3. Go into your **Scene** panel by pressing SHIFT+F2, and drag the *last two scenes* to the top of the list.

4. Double-click on the name of the first scene. Change it to `preloader` and then name your second scene `title`.

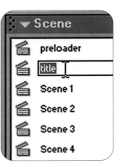

Getting started on the leica

Think of how the movie might start and what the first thing the viewer should see can be.

The original story tells us that a man is woken by knock on the door at 3 am, so the opening shot could simply show a guy asleep in a bed and, ideally, have a bright digital display in the background displaying the time. Another nice establishing shot could be the night sky and a silhouette of the house, *after* which we can show the man in his bed.

We can incorporate that establishing shot into our `title` scene. So, let's go into that scene, sketch in the silhouette and, using the Text tool with a boring font, slap in a title. We'll work on the look of the title and credits later in the section on **post-production**. Call the movie whatever you like, but don't give the punch line away in the title, e.g. *The Swing*.

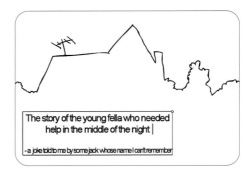

Scene 1: Digital clock

I've only called it `Digital clock` to avoid having to call it the 'bedroom scene'! In my version, this will be a very long scene because we need to give the audience some time to look at the scene before things start happening. After a while, we hear the knocking on the door, the guy wakes up and then he gets out of bed grumbling.

You might like to show the whole bedroom, but I'm keeping mine as simple as I can, so this will be a close shot, framing the clock and the guy's sleeping face. Any background will be black to avoid having to draw too much detail, but there will be the digital display showing up nice and bright. We want this one scene to tell the audience quite a lot.

There's not much to the drawings in my leica. You need little more than just a few rough lines to hint at composition and certain actions.

Scene 2: The hallway

Here, we see the grumbling man staggering up the hallway towards the door. Again, try to think about how we can cut down on the amount of drawing we need to do. Below I've sketched the rough layout of the whole hallway, but that's just for construction purposes, as I'm going for an entirely black background in this one with just a few slivers of light.

To remind me of the mood I want to portray in this shot, I've indicated some light and shadow here. Notice again, the very rough way in which I'm sketching these frames. This leica is the *rough* version, and you shouldn't be spending much time on any of it.

Scene 3: Opening the door

I'm showing this shot from outside the door. We'll see the door open, and while the young fella delivers his lines, we'll spend the entire time watching the reaction of the first man. He then slams the door, after which the young guy leaves the scene. This will save me having to animate the young guy's dialog at all, or even draw his face! How lazy am I?

127

Scene 4: Dismayed young fella

Aw, the poor guy. We'll watch him walk off into the foggy darkness now. This scene won't show much in the background, being foggy and dark, so we'll just roughly draw in the character and a streetlamp.

Scene 5: Back in bed

Here, we can use everything again from Scene 1, except you might like to change the time on the clock. Just go into your Scene panel (SHIFT+F2) select Scene 1 (or whatever you've called it) and click on the Duplicate Scene icon.

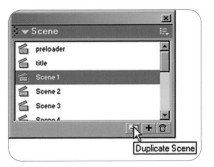

Your scene list will now have a copy of that scene, which you can drag into position just after Scene 4.

Once you have the copy in the correct position, double-click on the scene name and rename it `Back in Bed`. Now you can start changing the copied scene to suit the story. All the animation we used in Scene 1 can be re-used here, and the only things you'll have to change are the time on the clock, and maybe a guilty expression on his face or, in my case, a guilty eye. Even the animation where he gets out of bed can stay as it is.

I'll leave it up to you to rough out the remaining scenes, but with a bit of planning you'll find that all of your existing scenes or parts in the leica from here on in can be re-used.

Please be aware that if time and file size are your enemies, re-using animations is practical, but can cheapen your movie if you do it too much, or without planning. Check out hitchHiker: part two on my site and, if you look hard enough, you'll see where I've re-used various elements. I've done it a lot, but I've planned it very carefully, so it's not going to be obvious. Basically, re-use as much as you can get away with. It's not lazy, it's efficient and sensible. I'm encouraging re-uses in this small movie for the sake of workload, file size and sanity, but I'll leave it up to you to decide how much material you re-use in your own movie.

When all your rough scenes are done, you might like to start playing with the length and timing of each scene. You can test the movie as you go, watching how it flows and adjusting it as necessary. If you need some guidance, just have a look at `project_Leica.fla`.

Character, prop and set design

My advice here is simple: know your limits. If you're doing this for a client, and you have a team and/or a deadline, it's important to somehow limit the workload. If you're working on a personal project, then of course you set your own limits and deadlines, so go nuts if you're prepared to see it through.

This convoluted character *looks* entertaining, but with all this detail, he'd be a nightmare to animate.

Initially, I was regretting the design of the big scary guy in *hitchHiker*, but I've now found ways of limiting him. You can see in this screenshot how I've broken his face up into its separate layers.

For any substantial movie, it's essential that you design everything *before* you start work on the animation. You can tell what's happened when you see half a movie or comic book that looks awesome, only to see the point where the artist got bored or impatient and started to simplify everything (or worse, never finished!). With a little planning, they could save themselves a lot of grief by starting with a simplified design in the first place!

Limiting the character design

Quick and simple doesn't necessarily mean cheap and nasty. Decide on the look of your character first, and then work on the design. It's during this stage of the process that you need to find ways of limiting the workload. Often this can be as simple as cutting back on unnecessary character detail, such as a checked shirt or a convoluted logo on a jacket.

At other times, and in some cases *at the same time*, the animation itself can be limited. Indeed, limited animation is appealing in its snappiness and simplicity. A bit of planning at the storyboard stage and a few clever drawings in the Flash Library can save a lot of pencil mileage without lowering the quality. You'll find more on **limited animation** in the Character animation section a little later.

This character is fun to draw and simple to animate. This picture almost seems to tell a story by itself, and the design will lend itself really well to limited animation. Actually, I came up with this character just now and I really like him. You might see him on my site one day.

In the end, if your story, design, and animation come together well, your audience won't care whether the shirt is checked, plain, or Hawaiian.

Character design is discussed in detail in the section headed **Character animation**.

Limiting the background design

All this talk of limitations and cutting down your workload applies to props and backgrounds too. Sure, it's going to look great with lots of depth and detail, but how much is the audience really going to notice? How much is that fine detail going to affect playback on the viewer's machine?

Extra detail or movement in the wrong spot not only means more work, but also can be distracting and steal the scene. The audience should be looking where you want them to look, so it's up to you to direct their eyes. You might be proud of that huge background that took you 11 hours, but unless the background is the focus of the scene, you don't want your main character to be competing for audience attention.

In hindsight, I realize that a lot of work I did in *hitchHiker* was unnecessary. Many of the backgrounds were far too detailed and certain things I put in were just for the sake of it or to see if it was possible. That animating background cycle? What was I thinking?! On the other hand, there were some backgrounds that certainly lacked detail where it was needed. For example, there's a lack of detail in this scene, especially when compared to all the others; it looks like I've really rushed this one. Even the character is badly drawn.

One of the major design issues I decided for *hitchHiker: part two* quite early on (about halfway through my work on *part one*) was the use of 3D vehicles instead of freehand ones. I've never been much good at drawing machines. My good friend Swift 3D will not only make this quicker and easier to draw, but it'll make it look a helluva lot better.

Project 3: Design

The characters don't really need to be too complicated in our animation project. The old bloke will mostly just deliver dialog and frown a bit, so he'll only need a few drawings of his torso and head, as well as some separate eyes, mouths, and arms. In my version, we only need to make one symbol for the young guy. You'll see why in a second.

The backgrounds will also be quite simple. It's a dark foggy night, so we'll only need two dark interiors and two dark exteriors.

Open up `project_design.fla` from the download files to see the character and background designs I've come up with. Their simple design lends them well to lots of separate elements.

Go through your leica now or if you've chosen to use mine, open up `project_Leica.fla`. Look through it scene by scene and identify each different character pose. From this, you can set yourself a limit. For example, see if you can get away with doing *no more than three poses* for each character. Make changes to your leica if necessary, to accommodate the limited poses you'll work with.

After that, you should know roughly how many character drawings you'll need, and where they'll go, and you can get to work on those. Roughly sketch him into a frame, then use onion-skinning to clean him up in the next frame. Also, keep in mind that you need to put all his moving parts onto separate layers in the timeline.

Don't start adding any characters to your scenes yet. After you've designed both characters and their key poses, you can keep them in the Library and drop them into their scenes a little later, when we move on to the Character animation section.

Setting file size limits

We all know that working for the Internet imposes limitations on how large your file size can be. Macromedia Flash was built for such work, so some of the job is done for us, but with that comes the temptation to add more content. Finding the delicate balance between short download times and complex movies is a constant battle.

When I first decided to animate the story of the *hitchHiker*, I never meant for it to be in two parts, but I was almost halfway through when I realized that the SWF was already over 1MB – without sound! Since it was intended for the Internet, I decided to split it. This was good in a way, as it had already taken about eight weeks of my free time, and to take a break halfway was an unexpected 'yay!' It also gave the movie time to be viewed and enjoyed by a lot of people, which in turn fed the suspense and anticipation for the second part.

Although the need to keep the download small is something we should be constantly aware of when designing, it's not the only limitation. Even though broadband Internet is spreading like wild fire and the average connection will soon make the 56k modem a museum piece, bear in mind that it's the playback on the user's machine you also need to worry about. Even if someone with a slow connection sits patiently through your 2MB download, the choppy playback resulting from heavy use of gradients, alpha fades, and high detail will ruin the experience.

This scene from my series plays beautifully on television, but on a low-spec computer it plays like a slide show. You can see why.

I've become increasingly aware of the **Optimize** tool in Flash, and you'll notice that in my original *hitchHiker*, I was completely unaware of its existence (too excited to read the manual, you know how it is). One day I'll go back and optimize everything in the movie and we'll see that it's nowhere near its present 1.57MB.

Before I start on the animation, I'll look at the board and my designs, and then set myself a reasonable file size limit. For *hitchHiker: part two*, I've set myself a more realistic limit of 3MB. That's a pretty big file, I know, but for a four-minute movie with cinematic effects, quality dialog, sound effects, music, and some 3D vehicles and backgrounds, it ain't so bad.

A word on my sound

Sound effects and music are usually among the last things I add to a movie. However, dialog dictates animation and so it can be done anywhere from the leica stage of the process, to just after the character animation. I'll cover dialog and lip-sync in the Character animation section.

Now, I'm no master composer or sound technician, so I'm not about to write a section on sound and waveforms. I can, however, relate my experience so far with sound in Flash movies and how I get the results I need.

Free vs. quality

I gave up searching the Internet for high quality free sounds a long time ago. I found the process frustrating and exhausting; wading for hours through bad sound files, just to realize that I'm not going to find what I want.

What I finally recorded for *hitchHiker* with my tinny desktop microphone was probably better than most files I could have found for free on the Internet. Except for the match striking, the fire crackling, and the 'bling' sound when the old lady's car appears on the horizon, every sound you hear was done with my mouth and lips. Crickets, birds, cars, the old lady... yep, the microphone sure was glistening at the end of that day.

If you're happy with free sounds you can find on the Internet, then go for it. Otherwise, you can look over my personal recommendations for getting quality sounds:

- Buy one or two stock sound CDs, you know... the type with a thousand sounds on one CD?

- Search for and buy only the sounds you need at a site such as the excellent www.sound-effects-library.com.

- Call in some favors (thanks Kevin Peaty) or pay for a composer/sound guy to do the job (depends how important the job is).

- Record the dialog, music and effects yourself. For my dialog, I invested in a half-decent dynamic microphone and preamp. Armed with this and my soundcard's built-in recording program, I can record not only dialog, but also some generic sound effects from around the house. Other sound recording packages, such as Cool Edit and Cakewalk, are perfect for this type of thing.

- For my music I have a few silly little tunes flying around in my head and I put them through my little Midi Man Oxygen8 midi keyboard. Nice! (well, adequate anyway).

If you're willing to spend a little cash on your baby then you'll have no trouble getting hold of some fine quality sounds and music. For me, this far outweighs the sheer boredom of searching for free sounds, and the disappointment of hearing them spoil your movie. In fact, I highly recommend saving a little money for it, and getting the sounds you need, rather than settling for sounds that you don't even want.

Take a look at David Doull's Flash MP3 Jukebox chapter for some more advice on creating and buying sounds.

Project 4: Adding dialog to the leica

For the dialog in our project, I've provided the sound files for you and we'll cover the lip-sync in the Character animation section. I'll leave the music and sound effects up to you.

For now though, if you'd like to put your sound files into their scenes, open up `project_Leica.fla` and go to Scene 3, where the old guy opens the door.

Press F11 to open your Library. In there, you'll find four sound files: two for the old guy and two for the young fella.

1. In the `dialogue1` layer, select frame 15 and press F6 to add a keyframe here. This gives him time to open the door and see who's there, before he opens his trap.

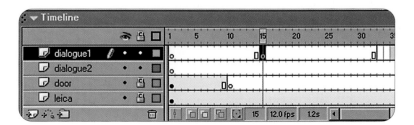

2. Now in the Library, select the `oldfella.wav` sound and press the play button in the top right corner of the preview window to hear the dialog. You should hear him say, 'Yes, what is it?'

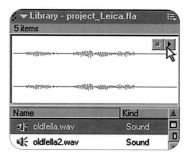

3. That's the one we want so, making sure the frame 15 is selected in the `dialogue1` layer, drag the sound from the Library onto the stage. The waveform is now starting from the frame you had selected, and is displayed in the timeline.

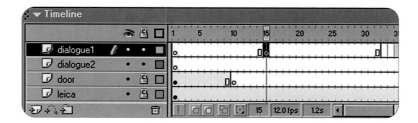

Now test the scene (CTRL+ALT+ENTER) and you'll hear the dialog in the context of the scene. You can start adding all the other sounds throughout the leica at this stage,, if you like, and it'll give you a better idea of how the dialog and acting can play out.

Environments

An environment is the world you create for your story. It consists of backgrounds, background elements, and effects. It's the place *in* which your characters exist, not just on or in front of. In this section, I'll show you how I go about constructing my environments, from the rough scratches you see in the `hh2_Leica.swf` to the finished backgrounds you see in the final movie. After this, we'll spend some time learning about the ways we can move our environments around to simulate camera moves.

Laying out your background

When laying out my backgrounds, I usually rough the basic components in one frame, then use onion-skinning to clean it up. In the download file `backgrounds.swf`, you'll see what I mean. Open up the file and you'll see the rough version of the background. Press the radio buttons to toggle between rough, clean, and color.

As you can see in the rough frame, I've loosely sketched the ground plane and the horizon, along with some indications of distance compression (the horizontal lines).

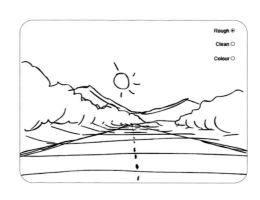

Although simple looking, this stuff is based on a decent understanding of perspective drawing, an invaluable skill with which I strongly suggest you become familiar, if you're not already. It's imperative, not just for background/landscape drawing alone, but also for things like character movement, prop animation and effects, such as light and shadow.

Perspective drawing is far too deep a subject for me to cover here, but if you want to get cracking on some awesome cityscapes and 3D environments, I'd recommend picking up a cheap book on perspective basics. There are thousands of them out there, and you can probably get one for next to nothing at a second-hand bookstore.

Rough to clean

When cleaning up my backgrounds, I use the **onion skin** to see my rough version underneath as a guide.

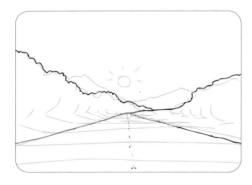

More often, I can clean up a background directly from the rough version, but sometimes it's necessary to do a 'fine rough'. That is, from my *really* rough version, I'll make a *less* rough version and then finally clean it up completely. My reason for this is that often my rough version is just a loose representation of where major elements might go, e.g. road and hills. In the fine rough, I'm nailing things down more carefully, such as the road, hills, trees, posts, fences, and so on, but without having to be extra careful with where I put the pen. Finally, for the clean version, I just trace everything carefully with the necessary tools to get the line I want.

Color

Over the next section, we'll look at re-using custom color palettes in Flash, and how to use a defined set of colors to create a specific atmosphere in your environment.

Saving and loading palettes

Being a movie that continues on directly from another, *hitchHiker: part two* will need the same or similar colors that I used in *part one*. In the movie, time is passing and the climactic ending takes place in the dead of night. Therefore, the tints and colors of my backgrounds and characters will be slowly changing scene by scene, mostly around sunset.

It's not vital that I use the same colors that I used in *hitchHiker: part one*, but they're a good point of reference. Instead of mixing all my colors again from scratch, I'm better off loading the same color swatch palette I mixed and used on the first movie. Besides, it's easier.

Press CTRL+F9 to open up your **Color Swatch** panel. Click the options icon and in the drop-down menu you'll see options to Add, Save, Delete, and Duplicate swatches, among other things.

If you've saved your palette from a previous movie and you'd like to use those colors in another movie, choose Add Colors… and browse to the folder where you have your CLR files stored.

Once the original *hitchHiker* palette is loaded and ready, I can finally get moving on full-color environments.

However, let's put environments aside for just a second. For an example in tints, I'm going to tint my character with early evening light, for which his 'daytime' skin colors just won't do.

Project 5: Using tint for custom colors

Open up `hh2_swatchMix.fla` and you'll see the line drawing of Chlu (pronounced 'clue'), the main *hitchHiker* character. There's a hidden layer called `bg`, but don't worry about that for now, we can unhide the sky when we've got something to compare it with. For now we'll just tint him with some lovely unique dusk colors.

Start by painting all his skin with his daytime skin color, as indicated in the legend beside him, so we have a point of reference for the evening version of his colors.

1. With the Eyedropper tool selected, click on the skin color in the model palette just off the stage. The hexadecimal representation of this color is #FFCC99.

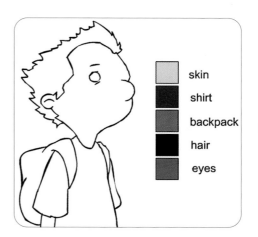

2. Color him completely with this daytime colors using the model palette I've prepared.

3. Drag a region around him with the Arrow tool (V), and convert him to a graphic symbol (F8).

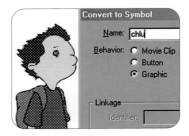

4. Make sure he's selected, go into the Property inspector, and choose Tint from the Color drop-down menu.

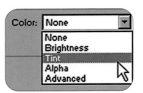

5. Pick a color that makes you think of evening light. You'll see that at 100%, Chlu is a silhouette of that color.

6. Drag the percentage slider down to about 15%.

There are our evening colors: skin, clothes, hair, everything! For a sneak preview, turn on the `bg`, `stars`, and `sky` layers.

7. Close down your test movie and save your version of this FLA. We'll be using it later in the chapter.

Now back to the project...

Project 6: Environments

We'll use onion-skinning to clean up our environments, as outlined earlier. It's a matter of preference whether or not you decide to do the 'fine rough' stage, so feel free to go ahead and clean directly from your loose rough if you like. These environments are in `project_backgrounds.fla`. Have a look through and see how I've cut corners.

1. The `title` scene is where we see a nice silhouette of the house. Silhouettes rock because they involve a filled outline – nothing more – and, as a nice added bonus, they are very atmospheric. Here's mine with some gradients to make it look foggy:

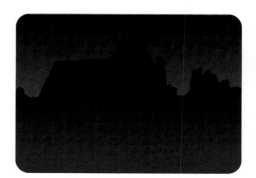

2. OK, the next scene (select Scene 1 from the Scene panel) is the shot of the man in bed, getting annoyed. Check out the FLA and you'll notice that the bedding, clock, and table are on separate layers. Also notice that the digital '2' is on its own layer. Later, we'll flip the '2' upside-down to get a '5'.

You don't need to finish the man's face yet, like I have here. I couldn't help myself. I've colored him with gray colors, and then given him a red tint of 4%.

3. In Scene 3, there is the man grumbling as he goes up the hallway. I'll be using lots of shadows here, because they are a nice, convenient excuse to skimp on detail, which means less workload and smaller file sizes.

4. Scrub along the timeline in this same scene to see the next shot. It's from outside as the front door opens, so the door will need to be on its own layer. I've decided to hold on to this shot while the young guy delivers his lines. It will save me from animating any dialog at all. Instead, we can watch the first man, and his reaction to the request. For this background, I've built the door and frame in Swift 3D and animated the door over two frames (frames 9 and 10 on the door layer). Quick, simple and looks great.

For the rest of the scenes, go through and clean up your backgrounds, keeping a lookout for opportunities to re-use material. Little secret: from here on you don't need to do another background.

How much depth and detail?

I was still getting a feel for Flash when I was working on *hitchHiker: part one* and, as I said earlier, much of what I put into those scenes was unnecessary. I spent a long time on the big vertically panning scene (shown here), and at times I was actually zooming into the stage by 1200% to add fine detail. That was just craziness, as most of it is completely lost with the movie dimensions of 550x400, and high detail like that can really slow down playback.

I'm working on a series at the moment intended for television, so its dimensions are 720x576. Even at these dimensions, I have to be careful about unnecessary work. Playback speed won't be a problem on TV but, for efficiency's sake, I need to be aware of what's going to show up on screen and how much I can get away with.

Simulating camera moves

I like moving the background around. You'll notice that there are many scenes in my movies where I try to keep the viewers absorbed by animating the viewpoint and moving the audience through my environments.

There are a number of generic camera moves. Pan, zoom, and truck are the three I use most frequently.

- **Pan** involves the camera pivoting left and right, and up and down. With a static background in Flash, this camera move is relatively simple to do using a motion tween.

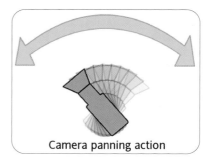

Camera panning action

- **Zoom** is the act of scaling up or down on a scene or background. That's all it is. When the camera zooms, its position doesn't change; its lens simply magnifies the image. Again, this is easy to do in Flash with a motion tween.

- **Truck** is a little more complicated as it is designed to show depth. Rather than just looking at the environment as if through a window, the camera *moves around within* the environment. Trucking is where the camera physically moves sideways, forwards, or backwards *through* and *across* the scene.

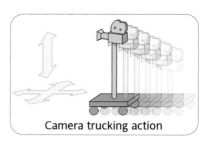

Camera trucking action

As an analogy, when you turn your head in any direction, your view is panning, and when you walk along your view is trucking. If you had telescopic vision, your view would be zooming.

Incorporating camera moves in scenes

Let's say you have a character talking away, and he has separate eyes, separate mouth, separate hair, and separate arms. He's acting up a storm, and you want to zoom in to him as well as pan across. This could involve carefully tweening every single element in the scene at the same rate, including the character and all his separate elements. What a nightmare!

The solution is quite simple, and you may have already thought of it. This is the method I use with complicated, multi-layered scenes in which I'd like to incorporate a camera move. Just put the entire scene, including character animation, into a movie clip. Now the scene itself can be panned and zoomed any way you like, not to mention rotating the scene, scaling, flipping, fading to black, or dissolving into the next scene.

Alternatively, you can put the character alone into a movie clip, and tween him across the screen at a different rate to the background, effectively simulating a camera trucking action.

Camera trucking

Trucking is achieved in Flash by tweening various elements in the scene at different speeds to give an illusion of depth to the environment. Those with an interest in Flash games may have heard of parallax scrolling, which is technically a camera truck.

Check out the scenes in *hitchHiker: part one* where we're in the car with the old lady. The background elements that appear closer to the car move the fastest; they zoom by. Those in the middle ground move past a bit slower to show that they are further away. The hills, way off in the distance, move very slowly.

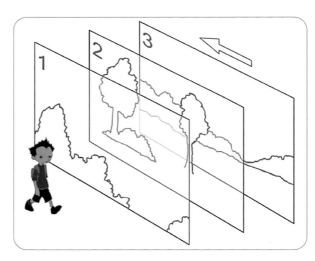

In this illustration, the numbered panes represent background layers in your movie, containing elements that tween at various speeds across the screen. 1 will tween the fastest and 3 the slowest. This is how the illusion of depth was achieved in the old lady scenes described above.

3D camera

In *hitchHiker: part two*, I'm combining a 3D camera move with a 2D background. The scene where the black van zooms past uses a 3D roadway and vehicle animated in Swift 3D, which are then imported into a layer in my Flash movie. If you open up `hh2_Scene18.fla` from the chapter files, the description will make more sense.

The only layers visible should be `Leica` and `vehicle`. `Leica` is a guide layer, so it won't show up when you test the movie.

In the `Leica` layer, I've drawn a really rough outline of where I need my hills and trees in the first frame of the scene, and again in the final frame. These two rough drawings were the foundation for the two separate 2D backgrounds. As the 3D road animation swings around, I manually placed each keyframe so the hills stay joined to the end of the road.

Notice as you scrub through the timeline, that the first background is glued to the point where the road vanishes into the distance, and the same goes for the second background as the other end of the road swings into view. As you can see by all the keyframes, I simply positioned each frame by hand, so the 3D road pretty much told me where my 2D background should go in each frame. When I animated the 3D elements in Swift 3D, I needed the van to almost fill the screen as it passes the camera, thus creating the perfect opportunity to swap backgrounds.

Here you can see the stage outlined by the bright green guides, my 3D van/road as it passes the camera, and my two separate backgrounds, as explained above. When you play the scene, it's a flawless transition.

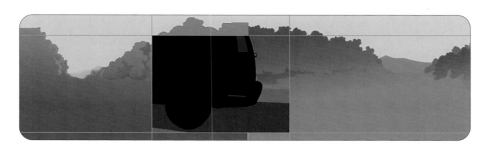

Character animation

This is what we've come for, the big one. Professional character animators train for years to get the results you see on the big screen. This subject doesn't involve drawing pictures alone, or making beautiful environments. Character animation requires a deep understanding of many essential individual areas. The neglect or misunderstanding of any of these areas can often result in second-rate animation. Some of these individual areas are: anatomy, drawing, perspective, volume, emotion, acting, comedy, timing and, of course, the tools used.

Character animation is an art that encompasses many other art forms and I can't promise to show you in a few pages all there is to know about character animation. However, this section will cover, in some depth, a few of the most requested topics I've received: **Design and Construction**, **Dialog**, **Walk**, and **Run Cycles**. I'll explain some basics of each, and we'll put some of them into practice in our animation project.

After all this, I'll explain the differences between two of the major animation styles and why they're the major ones, which hopefully will help you on your way to designing, animating, and uploading your own epics. Here goes...

Design and construction

The look of my character in *hitchHiker* is based on a cartoon version of myself (I guess that's why he's instantly likeable!). I decided on that design because I found him easy to draw. It's important that you enjoy drawing your character. Try to come up with a design that makes you want to draw him a lot. You'll find that the more comfortable you are with drawing him/her/it, the more fun you'll have animating him/her/it.

I'll show you here how my main character is constructed, and hopefully from this you can see how a few simple lines can define the basic shapes to build on.

Being able to draw him without feeling like it's a major chore is a big plus, and I find that the more fun I have making a movie, the better the end product!

Let me say here that it's always nice to see a drawing done by someone who knows a bit about anatomy. Grab a book on human anatomy (not on cartooning!) and study a bit about the form of real humans. If your character's a dog, look at some dog books. A robot? Get your hands on some robot or machinery books. All this will go a long way to helping you make your characters appear lifelike in design and movement.

If you're stuck for ideas in your character design, you might start by sketching some basic shapes such as squares, circles, pear shapes, triangles, and so on. Add some rough lines or other shapes for eyes, mouths, limbs, and other features. If you see something you like, build on it, and you'll probably surprise yourself when something completely original flies out the end of your pen.

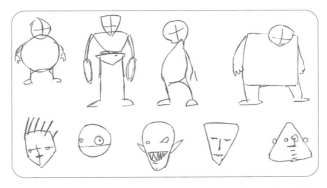

Start with primitive shapes. The cross in the middle of the face is indicative of eyeline and center of head, and it's a good habit to get into. It keeps things as simple as possible while showing head direction and tilt. Try to refrain from adding any features at this stage. Instead, just draw a lot of primitives with those eye and center lines.

Soon enough, something will leap off the page at you, and you can work on it. Again, try not to add more features, just get cozy drawing the same basic form in lots of different poses. The more comfortable you are drawing its primitive form, the more natural the other features will come.

Once you have a character that you're comfortable with, there's nothing to stop you from using it in everything you do. Drawing him a lot is like getting to know him, and you'll find that you're learning more about your own character every day if you're constantly constructing and posing him.

Dialog

Quite simply, nine mouthshapes are all you'll ever need for Flash animation dialog. One mouthshape can safely cover a wide range of phonetic sounds. For example, S, T, and Z can all be sounded with the same mouthshape.

In this table you can see the phonetic sounds and their corresponding mouthshapes. If you really want to streamline things, just keep these separate mouths in your Library and drop them onto your character's face as he speaks.

A		E, G, H, R		O	
B, M, P		F, V		oo, W	
D, J, N S, T, Z		L		'th'	

Of course, there are a million mouthshapes if you want to find them. 'Ch, Sh, J' is one I could have included, but they may be safely represented by the S, T, Z mouthshape shown above.

Before we go any further, a couple of don'ts:

- Be very careful not to go overboard with lip-sync. It looks quite silly if there's a mouthshape for every single letter of the word being spoken unless your character is enunciating. For example, spoken naturally, the mouthshape order for the word 'animation' would go like this: *a n m a sh n*. However, this would just look silly: *a n ee m a ee sh o n*. I mean, really... who talks like that? You'd get cramps in your face after just a few words.

- Never use the 'L' mouthshape for the 'N' sound. I've seen it done and it's horrible. Sure, your tongue may touch the roof of your mouth when you say it, but 'D' is closer to 'N' than 'L' is. Besides, how many people do you know hold the 'L' mouthshape when they say 'N' naturally? Go on, say 'Never known a nutter named Ned'. Animate that with the 'L' shape all over the place, and I guarantee it'll look like 'Lever lowl a lutter lamed Led'.

Project 7: Lip-sync

In this little exercise, you'll synchronize the animation of a big ugly mouth with a dialog track, so make sure your speakers are turned on.

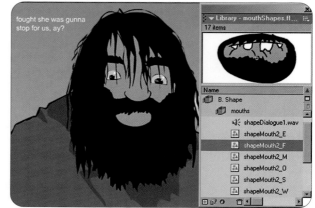

Open up `hh2_mouthShapes.fla` from the download files. When you open the movie, you'll see the big guy from *hitchHiker* with no mouth. Open your Library (F11) and you'll see several mouthshapes as graphic symbols, plus a sound file in there.

Before we go any further, you might like to look over the movie and its layers. For a start, click the hide layer icon on the `mask` layer. Now hide his `shapeHair1` layer. Scary isn't he? If you hide a layer at a time, you'll see how the big guy is split into his layers ready for acting and dialog. His eyes are kept separate too so that he can blink, squint, frown and look around without the need to move anything else.

OK, now let's make him talk.

1. Select frame 10 of the `dialogue` layer and hit F6 to create a keyframe. With this keyframe selected, drag the sound called `shapeDialogue1` from the Library, and drop it on the stage. Starting the dialog at frame 10 gives us a little pause at the beginning of the scene so he doesn't start yammerin' straight away. You'll see that the waveform is now in the timeline.

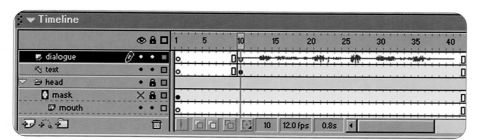

2. Select your sound in the timeline by double-clicking on it. Then, open the SYNC drop-down menu in the Property inspector and set it to STREAM.

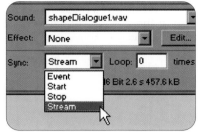

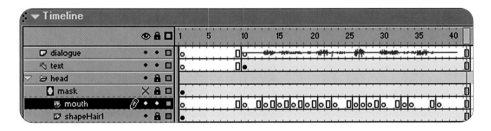

3. Go back to your timeline and drag the playhead slowly from frame 1 to the end. Much the same as you *see* frames pass by as you scrub them, you will now *hear* each frame as you pass over it. Listen to the sound he makes and picture his mouthshape as he says it.

You might find yourself mouthing the words as you listen, which is excellent. Take notice of the shapes you're making with your own mouth. Professional animators always have a mirror at their desk primarily for mouthshape reference (and secondarily for personal skin maintenance).

4. So, as you scrub the timeline, listening to his sounds, note at which frames his mouthshape will change. Select those frames, one at a time, and make them keyframes (F6). These keyframes are where you'll be dropping mouthshapes very soon. When you've finished this step, your mouth layer should look something like this:

5. Good stuff. Now start dragging and dropping the mouthshapes from the Library and onto the mouth layer. Don't worry too much about placing his mouth on the exact same spot every time, as it always looks less mechanical if it's slightly different from frame to frame. When you have the whole line of dialog covered with mouthshapes, test the movie (CTRL+ENTER). Now call your entire household in and show them what you've just done.

There are some fine-tuning points that I don't have time to go into here, but in the download file for this chapter I've added some finishing touches to the lip-sync with some tweening, and the file's called `hh2_shapeDialogue.fla`. This is its timeline:

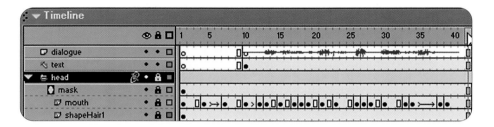

Have a look at what I've done here, then go back and try your own fine-tuning. You could even try to sync his mouthshapes with other dialog recordings. In fact, why not drop part of a song in there, and have the guy singing it? Better yet, build your own character from scratch, with its own mouthshapes and see what you can come up with!

To avoid that cardboard-cutout Flash character look, see if you can come up with some ways to liven the guys up. For instance, the old guy and his mouth could be placed together inside a movie clip, which, on the main timeline may then be shifted very subtly as he talks. For the young fella, you might like to create a small movie clip of subtle steam puffs, so that when he is talking, you can synchronize the steam puffs with his dialog! That way, we don't see his mouth moving, but the audience will know it's him who's talking, as well as the fact that it's freezing cold outside.

A lot of people find it hard to get their head around what you've just learned. Simple though, isn't it?

Walk and run cycles

Character walk cycles are the most frequently requested files from me, so here I'll outline walk and run cycles from various angles. Before I go into it though, I should mention that walks and runs should be used sparingly. They can be a lot of work, and sometimes unnecessary. A walk or run can be adequately portrayed showing only the upper body, with swinging arms and up and down motion. See `hh2_chluRun.fla` for an example.

Walk

OK then, so you really want to see his legs? Here we go. Take a look at `walk.fla` (in the `misc` folder, in the download files) and scrub along the timeline. I've animated four angles: profile, three-quarter, front, and back, and contained them in their own layer folders. Within each folder, I've hidden the layers containing all the inbetween drawings, so as you scrub the timeline you'll only see the **keys** (the four major positions of the legs in a walk cycle). Feel free to unhide those layers, but I suggest you familiarize yourself with the keys first, as understanding these few major positions will help you in the long run.

You'll notice that these walk and run files contain very rough drawings. I'm showing you *basic* construction here, so you can apply them to any character. This straightforward stickman concept may be easily applied to a wide range of characters.

The trick to understanding a walk cycle is to first understand how each leg moves through its cycle, what it is doing, and the role it plays in stopping the guy from falling on his face. I once heard a walk referred to as a controlled fall. When you take a step forward, you are using gravity to drive your momentum, and it's when you put your leg out in front of you that you stop the fall. Picture a drunk man, barely controlling his fall/walk. If, at any moment, his leg is too slow to catch that fall, he's on his side with a puzzled expression and drink everywhere.

Open the `profile` layer folder in the `walk.fla` timeline to see the drawings. You'll see the `keys` and `inbs` layers (hidden). Don't try to learn all the inbetween positions yet. If you familiarize yourself with these keys, the inbetweens will almost draw themselves.

Here are the four major keys in a walk cycle:

1. The first major key has the right foot planted firmly. All the weight of the body is moving over it, and the left leg is swinging through.

2. The next key has both feet touching the ground in mid-stride, with the left foot in front.

    This repeats with the other leg.

3. The third major key has that left foot planted, and the right leg is swinging through.

4. The fourth key has both feet touching the ground again, but now the right foot is in front.

Once you've got these four keys, there's your walk cycle! Keep these four keys in mind, study the positions of the legs, practice them, and you'll never forget how to animate a walk. If timed correctly, these keys can be all that's required for a limited walk cycle. To make the walk less limited, or to make it slower or smoother, simply add inbetweens and adjust the timing of each key.

Also note that if you're animating a silhouette or shadow of a character walking in direct profile, he only has two major keys, and half as much animation! I'll leave you to figure out why.

Run

Open up `run.fla` and again you'll be presented with a cycle from four different angles: front, back, profile, and three-quarter. Within their separate folders, I've put all the keys on one layer, and the inbetweens on another. (Please note that the arm positions are in the download files, but I haven't included them in this chapter, as they are relatively simple to learn.)

Drag the playhead across the frames and pause a moment to study the position of his legs on each keyframe. As with the walk cycle, there are only four keyframes in a run cycle and, if you memorize these, it all becomes part of your CV. Once again, if you'd like to see the animation with all the inbetweens, unhide the `inbs` layers.

Here are the major keys of a run cycle:

1. The first key has the left leg straight, with its heel just touching the ground, out in front. The heel of his right foot is almost kicking him on the backside.

2. The second major key shows that the left leg is directly under the body, taking all the weight. The right leg is swinging through to the front.

Again, this all repeats with the other leg.

3. In the third key, it's the right leg that is straight now, its heel touching the ground, and the left leg is now doing the bum kicking.

4. This is the same as the second key, but with the right leg under the body this time, and the left leg swinging through to the front.

Anyone see a pattern? Just remember that there are only two keys to each leg. Memorize the positions for one leg, and the other is a mirror image. Simple! In fact, I'll show you now how I construct the run cycle from the three-quarter view, using the mirror image concept as a guide. When drawing his opposing keys (1 and 3, 2 and 4), imagine a mirror splitting him down the middle.

Run Key 1

Run Key 2

Run Key 3 - Mirror of 1

Run Key 4 - Mirror of 2

Project 8: Character walk

The only real visible walking cycle in my project leica is where the young guy walks off into the fog. In line with the walk cycle steps outlined above, I've animated a rough version of his cycle and converted it to a movie clip. In the `project_designs.fla` Library, you'll see a movie clip called `mc.walk`. Double-click on it in the Library and have a look at its timeline.

I've deliberately left this rough so that you can fill in the detail and form you need. As you clean up this rough animation, when you're animating the young fella in the scene, frequently refer back to the `walk.fla` animation and use it as a guide.

The other walk in the movie is cheated. Look at `project_backgrounds.fla` and navigate to Scene 2, where the old guy is walking up the hallway. Hide the `bg` layer (the background) to see what I mean. There's no walk there at all! Don't you just love shortcuts?

Limited and full animation

Let me start with a short explanation of the **full** animation style, which you are likely to see in animated feature films and some animated television productions.

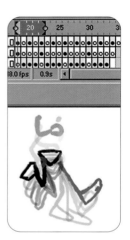

Full animation involves a lot of work and, while very versatile, is quite an unrealistic choice if you're short of time or money. It involves drawing every single frame of a character's, or effect's, movement. For example, in Flash, if I were to animate a walk cycle in the full animation style, the timeline would be full of keyframes. Note that in `walk.fla` and `run.fla` I've animated them fully.

In feature and television animation, the frame rate is generally 24 fps. In a typical character acting scene, a drawing is made for every two of these frames, referred to in the industry as **working on twos** or **doubles**. This means that in every second of animation, there are at least 12 separate drawings. To smooth out certain character movements, such as subtle expression changes, or some fast whipping action, it is often necessary to add **singles**, in which case there can be as many as 24 drawings for every one second of film.

The full style of animation is employed when it's necessary to show 3D movement, such as that of a character turning his head, and the progressive change of angle needed in each frame between the two key poses.

As another example, you might want to show a character's hand slowly turning over and opening to reveal a coin. This is also a scene that requires each frame to be drawn individually, to show every different angle of the hand as it rolls from one position to the other.

Limited animation is, as the name implies, an animation style that is designed to achieve maximum effect with minimum effort. A walk cycle in the limited animation style only involves drawing keyframes, with inbetweens inserted sparingly.

The ideal way to limit the hand-and-coin animation above would be to simply draw the hand already open with the coin visible at the beginning of the shot, rather than animate the rotation. This way, only one drawing is required for the entire scene. It's this kind of limitation decision that requires a bit of thought and planning, and therefore should be considered in the early stages of the design process.

Why am I telling you all this? Well, it's this limited style that lends itself beautifully to Flash. In limited animation, it is primarily the pencil mileage, file size, and the workload in general that is saved on, which is perfect and more often necessary for us Flash users.

To illustrate the difference between limited and full animation, I've provided a file called `styles.fla`. Open it up:

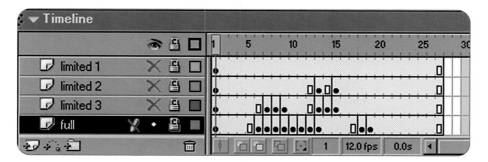

Keep all of the `limited` layers hidden for now and scrub the playhead along the timeline. Notice that in the `full` layer, I've done a complete drawing for every angle of the rolling hand. This not only means a great deal of drawing work, but also a lot of thought and rough sketching goes into the construction of each angle shown. If you want to see my construction drawings, check out the `construction` layer.

It would be impossible for Flash to tween this rolling action, so my limited solutions would be as you can see them in the `limited` layers. Unhide them one at a time and scrub the timeline to see how the same action may be limited in different ways.

You may find that it's feasible for your movie to be a hybrid, containing both styles; limited animation for most of the movie, with certain important scenes fully animated. For example, if you decided early on that you *absolutely must have* that hand rolling over slowly, opening to reveal the coin, you could do so, marking it as one of your important or special scenes.

Despite all this talk of limitations, you may have a lot of time and patience and decide that the full style is how you'll go for your entire project. There's nothing stopping you from doing this. Indeed, I've done it recently myself for my series, and I'm delighted with the results. It's simply a matter of making a brave decision at the beginning of the project and having the willpower to see it through.

There is far more to the art of limited animation than I can cover here, but if you'd like to learn more about character animation in general, there are truckloads of books available. Disney's *The Illusion of Life*, by Frank Thomas and Ollie Johnston (ISBN: 0786860707) is considered by professionals everywhere as the animator's bible, so get your hands on a copy of that if you're serious. Best of luck on your character animation quest!

Effects

The clever use of effects will give your Flash movie that big-budget, professional quality. I strongly believe effects are essential for a high-class finish, and this stuff grabs and holds audience attention like nothing else can. Flash effects should be very carefully planned at the design stage, and realistically should come near the end of the production process because they can often be bandwidth-heavy and processor-intensive.

Consider how much file space you can spare and whether or not it'll hurt to add some effects. I find that lighting effects especially are well worth the extra KB, and it's what separates a cartoon from a more believable, more lifelike, character in a realistic environment.

Light and shadow

As with character animation, there's a lot to study in the world of effects animation and I could write volumes about it, but in this section I'll only have the space to concentrate on light and shadow effects. Light and shadow are what I consider to be the most important effects of all, and should be seriously considered for your movie.

If you must sacrifice some areas of your design and animation in order to make room for some light and shadow effects then, in my opinion, it'll be well worth it. There is an astounding difference between a piece of Flash animation with light and shadow, and the same animation without it:

Without lighting effects: a cartoon

With lighting effects: dimension, volume, ATMOSPHERE

This is the piece of artwork that makes all the difference:

The effects illustrated above are referred to in the animation industry as **tones**, **highlights**, and **shadows**.

The **tone** is the shady area of an object that the light cannot reach. It's always on the same side as the shadow. Imagine a ball in the sunlight, and see the dark side, or the tone. The tone effect in your movie is what can make a flat image appear to leap from the screen, giving it the appearance of possessing volume.

The **highlight** is the reflection of the light source. Imagine a billiard ball and the spot of light on its surface.

Compare the two earlier screenshots of the character with and without lighting effects. The eyes in the second shot appear wet, thanks to those two tiny spots of brightness (the highlights), which give the eyes their clear and glassy look. They also tell us that the eyes are not just colored circles, but moist little orbs.

I'm sure this won't be news to many people, but **shadows** are the result of something blocking the main light source. The tricky thing with creating shadows is getting the perspective right, and as I mentioned earlier, it helps if you have some understanding of perspective basics. We'll look more at shadows in perspective in more detail next.

Shadows: light source and direction

Before you start work on any light and shadow effect, it's a good idea to nail your light source and direction, even if it's not going to be visible in the movie itself. For example, before I started on this drawing, I drew the red arrow just off the stage to indicate the position of the light source and its direction.

This icon constantly reminds me that I need to ensure the light and shadow always comes from the same place, so that my lighting effects don't clash. To further illustrate this point, in the left-hand drawing below, the effects are contradicting each other. According to his shadow on the wall, the light is coming from the left of frame, but contrary to that, the tone on his face suggests a light source from the right of frame. The example on the right, shows the correct lighting.

Wrong: Contradictory lighting effects, conflicting shadows.

Right: Correct lighting, with consistent light source and direction.

Shadows: in perspective

Shadows in perspective can portray miles of depth in your backgrounds all by themselves. For example, look at this screenshot from *hitchHiker: part two*:

Can anyone tell I love doing nightscapes? If you have a large flat area of color, you can illustrate depth and distance by drawing the shadows correctly. Distance compression affects everything in the scene. In the right hand image, you can see how perspective affects the leaves and trees, as well as the more subtle details like highlights and shadows.

OK, I'm about to go into a bit of an analysis into how perspective affects shadows, and how shadows are affected by perspective. Bear with me, as knowing this stuff can help you give your movie unrivalled class.

To start with, let's examine how the proximity of a light source to an object affects the size of its shadow. Remember when you were a kid making shadows on the wall from your bedside lamp? The closer your hand was to the lamp, the larger the shadow on the wall. That's because light *moves* in perfectly straight lines, and therefore shadows are *traced* in perfectly straight rays.

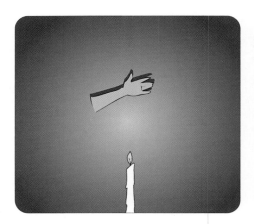 

If the shadows weren't creepy enough, it's a disembodied forearm!

Shadows cast by the sun always run parallel here on earth. As illustrated in this diagram, the sun is one massive light source and, being mere specs in the solar system, our tiny bodies, even our tiny mountains, cast only tiny shadows in this great stream of light.

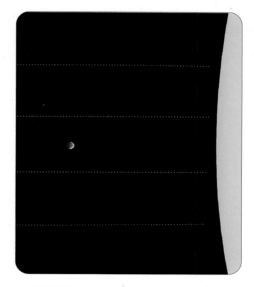

Now imagine a group of tall cylinders, such as telegraph poles standing on a flat surface. Let's take a view of these poles from the top, looking directly down on them like a map. If it was late afternoon, we may see the poles casting shadows something like this:

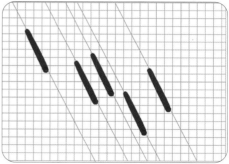

The green lines indicate the parallel direction of light rays from the sun. Now let's look at the same landscape from a lower angle:

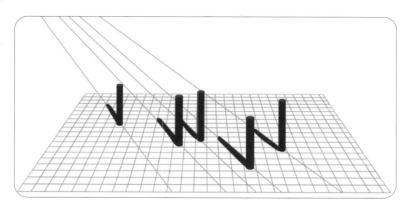

Notice how everything recedes in perspective, even sunlight shadows. Next time you're awake at sunrise (or if you're like me and more likely to see a sunset), notice the long shadows on the ground and how they look in perspective. To further illustrate my point, think of a photograph where long shadows reach toward the photographer.

OK, so it's not a photograph, but you get the idea!

Shadows from the sun always run parallel to each other, but I've known people to be under the misconception that shadows in perspective should always be *drawn* parallel. Nope: perspective diminishes all things towards a vanishing point. Imagine what would happen if we were to run our shadows parallel in perspective, as in the left-hand image below. These shadows in perspective have been *drawn* parallel to each other; again the green lines are indications of light rays. Now, see how according to the top-down view in the right-hand image, that it can't possibly be sunlight:

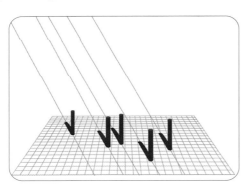 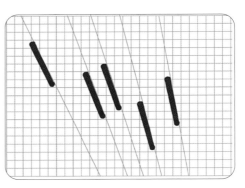

As shown by the green lines, the pole shadows here are fanning out, which tells us that it can't be sunlight, but a much closer light source. To illustrate this example with animation, I've provided `longShadows.swf` in the download files, in which you can see how some fixed shadows appear from a moving camera.

I'm telling you all this simply to drive the point home that although sunlight shadows *do* run parallel, in perspective they aren't *drawn* parallel. Perspective diminishes *all* things to a point.

Project 9: Character shadows in Flash

The new Free Transform tool in Flash MX is a godsend for effects animators. You can instantly think how a character shadow may be created using a duplicate of the character and smearing it all over the ground plane, or any other plane. Let's walk through those steps now.

1. Open up the download file `hh2_castShadow.fla` and you'll see Chlu standing near a wall. We're going to cast a shadow from the light source indicated by the red arrow.

2. Drag a region around him using the Arrow tool (V), then press CTRL+C to copy him.

3. Select frame 1 in the shadow layer and Paste in Place by pressing CTRL+SHIFT+V.

4. Lock and hide the chlu layer so we don't accidentally ruin him, then back in the shadow layer, select frame 1 again so the graphic of our character is selected.

5. Go to the Fill Color picker in the Colors section of the Tools panel and choose a shade of gray that you think is suitable for a shadow. The character should now be a complete silhouette of that color.

6. Now it's time to play. Unhide (but don't unlock) the chlu layer.

7. Choose the Free Transform tool (Q) , and then select the Scale modifier. Scale the shadow up a bit, to give it some drama.

8. Next, shift the whole shadow down so that the top of the shadow's head is almost level with his eyes. In just a minute this will be consistent with our light angle, as indicated by the red arrow.

9. With the shadow selected, press SHIFT+RIGHT ARROW, until the shadow is positioned away on the right from the character, like so:

10. According to the light source and the wall angle, we should stretch and skew this shadow slightly. So, making sure that the shadow is still selected, select the Free Transform tool and the Distort modifier. First, drag the right-hand side of the bounding box to the right so he gets fatter.

11. Now push the top left-hand corner of the shadow up a bit, and the top right-hand corner down a little, so that the angle is consistent with that of our red arrow at the top left of the stage.

12. Looking good. We'll have to do something about his leg shadows now though. Grab the Lasso tool (L) and select **Polygon** mode in the Options areas of the Tools panel. Make a straight-edged selection along the base of the wall and around his leg-shadows.

13. Finally, using the **Rotate and Skew** and the **Distort** modifiers, play around with the shadow, using something like the following sequence:

Now smile real big and squeal.

If you're confident with your pen, it can be much quicker to draw the shadow than to go through all of those steps, but your freehand results are likely to be much less accurate.

Also, as mentioned earlier, shadows and other effects *will* add to your file size, so be careful how and where you use them. If you decide that you must have them in, you may need to optimize them (CTRL+SHIFT+ALT+C) using multiple passes, to lower their byte-count.

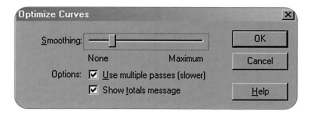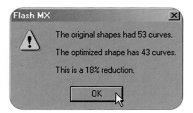

Note also, for walk or run animation movie clips, you can have two instances of the same movie clip onstage, with one of them skewed and silhouetted acting as the shadow, which will synchronize perfectly with the character animation, because it is the same symbol.

Play with the Envelope modifier of the Free Transform tool if you'd like to conform a shadow to an undulating surface, such as a boulder or a rolling field.

Project 10: Tones

There are a couple of effective ways to do tones. I prefer the longer way of mixing darker colors for each area of the character's palette. This method works very well for full animation with lots of inbetweens, but is equally efficient for limited animation.

There is another way that is very effective but is much quicker, especially for limited animation; I call it the **masked tone**.

In the following exercise, you'll add a masked tone to a character to give him some volume and form.

1. Open up your `hh2_swatchMix.fla` that you saved earlier. Of course, thanks to you, he's got some excellent evening colors now, but all the same he's a fairly uneventful character so far. He still looks very flat, as if he's a cardboard cutout printed on matte paper. So, let's give him some volume and gloss. Add another layer to your timeline and call it `tone`.

2. Add two keyframes (F6) to frames 1 and 2 of this new layer, and extend all the other layers to frame 3 by inserting blank frames (F5). Next, select frame 2 in the `chlu` layer and press F7 so he's only got one frame. This is that so we can use onion-skinning effectively.

3. Select frame 2 of your `tone` layer, and turn on onion-skinning. Make sure the onion skin handle is far enough across to show the character throughout the onion skin.

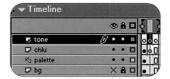

4. Start by doing a rough version of the tone in frame 2. Think about how you'll show volume, with his round cheeks, skinny neck, and possibly some folds in his clothing. Draw only the demarcation line (the tone boundary on his skin where you want the darkened areas to start).

5. When you've done that, go to frame 3 with onion-skinning turned on and clean up your rough, then loop the two ends of that line so that you have a contained area.

6. Fill that area with paint and you should have something that looks like this:

7. Go into your Color Mixer panel (SHIFT+F9) and make a black fill color that has an alpha of approximately 20%.

8. Grab the Paint Bucket and fill your looped tone with your new see-through paint. If you look at the character now, you'll see he has a nice shadowy bit, but the huge, ugly blob of the loop is still there.

9. You can cut this blob off manually, or you can mask it off. Here's how I mask it. First create a new layer and call it mask. Now, using the Arrow tool (V), select the entire character graphic (NOT the tone) and convert him to a graphic symbol (F8).

10. Press CTRL+C to copy the graphic and then paste it in place (CTRL+SHIFT+V) in the mask layer. Right-click on your mask layer, and choose mask from the drop-down menu. The mask layer automatically takes your tone layer under its wing, and the ugly tone loop will be masked out. Delete the two keyframes you added to the tone layer earlier, so that your tone fills the whole layer.

11. Now add some highlights to his eyes, unhide your background layers, and... yum!

Not only does the character now have some volume and realism, we've also brought some serious atmosphere into the shot. (If you like, you can compare your movie with hh2_swatchMixdone.fla in the download files.)

Highlights

A highlight may be defined as the *reflection of the light source*. They can appear not only on shiny surfaces, such as eyeballs and bubbles, but on less reflective surfaces too. In *hitchHiker*, I show the volume and form of trees and bushes using the same principles used to highlight a character's eye.

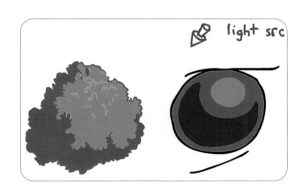

In this simplified bush, you can see the similarities in the treatment of highlights and tones to show volume and form in the bush and the eye.

To add a highlight to an eye, I simple choose an appropriate highlight color, zoom in on the eye and use the Brush tool with a large sized brush to make a dot in keeping with the light direction.

Effects summary

The effects in our project needn't be anything spectacular, as we're telling the story in fairly low light and in fairly ordinary environments, but this isn't to say we're limited with what we can do. There are plenty of opportunities throughout to have a nice effect here and there, such as the highlight in the old guy's eye, the shadows in the hallway, the fog under the streetlamp, and the steam puffs mentioned in the lip-sync section.

Have a look around the movie and use your imagination!

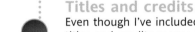

Post-production

In this final section, we'll look at some of the finishing touches you can apply to your Flash animations.

Titles and credits

Even though I've included this subject in the post-production section, it doesn't matter whether you make your titles and credits scenes first or last. In fact, there's nothing stopping you from working on them when you're halfway through the movie and need a break from drawing.

The title scene is your chance to do something interesting, and even mind-blowing, to get your audience hooked before any of the characters appear on-screen. Having said that, you may like to integrate some character animation into your title scene or, on the other hand, incorporate some titles into your first scene of the actual movie.

That's not to say you can't do something amazing with text. There's a chapter in this book on text effects and animation, and you'll learn a lot in there about the endless possibilities of text manipulation in Flash MX.

For my own part, the following is what I regard as a particularly important point to consider in the titles and credits creation process.

Theme

I believe the preloader, titles, and credits are important parts of the movie, and as such should follow a common theme throughout. It's for this reason that I'm using the exact same titles scene from *hitchHiker:part one* for *part two*, with some obvious changes.

The way my *hitchHiker* titles came about was that I initially wanted a view from a driver's seat, with road signs going past. Each of these road signs would have had some text with titles and credits, and being at night, the headlights for the car would have lit up each sign as it flew by. After all the credit signs had gone by, we'd see our *hitchHiker* character go past in the same way.

In the end, I decided on a simplified version. The movie starts in complete darkness, and as cars go past, the headlights light up the titles.

This was achieved by simply tweening the brightness values of the text from black to white, and back to black again, as the pool of light moved through. The shadow of the text was a skewed instance of the same black text symbol, which needed some keyframing and manual positioning to make it work the way I wanted it to.

Having the constrain point of the symbol at the base of the text ensured that the shadow remained rooted to the base of the main text as it moved.

Open `hh2_titles.fla` in the download files and have a look around.

Credits

Most people leave the cinema when the credits start rolling. Why? Credits are boring. It's only fairly recently that filmmakers have begun to feature outtakes or extra scenes while the credits are rolling. We don't have to go so far in our Flash movies, but it's certainly something to ponder.

I've come to this fairly loose conclusion: people don't lose interest until the screen goes black. So, if the story allows, don't fade to black until the credits have finished! Suppose your final scene shows your character walking slowly into the sunset. This is the perfect opportunity to roll credits and have people take notice. If the animation isn't distracting, then I guarantee the audience will read your credits.

Project 11: Titles and credits

I've decided on a title for the joke, and it's simply 'A Little Help', which gives nothing away. For simplicity's sake, let's just stick the title there in a nice font with an appropriate color, and fade it on then off again. Open the `project_titles.fla` and you'll see what I've done.

In keeping with the style of the titles, I've made the credits with the same font and a nice color taken from the fog gradient in the opening shot. Again, I'm using the ancient, tried-and-true method of fading in and fading out the text. Test your `titles` scene (CTRL+ALT+ENTER) to get an idea of how long your credits will need to be on-screen, so the viewer can read them, and then adjust the timing if necessary.

The possibilities of text manipulation are only limited by your own imagination; don't forget to check out the text animation chapter in this book for more inspiration.

Preloader

The *hitchHiker* story does have a preloader, but we'll not go into my method here as there is a dedicated chapter on preloaders at the start of this book by Todd Yard. However, if you are interested in looking at the *hitchHiker* preloader, you can download a short tutorial on it from the friends of ED web site.

Summary

In this chapter, we've covered quite a lot of ground on animation with Flash MX, looking at the inspiration, story, and storyboard stages of the production, then building the environments in which our story plays out. We've also covered the design and construction of our characters, moving them around within their environments and bringing it all to life with a little effects magic.

Finally, in the post-production section we learned about adding titles and credits, and discussed their important role in telling our story.

I've purposely left the project file unfinished. It's yours, and hopefully now you have all the skills you need to finish it yourself. Good luck! When you finish it, post a link on the friends of ED forums, I'd love to have a look!

About the Author
Chad Corbin

Chad Corbin is the designer/programmer behind lo9ic.com, an award winning Flash web site recognized for technical excellence and innovation.

Most recently, lo9ic.com was awarded a Bronze Medal in the ID Magazine, Interactive Media Review.

The majority of the experimental works displayed on lo9ic.com concentrate on using 3D effects and mathematics to create interfaces and interactions.

Chad attended Cornell University where he received a degree in Mechanical Engineering. After graduating, he taught himself Flash, HTML and JavaScript, and began his career as a web designer/developer.

Chad now lives in Boulder, Colorado where he works as a web designer/developer for Wall Street on Demand.

"Lo9ic gives me a place to experiment and try things that I don't get to try at work. It's where I get play with the ideas that pop into my head late at night when I should be sleeping."

"I'm really interested in exploring interaction and information display problems with my experiments. Using 3D has added to the complexity or the problems, but has opened up all sorts of new possibilities."

"I had always wanted to be in engineering, so it's a little ironic that all of the math, programming and problem solving techniques I learned in engineering school prepared me for a career in web design, especially since barely any of this stuff existed when I started college."

Dynamic Drawing

Macromedia Flash MX includes a whole host of new features that allow us to dynamically draw shapes at runtime, without needing to duplicate movie clips or attach movies from the Library. This is a huge step forward for Flash as an animation and application programming environment because it gives us the power to create dynamic effects in timeline-based movies, or create single frame movies that are built entirely from ActionScript. Fortunately, the engineers at Macromedia have made it much easier for us to tap into this new capability by providing us with new ActionScript methods.

Over the course of this chapter, we'll investigate the **drawing API**, the new dynamic drawing methods in Macromedia Flash MX, learning how to dynamically draw lines, curves, solid fills, and gradient fills. In addition, we'll discover how to create movie clips and transform movie clips into buttons at runtime. These methods, theories, and techniques will all be combined in the creation of our final project, an interactive sequence of 3D shapes and images dynamically generated using ActionScript and XML, which we'll build from the ground up:

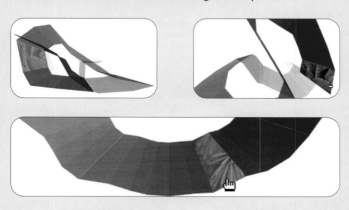

The drawing API

In this first section, we'll look at each of the new drawing API methods in turn, covering all of the parameters along the way. Each of these methods also has a practical example to illustrate them in action. As we go along, you can test the ActionScript in a movie of your own simply by creating a single frame movie and adding the ActionScript listed in the example (all of these new drawing API tools are ActionScript-based, so we'll be spending all of our time in the Actions panel). For the purposes of this tutorial, we'll be working in **Expert Mode** in the Actions panel (CTRL+SHIFT+E).

Also, you can view the finished code by downloading the example FLA files from the friends of ED web site. I encourage you to spend a few minutes with each example, playing around with the code to see how it behaves. Don't be afraid to experiment: experimentation is really the only way to truly learn how each method works in practice.

Drawing lines

Thanks to the addition of the drawing API in Flash MX, we cannot only draw lines at runtime, but also control a line's thickness, color, and transparency (alpha) using a few simple ActionScript methods.

Drawing a straight line with lineTo()

We're going to create a line that is 100% opaque red with a 6pt weight, extending diagonally from the top left corner of the stage (0,0) to the bottom right corner (550, 400). (This is `straight_line.fla` in the download files.)

1. Open a new movie and select frame 1 of the default layer. Open the Actions panel (Window>Actions / F9), and set the `thickness`, `rgb`, and `alpha` parameters of the line using the `lineStyle()` method by adding this line of ActionScript:

    ```
    this.lineStyle(6, 0xFF0000, 100);
    ```

2. Next, set the end point of the line using the `lineTo()` method:

    ```
    this.lineTo(550, 400);
    ```

3. Test your movie:

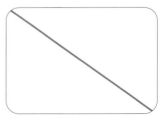

To get a feel for how the `lineStyle()` and `lineTo()` methods work, try changing some of the parameters in this example. For instance, try changing the end point, color, or thickness. Can you make a line that's blue, 50% opaque, and 8 pixels thick? What happens if you add more lines to the drawing?

> *It's worth noting that when no movie clip or timeline is specified for the drawing to be placed in, Flash will place the drawing in the root timeline.*

For reference, here are the ActionScript definitions for the `lineStyle()` and `lineTo()` methods.

Method

```
mc.lineStyle(thickness, rgb, alpha);
```

Parameters

- `mc` can be the instance name or path to any movie clip in the Flash movie, and is where the drawing will occur.

- `thickness` sets the width of the line and can be any number between 0 (hairline thickness) and 255 pixels wide. Also, the end of the line is curved rather than blunt.

- `rgb` sets the color of the line and takes the form of any hexadecimal color code. For example, you would use `0x000000` for black, and `0xFFFFFF` for white.

- The `alpha` parameter sets the transparency of the line and can be any number between 0 (totally transparent) and 100 (fully opaque).

Method

```
mc.lineTo(x, y);
```

Parameters

- `mc` can be the instance name or path to any movie clip in the Flash movie. `mc` is the name of the movie clip in which the drawing will occur.

- `x` and `y` are the end point coordinates of the line, relative to the coordinates of `mc`.

Drawing curves

Another useful tool in the drawing API is the ability to draw curves at runtime using the `curveTo()` method. Creating a similar effect in previous versions of Flash was very difficult, to say the least. This new method has opened up all sorts of possibilities for those of us who like to play in the Actions panel and will undoubtedly change the way many Flash movies are created. The method for creating curves is very simple, as we'll see in the following example.

Drawing a curve with curveTo()

Let's create a curve that's 4 pixels thick and 100% opaque blue. It will extend from the top left corner of the stage (0,0) curving towards (550,0), and finally ending at the bottom right corner of the stage (550, 400). (For reference, this is `curve.fla`.)

1. Start a fresh new movie (CTRL+N). Just as we did in the last example, begin by setting the thickness, rgb, and alpha of the line using the lineStyle() method:

        this.lineStyle(4, 0x000066, 100);

2. Set the anchor point and end point of the curve using the curveTo() method:

        this.curveTo(550, 0, 550, 400);

3. Finally, test your movie (CTRL+ENTER). You should see the blue curve like this:

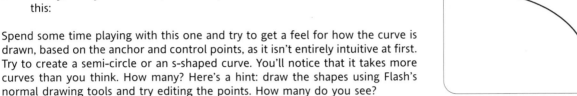

Spend some time playing with this one and try to get a feel for how the curve is drawn, based on the anchor and control points, as it isn't entirely intuitive at first. Try to create a semi-circle or an s-shaped curve. You'll notice that it takes more curves than you think. How many? Here's a hint: draw the shapes using Flash's normal drawing tools and try editing the points. How many do you see?

Here are the method and parameters to help you along:

Method

        mc.curveTo(controlX, controlY, anchorX, anchorY);

Parameters

*   mc can be the instance name or path to any movie clip in the Flash movie and is the place in which the drawing occurs.

*   controlX and controlY are the control point coordinates of the curve (relative to the coordinates of mc), determining the direction and amount of curvature of the curve.

*   anchorX and anchorY are the end point coordinates of the curve, relative to the coordinates of mc.

Drawing solid fills

You may have been waiting for something like this one for a while; I know I have! After all, what set of dynamic drawing tools would be complete without a method for creating fills? As you might have guessed, Flash MX includes such a method and, when used in conjunction with the lineTo() and curveTo(), gives us the ability to fill any shape we can dream up with color.

Drawing a solid fill with beginFill()

In the following example (solid_fill.fla), we'll use the beginFill() method to create a shape with a green fill, that's 100% opaque, and also has a transparent outline.

1. In a new movie (CTRL+N), go into the Actions panel (F9) and set the `rgb` and `alpha` values of the fill using the `beginFill()` method:

    ```
    this.beginFill(0x33CC33, 100);
    ```

2. Draw the curved lines to bound the solid fill using the `lineStyle()` and `curveTo()` methods:

    ```
    this.lineStyle(0, 0x000000, 0);
    this.curveTo(275, 200, 550, 0);
    this.curveTo(275, 200, 550, 400);
    this.curveTo(275, 200, 0, 400);
    this.curveTo(275, 200, 0, 0);
    ```

    You may have noticed that the first line of the above ActionScript isn't strictly necessary for this movie to function properly, but it's useful to note what it is doing: it is setting a line style that has a hairline thickness, is black, but has an alpha of 0. This third parameter value is what makes the outline completely transparent.

3. Complete the fill using the `endFill()` method:

    ```
    this.endFill();
    ```

4. Test your movie (CTRL+ENTER). You should see the filled green shape like this:

    Try altering the parameters of the fill and the curves used to bound the fill to see what effect this has. Also, try crossing over the curves to see how you can create negative spaces in the fill.

    For example, this drawing was produced simply by editing the parameters in bold:

    ```
    this.beginFill(0xFF33CC, 100);
    this.lineStyle(2, 0x000000, 100);
    this.curveTo(275, 200, 0, 550);
    this.curveTo(275, 200, 550, 400);
    this.curveTo(275, 200, 0, 400);
    this.curveTo(275, 200, 0, 0);
    this.endFill();
    ```

You can even experiment with adding loops and random numbers to create abstract shapes.

Once again, here are the method and parameters to help you out:

Method

```
mc.beginFill(rgb, alpha);
```

Parameters

- `mc` can be the instance name or path to any movie clip in the Flash movie, and the movie clip in which the drawing occurs.

- `rgb` sets the color of the fill and can be any hexadecimal color code: `0x000000` for black, `0xFFFFFF` for white, and so on.

- `alpha` sets the transparency of the fill and can be any number between 0 (fully transparent) and 100 (fully opaque).

Drawing gradient fills

As well as drawing fills of solid color, we can also create fills containing linear and radial gradients. While these types of fills may be the most difficult to learn and master, the visual effect is identical to the gradient fills you can create using the Color Mixer panel. After some time and experimentation, you should be able to dynamically generate both linear and radial fills to produce the exact effect that you are looking for.

In the following examples, we'll take a look at how to generate both types of fill using the `beginGradientFill()` method but, because it is more complicated than the previous methods we've looked at, it's probably useful to examine the methods and parameters first:

Method

```
mc.beginGradientFill(fillType, colors, alphas, ratios, matrix);
```

Parameters

- `mc` can be the instance name or path to any movie clip in the Flash movie and is the clip in which the drawing will occur.

- `fillType` sets the type of fill, which can either be `"linear"` or `"radial"`. The `fillType` parameter is entered as a string, so remember to use quotation marks around the type of fill you want.

- `colors` is an array of color values given as hexadecimal color codes.

- `alphas` is an array of alpha values, each between 0 and 100, that determines the transparency of the color in the corresponding slot of the `colors` array.

- `ratios` is an array of numbers, each between 0 and 255, that determines the center of each color in the corresponding slot of the `colors` array. In linear fills, a ratio of 0 corresponds to the left boundary of the fill and a ratio of 255 corresponds to the right boundary of the fill. In radial fills, 255 corresponds to the center of the fill and 0 corresponds to the outer edge.

● matrix is an object that takes either of these two forms:

{a:#, b:#, c:#, d:#, e:#, f:#, g:#, h:#, i:#}

where the variables a through to i define a 3x3 transformation matrix, which scales, skews, and rotates the gradient fill. (# represents a numeric value.)

{matrixType"box", x:#, y:#, w:#, h:#, r:#}

where matrixType always equals "box" and x and y define the x and y coordinates of the upper left corner of the fill. The parameters w, h, and r define the width, height, and rotation of the fill.

The first form of the matrix parameter is by far the strangest looking. Certainly, the most difficult aspect of the begingradientFill() method is determining the values to enter into this form of the matrix parameter. The documentation on this matrix form is sparse so I spent some time experimenting, plugging in various numbers to see what happened. This is what I discovered:

Matrix Parameter	Property
a:	the width of the gradient in pixels
b:	the y skew of the gradient
c:	always equal to 0
d:	the x skew of the gradient
e:	the height of the gradient in pixels
f:	always equal to 0
g:	the x offset of the gradient in pixels
h:	the y offset of the gradient in pixels
i:	always equal to 1

When this matrix form is used it scales, offsets, and skews a 2-pixel square fill centered at (0,0). This means that in order to fill a 100-pixel square, centered at (200, 200), you would enter 100 for a and b, and 200 for g and h. However, because there is no variable for rotation, you have to use the skew variables to fake a rotation. Unfortunately, this is not a very reliable method and the outcome is difficult to control.

The second form of the matrix parameter, also known as a **Box transform**, specifies the gradient as a box shape, whose parameters are stored in an Object object called matrix. Although this object is called matrix, it isn't really a matrix at all, so you only have to think of it as an object with properties that define the fill. Your matrix object must have a number of properties, and these describe the bounding box of your gradient pattern. It's important to realize that these do not define the fill area, simply how the gradient will look.

The gradient bounding box will have the gradient running along the direction of the arrow, starting from the corner point (x, y), *not* the center of the box.

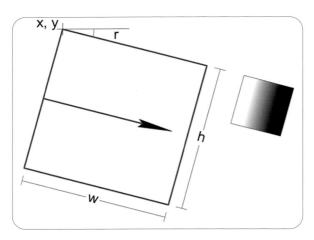

- `matrixType` must be "box" if you wish to rotate the gradient accurately.

- `x` and `y` are the coordinates of the corner point of the gradient bounding box.

- `w` and `h` are the width and height of the bounding box.

- `r` is the angle of rotation of the box, and is measured in radians.

Drawing a linear gradient with beginGradientFill()

In this example, we'll create a linear gradient from blue to yellow, scale it to fit the stage, and rotate the gradient by 45 degrees. We'll also be using the Box transform form of the `matrix` parameter (the source file is `linear_gradientFill.fla`).

1. In a new movie, set the `fillType`, `colors`, `alphas`, and `ratios` parameters of the fill:

    ```
    this.fillType = "linear";
    this.colors = [0x0000FF, 0xFFFF00];
    this.alphas = [100, 100];
    this.ratios = [0, 255];
    this.rotation = 45;
    ```

2. Next, set the `matrix` parameter:

    ```
    this.matrix = {matrixType:"box", x:0, y:0, w:550, h:400, r:rotation*
    ➡(Math.PI/180)};
    ```

    As `r` (the angle of rotation of the gradient) is measured in radians, there is a small calculation at the end of this line to convert the value of `rotation` from degrees into radians.

3. Now set the gradient with the `beginGradientFill()` method:

    ```
    this.beginGradientFill(fillType, colors, alphas, ratios, matrix);
    ```

4. Draw the lines or curves to bound the solid fill using the `lineStyle()` and `curveTo()` methods (note that we're making the outline transparent again here and that the boundaries are the same size as the default stage in Flash):

```
this.lineStyle(0, 0x00000000, 0);
this.lineTo(550, 0);
this.lineTo(550, 400);
this.lineTo(0, 400);
```

5. End the fill using the endFill() method:

```
this.endFill();
```

6. Finally, test your movie (CTRL+ENTER) to see the linear gradient fill in effect.

Drawing a radial gradient with beginGradientFill()

In this next example (radial_gradientFill.fla), we will create a fully opaque, pink to blue radial gradient. The gradient is centered on the stage, and we'll use the {matrixType...} form of the matrix parameter again.

1. In a new movie, set the fillType, colors, alphas, ratios, and matrix of the fill using the beginGradientFill() method:

```
this.fillType = "radial";
this.colors = [0xFF99FF, 0x330099];
this.alphas = [100, 100];
this.ratios = [0, 255];
this.matrix = {matrixType:"box", x:0, y:0, w:550, h:400, r:0};
this.beginGradientFill(fillType, colors, alphas, ratios, matrix);
```

2. Draw the transparent lines or curves to bound the solid fill, using the lineStyle() and curveTo() methods:

```
this.lineStyle(0, 0x00000000, 0);
this.curveTo(550, 100, 450, 175);
this.curveTo(550, 100, 450, 400);
this.curveTo(550, 100, 0, 400);
this.curveTo(550, 100, 0, 0);
```

3. End the fill using the endFill() method:

```
this.endFill();
```

4. Now test your movie (CTRL+ENTER). You should see a radial gradient fill like this:

It's definitely worth spending some time experimenting with the parameters of this method. Try using three, four, or five colors by adding elements to the colors array.

This colors array contains three colors and produces the following effect:

```
this.colors = [0xFF99FF, 0x330099, 0x99FFCC];
this.alphas = [100, 100, 100];
this.ratios = [60, 200, 60];
```

Try changing the `alphas`, `ratios`, and `matrix` values, remembering that the number of elements in the `alphas` and `ratios` arrays must always match the number of elements in the `colors` array, otherwise your drawing will not appear.

In this image, I've changed the ratios array to `this.ratios = [150,100];`

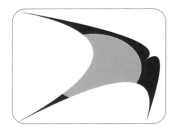

Try moving the radial gradient away from the center of the shape, by altering the `x` and `y` values in the matrix like this:

```
this.matrix = {matrixType:"box",x:180,y:60,
➡w:550,h:400,r:0};
```

It may take a while to get the hang of this, but the power that comes with learning how to use it properly will enable you to create any gradient you could ordinarily draw using Flash's manual drawing tools.

Moving the drawing position

If you experimented with any of the previous examples, you may have noticed that lines and curves are always drawn from (0,0) initially. Also, the drawing then continues from the end point of whichever line or curve was drawn last. But what if you wanted to draw separate lines or curves? Flash MX has the `moveTo()` method for this exact purpose, enabling you to move the current drawing position and create separate lines, curves, or fills.

Method
```
mc.moveTo(x, y);
```

Parameters

- `mc` is the instance name or path to the movie clip, and is the movie clip in which the drawing occurs.

- `x` and `y` are the new drawing position coordinates relative to the coordinate system of `mc`.

Clearing the drawing

Once a drawing on the screen is created, it remains visible throughout the life of the movie, or until its parent movie clip is hidden or removed. This is because the drawings are not tied to any particular frame on the timeline. However, the drawing API contains a useful method called `clear()` that erases any graphics created using the drawing API methods:

Method

```
mc.clear();
```

Parameters

- `mc` is the instance name or path to the clip that you want cleared.

Notes on the dynamic drawing tools

- You can reset the line style by calling the `lineStyle()` method with no parameters. Also, to draw a line quickly , you can just use one parameter (which is a number specifying line thickness). For example, `lineStyle(2)` will draw a black line with a thickness of 2, which is useful for drafting things quickly.

- The `clear()` method removes all line style information and sets the drawing position back to (0,0).

- Using the `moveTo()` method between `beginFill()`, `beginGradientFill()`, and `endFill()` methods will erase sections of the fill.

- Each successive drawing within the same movie clip is drawn on top of the previous one, giving the impression that the drawings are stacked.

Creating movie clips and buttons

In addition to the new dynamic drawing methods, Flash MX also enables us to create empty movie clips. One particular use for this is to transform them into buttons. This new functionality decreases our reliance on exported Library items and duplicated movie clips, allowing us to create objects and interactions at runtime using ActionScript alone.

Creating empty movie clips

The `createEmptyMovieClip()` method can be used to create new, empty movie clips within any movie clip present in your movie, or at the _root level. These movie clips have the same properties as movie clips created using the Insert>Convert to Symbol… menu command, but with one exception: they only have one frame. Despite this difference, you can assign variables, change properties, and even define functions and events to the dynamically created movie clips, treating them just like any other movie clip.

In this example (`createEmptyMovieClip.fla`), we'll create an empty movie clip to contain a dynamically drawn image.

1. Create the empty movie clip using the `createEmptyMovieClip()` method and position the clip in the center of the stage:

    ```
    this.createEmptyMovieClip("myDrawing", 1);
    myDrawing._x = 275;
    myDrawing._y = 200;
    ```

2. Set the line style of the movie clip and draw a picture:

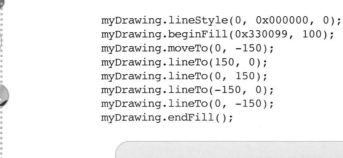

```
myDrawing.lineStyle(0, 0x000000, 0);
myDrawing.beginFill(0x330099, 100);
myDrawing.moveTo(0, -150);
myDrawing.lineTo(150, 0);
myDrawing.lineTo(0, 150);
myDrawing.lineTo(-150, 0);
myDrawing.lineTo(0, -150);
myDrawing.endFill();
```

> *Note that any drawings created with these methods use x and y coordinates relative to the center registration point of the movie clip in which the drawing is made. This means that when we use negative values for the x coordinate, we are drawing to the left of the center of the movie clip. Likewise, if we use a negative value for the y coordinate, we are drawing above the center of the movie clip.*

3. Finally, test your movie (CTRL+ENTER). You should see a drawing like the one illustrated here.

   Now that you know how to create one movie clip, try creating several more using different colors or shapes to fill them. You may also want to try nesting movie clips inside each other. As a challenge, see if you can figure out a way to animate the movie clips using a movie event such as `onEnterFrame`.

Here are the parameters for the `createEmptyMovieClip()` method:

Method

```
mc.createEmptyMovieClip(instanceName, depth);
```

Parameters

- `mc` is the instance name or path to the movie clip in which you want to create the new empty movie clip.

- `instanceName` is the instance name of the clip to be created.

- `depth` is the layer in the stacking order on which you want the new movie clip to reside.

Transforming movie clips into buttons

There is no method in Flash MX to dynamically create buttons in the same way as movie clips. However, by assigning **button events** to movie clips, you can transform the behavior of a movie clip so that it acts just like a button. What's really amazing about this feature is that the events can be turned on or off while the movie is playing, allowing you to change the behavior of a movie clip to a button and back, depending on the user's actions. This makes it possible to create interfaces that can be enabled or disabled without resorting to creating a separate frame for each button state.

Creating a button with button events

In this example (`buttons.fla`), we'll take a movie clip drawn using a combination of the drawing API methods that we've looked at already, and from this we'll create a button that changes color according to the `onRollOver` and `onRollOut` event handlers.

1. In a new file (CTRL+N), create the empty clip using the `createEmptyMovieClip()` method and position the movie clip in the center of the movie:

    ```
    this.createEmptyMovieClip("myDrawing", 1);
    myDrawing._x = 275;
    myDrawing._y = 200;
    ```

2. Next, define a function that will draw a shape in the movie clip `myDrawing`, with the color specified in the `myColor` parameter:

    ```
    function setColor(mycolor) {
        myDrawing.clear();
        myDrawing.lineStyle(0, 0x000000, 0);
        myDrawing.beginFill(myColor, 100);
        myDrawing.moveTo(0, -150);
        myDrawing.lineTo(150, 0);
        myDrawing.lineTo(0, 150);
        myDrawing.lineTo(-150, 0);
        myDrawing.lineTo(0, -150);
        myDrawing.endFill();
    }
    ```

3. After this function, define the `onRollOver` and `onRollOut` event handlers for `myDrawing`:

    ```
    myDrawing.onRollOver = function() {
        setColor(0x660000);
    };
    myDrawing.onRollOut = function() {
        setColor(0x666600);
    };
    ```

4. Call `setColor()` to draw `myDrawing` in its default color:

    ```
    setColor(0x666600);
    ```

5. Test your movie (CTRL+ENTER). If you roll over the shape, it should change color and return to the original default color when you roll out:

This technique could be used to create buttons from external images that are loaded at runtime or from dynamic text blocks from XML, eliminating the need for transparent buttons. Complex buttons that change shape, color, and animate without being interrupted by mouse events are also possible. For additional practice, see if you can figure out a way to use loops to create a multi-button menu.

```
mc.onPress
mc.onRelease
mc.onReleaseOutside
mc.onRollOver
mc.onRollOut
mc.onDragOver
mc.onDragOut
```

To the right is a list of the different possible button clip event handlers you can use to detect user activity, and hence animate your movie clips as required.

Notes on dynamic movie clip and button creation

- Empty movie clips can be nested inside each other.

- Empty movie clips are automatically placed at (0,0) inside the movie clip where they are created.

- Empty movie clips only contain one frame.

- Whenever the mouse is rolled over a movie clip that has a button clip event handler, the arrow cursor will change into a hand.

- The button states of 'up', 'over', 'down' and 'hit' need to be programmed into the movie clip, using the button clip event handlers, in order to change the color or shape, for example.

- Setting the `enabled` property of a movie clip to `false` will disable the button. You can do this using `mc.enabled = false;`.

Dynamically drawn masks

Combined with the drawing API tools, dynamic masking gives us the to power to create many new visual effects. What is especially great about this new feature is that it allows you to create very complicated masked movie clips, where both the mask *and* the contents of the masked movie clip are animated. Masks can be generated at runtime with the drawing API tools, and then set to mask movie clips (which could also contain further nested masked movie clips).

Creating a mask with setMask()

In this example (dynamic_masking.fla), we'll create two new movie clips, draw a shape in each, and then set one movie clip to mask the other.

1. In a new movie (CTRL+N), start by adding the following line of ActionScript to create a new movie clip called drawing:

    ```
    this.createEmptyMovieClip("drawing", 1);
    ```

2. Draw a filled shape inside drawing:

    ```
    drawing.beginFill(0x6600CC, 100);
    drawing.curveTo(275, 200, 550, 0);
    drawing.curveTo(275, 200, 550, 400);
    drawing.curveTo(275, 200, 0, 400);
    drawing.curveTo(275, 200, 0, 0);
    drawing.endFill();
    ```

3. Test your movie (CTRL+ENTER) to see the shape you've just drawn:

4. Close down the test movie and continue your code by adding this next line to create a new movie clip called mask. This will sit on the second level of the stacking order.

    ```
    this.createEmptyMovieClip("mask", 2);
    ```

5. Add the following drawing API code to draw a rectangular shape that will act as the mask shape in the mask movie clip:

    ```
    mask.moveTo(50, 50);
    mask.beginFill(0x6600CC, 100);
    mask.lineTo(500, 50);
    mask.lineTo(500, 350);
    mask.lineTo(50, 350);
    mask.lineTo(50, 50);
    mask.endFill();
    ```

6. Now we use setMask() to make the mask movie clip mask the drawing movie clip:

    ```
    drawing.setMask(mask);
    ```

7. Test the movie (CTRL+ENTER). You should see this effect, with the rectangular mask movie clip masking the four corners of the drawing movie clip:

The setMask() method actually improves upon the standard masking technique, allowing you to generate effects that would otherwise be impossible. We can dynamically nest masks inside of masked movie clips to create a layered masking effect. Even better, you can control and animate the masks just like any other movie clip, by using all of the MovieClip object properties you have worked with before. Very complex, randomized, image transitions can be programmed, making each transition unique. Using the method we've just looked at, try nesting and animating both the mask and masked movie clips to see what new effects you can create.

Here's the actual syntax for the setMask():

Method

```
mc.setMask(maskMovieClip);
```

Parameters

- mc is the instance name or path of any movie clip in your movie that will be masked.

- maskMovieClip is the instance name or path of any other movie clip, which will mask mc.

Notes on dynamic masking

- You can dynamically remove a mask by setting maskMovieClip to null like this:

  ```
  mc.setMask(null);
  ```

- A mask movie clip cannot be set to mask itself.

- Mask movie clips can only be applied to one movie clip at a time.

- Device fonts rendered inside of the masked movie clip will still display, despite being masked.

Putting it all together

Now that we're ready to build the final project, go ahead and open the file `final_project.swf` and spend a few minutes playing around with the movie. You'll notice that a sequence of red shapes seems to follow the mouse, twisting and rotating in 3D space, replicating and eventually fading away. If you click your mouse, the movie pauses, and if you roll over the shapes you should see an image appear, masked by what used to be the red shape that the mouse is over. Moving your mouse away from the image returns the shape to its original color, hiding the image. Clicking once again sets the movie back in motion.

 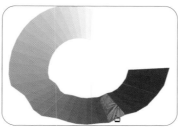 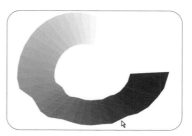

Open `final_project.fla` from the download files and take a look at the code in its final form. This is what we'll build during the rest of this chapter, taking the dynamic drawing techniques that we've learnt so far and applying them to this project. We'll also incorporate some simple 3D, XML, and external JPG images, to add to its use as a dynamic application. Don't worry if you haven't seen how to create 3D effects, use XML, or dynamically import images at runtime before; I'll cover each of these techniques in turn as we go along. It may seem like a lot of code now but, as we get stuck in, you'll see that it's fairly simple.

So how will we build our project? You may have begun thinking about how we will tackle the problem, but if not, that's OK. At the very least, I hope you have a solid understanding of the techniques we'll be using.

The approach that we'll take in building this effect is the same approach that I use whenever I work on a new project: I always start with a list of ideas of how I might achieve the final effect I'm looking for. Even for simple projects, or simply when experimenting, I figure out how I want to make the movie and write down a few sentences or thoughts about how I will execute the idea. For more complex projects, and especially on client work, forming this list becomes even more important and I end up writing down even more ideas. The list doesn't need to be an exact blueprint for the code you are going to use; it can simply be a couple of ideas of what you want to achieve.

Imagine for a moment that the movie you've just seen had not yet been created; how would you describe the steps involved in creating the effects you've seen? Well, there are lots of ways to approach the problem, so we just choose one that suits us and start listing our ideas. To help the process along, I've created a list that I hope will accomplish our goal. Hopefully, by examining the list below, you'll get closer to understanding why I've structured the code the way it has been in `final_project.fla`.

So, here's what we're going to do:

1. Make a movie to contain all of the movie clips that we'll create.

2. Load JPEG images into the movie from an external source. Keeping the images external makes it much easier to update the images at later date.

3.   Draw some shapes that respond to the user's mouse position by displaying one of the images. Using the shape to mask the image would be interesting.

4.   Make these shapes spin around as if in 3D space, with the mouse controlling the amount of rotation and movement.

5.   Create a loop that automatically generates the shapes and connects them to the previously drawn shapes.

6.   Build in a method that stops and starts the motion. A mouse click will work fine here.

With these points in mind, we'll work down the list, using it as a skeleton plan for writing the functions that make up the movie. We'll spend the rest of the chapter building this effect, doing so in separate sections so that you can see how the code is formed and structured. Remember, you can always refer to `final_project.fla` to compare your own movie.

Initializing the movie

As I thought about the items in the list above, I recognized that we'd need global variables and a place in the movie to initialize them. I like to initialize these variables together in one place, just in case I ever want to quickly re-initialize them later on while the movie is running.

1.   In a new movie (CTRL+N), add the following code to frame 1 of the default layer:

```
function initMovie() {
    objs = 0;
    max = 30;
    perspective = 300;
    this.createEmptyMovieClip("theScene", 1);
    theScene._x = 275;
    theScene._y = 200;
```

We'll need to count the number of mask movie clips on our stage as we create them, so we've defined an `objs` variable to act as a counter. We'll also want to cap the number of movie clips in the movie to keep it running smoothly, so we've defined a variable called `max` to set this maximum number. And, since we'll be dealing with 3D at some point, we've created a constant called `perspective`, which will be used in the 3D calculations later on. Finally, we'll need a container for all the masks and image movie clips, so we've created an empty movie clip called `theScene`, placing it at the center of the stage.

2.   Add the following lines to complete `initMovie()`, the initialization function:

```
    XMLdoc = new XML();
    XMLdoc.ignoreWhite = true;
    XMLdoc.onLoad = processXML;
    XMLdoc.load("imagelist.xml");
}
```

Here, we've created a new XML object with the `new XML()` method, and set the `ignoreWhite` property to `true`. This property tells Flash to ignore any extraneous tabs, spaces, and carriage returns in the XML (these extra characters are often present in XML, since it makes reading and writing XML much easier). We've also defined an `onLoad` event for the XML object, which will automatically be called whenever the external document loads. Finally, we've instructed Flash to load in the `imagelist.xml` document using the `XML.load()` method. This is a simple file containing a list of the file names of the JPEG images we'll be using.

That's the movie initialization set up. Let's move on and look at what Flash does with the XML document that we've just loaded.

Processing the XML

1. This XML document is included in the download files as `imagelist.xml`. Go ahead and open the document in a text editor program to see what it looks like:

If you are new to XML, you can simply think of it as a glorified HTML document with a top-level tag (a **node** or **first child**), containing nested tags (**child nodes**) between them. In our document, the `<imageList>` tag is our first child and each `<image>` tag within it is one of its children. Also notice that each `<image>` tag contains a `src` attribute. Attributes can be any `name="value"` pair and can be used to provide additional information about each node.

Since XML is structured data, we'll have to use any knowledge we have of the structure to write a function that processes the data in a way that is useful. We need a function that can perform the following operations:

- Go through all the children of the XML document.

- Locate the information in each child and use it to create empty movie clips.

- Populate these movie clips with the image specified in the `src` attribute.

2. Back in Flash, let's write a function that can do all of this for us. Directly beneath the previous function, add this `processXML` function:

```
function processXML(success) {
    if (success) {
        for (i=0; i<this.firstChild.childNodes.length; i++) {
            theScene.createEmptyMovieClip("image_"+i, i);
            theScene["image_"+i]._x = 2000;
            theScene["image_"+i].loadMovie(this.firstChild.childNodes[i].
            ➥attributessrc);
        }
    } else {
        getURL("javascript:alert('XML load failed.');");
    }
}
```

The `XML.load()` method (called in the `initMovie` function we've already written) returns the **load status** in addition to the actual XML itself. This status, which we are calling `success`, is passed into our function and checked to determine the existence of the XML. If the XML *does not* exist, we'll generate an alert message using a `javascript:` call in the `getURL()` method. If the XML *does* exist, we proceed with the processing.

In the third line of the previous code, we've set up a loop to go through the XML. We start with an index of 0, and loop through as many times as there are children in the `<imageList>` tag. Remember that the first child of our XML is the `<imageList>` tag, so `this.firstChild.childNodes` are the children within the `<imageList>` tag. In Flash, the `childNodes` attribute actually represents an array of the children, allowing us to easily find out the length, and thus count the number of children.

Inside of our loop, we create an empty movie clip within `theScene` for each `<image>` tag in the XML, naming the movie clip according to the index. Then, we position the movie clip off stage (at `_x = 2000`) so that when the image loads in, it is not visible.

Finally, we take the `src` attribute of each `<image>` tag, using it as the name of the external image to load into the empty movie clips. Again, we use the fact that `this.firstChild.childNodes` acts as an array to tell Flash which `<image>` tag to look at for the attribute.

Creating the mask movie clips

Now that the images are loaded in, we'll move on to creating the movie clips that mask the images. This will be achieved with the `createMaskClip()` function and, since we'll be using it a lot, we need to make it as generic as possible. To do this, we first decide what types of attributes each mask movie clip needs to have. We need to tell the function where the movie clip will be created and what its name and depth are, so we define `myPath`, `myName`, and `myDepth` parameters. We also need to tell the function which image the mask will be applied to, so we define the `myImage` parameter. Finally, since our mask will be living in a 3D space, we define `myX`, `myY`, and `myZ` parameters for the x, y and z coordinates. Unlike the 2D space that we are used to when working in the drawing window, we require the extra z coordinate to give our objects depth. Think of this coordinate as a distance measured into the screen.

1. Begin by defining this function underneath all of the previous code in your movie:

```
function createMaskClip(myPath, myName, myDepth, myImage, myX, myY, myZ) {
```

2. Now that the parameters are defined, we can begin writing the function itself:

```
this[myPath].createEmptyMovieClip(myName, myDepth);
this[myPath][myName].image = myImage;
this[myPath][myName].x = myX;
this[myPath][myName].y = myY;
this[myPath][myName].z = myZ;
```

The first thing we do here is to create an empty movie clip using the `createEmptyMovieClip()` method, setting its path, name, and depth to the `myPath`, `myName`, and `myDepth` parameters. Next, we take and set the `image`, `x`, `y`, and `z` variables in the newly created movie clip using the remaining parameters.

To make our movie interactive, we want these mask movie clips to react to the user's mouse. To do this, we'll define `onRollOver` and `onRollOut` event handlers for each mask. This has the added benefit of making the hand symbol appear whenever the mouse hovers over one of the masks.

3. Add the following code that will execute when the user's mouse rolls over the mask movie clip:

```
this[myPath][myName].onRollOver = function() {
this.myBounds = this.getBounds(this._parent);
this._parent[this.image]._x = this.myBounds.xMin;
this._parent[this.image]._y = this.myBounds.yMin;
this._parent[this.image]._xscale = Math.abs(this.myBounds.xMax-
➥this.myBounds.xMin)/2;
this._parent[this.image]._yscale = Math.abs(this.myBounds.yMax-
➥this.myBounds.yMin)/2;
this._parent[this.image]._visible = true;
this._parent[this.image]._alpha = this._alpha;
this._parent[this.image].setMask(this);
};
```

The onRollOver event handler triggers a number of actions for the mask movie clip and the image that it covers. The second line measures the size of the mask using the getBounds() method, and uses these boundaries to set the position and scale of the image clip to be masked. The visibility of the image movie clip is turned on and the _alpha property of the image movie clip is set to the current _alpha of the mask (you'll see why we're using the _alpha property later). Finally, the mask movie clip is set to mask the image movie clip using the setMask() method.

4. Lastly, close the function by adding the actions for the onRollOut event handler:

```
this[myPath][myName].onRollOut = function() {
this._parent[this.image].setMask(null);
this._parent[this.image]._visible = false;
};
}
```

These closing lines define the onRollOut event handler for the movie clip. This event tells the movie clip to remove the mask and hide the image, returning everything to the state it was in before the onRollOver event handler was triggered. Don't forget to include the closing brace for the function.

Creating the 3D effects

Now comes the math. What we need to write next is a function that will take a point and rotate it in 3D space.

1. Underneath all of the previous code, add this getNewPoint() function:

```
function getNewPoint(myX, myY, myZ, myXangle, myYangle) {
    tmp = myZ*Math.cos(myYangle)-myX*Math.sin(myYangle);
    Xpos = myZ*Math.sin(myYangle)+myX*Math.cos(myYangle);
    Ypos = myY*Math.cos(myXangle)-tmp*Math.sin(myXangle);
    Zpos = myY*Math.sin(myXangle)+tmp*Math.cos(myXangle);
    return [Xpos, Ypos, Zpos];
}
```

This diagram illustrates the basic process:

We start with a point (the black dot) defined in the (X,Y,Z) coordinate space by the variables **x**, **y**, and **z**, and define two angles, **Xangle** and **Yangle**, and their directions of rotation. Next, using the point, our two angles, and 3D transformation equations, we calculate **new x**, **new y**, and **new z** and draw the point in this new location.

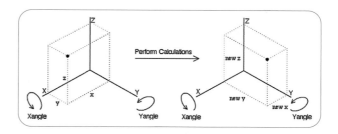

To make life easier on all of us, I won't to go into the details surrounding the derivation of the 3D equations shown above; the subject could easily consume an entire chapter all by itself. What I will say, however, is that these equations result from a lot of trigonometry and matrix mathematics figured out a long time ago by some really smart people. As such, all we have to be concerned with is the result! So, using these equations, we calculate the new position of the points (Xpos, Ypos, and Zpos in our function) and return the results in an array.

Since this function is written specifically to be as generic as possible, you could take it as it is now and place it in your own projects. Try it out. You'll be surprised at how easy it is to make 3D effects.

Rendering the mask movie clips

Back in the createMaskClip() function, we created the mask movie clips and gave them some properties and actions, but they will all remain empty unless we write a function to draw them. This is our next task.

1. Begin by defining this function, underneath all of the previous code:

    ```
    function renderObj(obj, myX, myY, myAlpha, myTarget) {
    ```

    The function needs to know the name of the mask movie clip that is being drawn so that it can modify its properties. It also needs to know the name of the preceding mask clip to determine the shape of the drawing. By knowing the name of the preceding mask clip, we can get the x and y position of the preceding mask and draw the new mask so that it meets with the preceding mask's edge. This creates the continuous 'joining-up' effect.

    We define obj and myTarget as parameters containing those names (both are actually references to the movie clips, which Flash treats as pointers). We also define the position where we want the mask to be moved with myX and myY and the _alpha value of the movie clip with myAlpha.

    Remember when we set the _alpha of the image with the onRollOver event handler? We did this because we wanted to give the image the same level of transparency as the mask (the _alpha level of the red shape when it's fading away). We apply the same _alpha values so that the images also fade away simultaneously, preserving the desired effect.

2. Now add the following lines of code to the function:

    ```
    obj._x = myX;
    obj._y = myY;
    obj._alpha = myAlpha;
    ```

Here we are taking and moving the mask (referenced by `obj`) to the coordinates (`myX`, `myY`) and setting the `_alpha` level with `myAlpha`.

3. Next, add this drawing API code and conclude the function:

```
obj.clear();
obj.beginFill(0x660000, 100);
toX = (myTarget._x-obj._x);
toY = (myTarget._y-obj._y);
obj.lineTo(toX, toY);
obj.lineTo(toX-myTarget._x/2, toY-myTarget._y/2);
obj.lineTo(-obj._x/2, -obj._y/2);
obj.endFill();
}
```

This clears whatever drawing may already exist within the movie clip and begins to draw. The shape is derived from the relative positions between `obj` and `myTarget`. The result creates the illusion that all of the movie clips are connected in a continuously fading ribbon of color.

Controlling the movie

Looking back at our original code structure list, you can see that we're almost done. The only major hurdle left is to write a function that controls the execution of the movie. Now, we'll rely on our previous work and pull all of these functions together to make our project come to life in the `run()` function.

1. Underneath all of the previous code, add the following lines of ActionScript:

```
function run() {
    objs++;
    createMaskClip("theScene", "obj_"+objs,objs+XMLdoc.firstChild.
➥childNodes.length,image_"+objs%(XMLdoc.firstChild.childNodes.length-1),
➥theScene._xmouse, theScene._ymouse, 100);
```

We start by calling the `createMaskClip()` function that we wrote earlier, passing into it all of the parameters we defined above. New mask movie clips will be created in `theScene`, with names based on the `objs` counter. The depth of the movie clip is calculated by adding the number of image movie clips that were loaded in, plus the number of mask movie clips already present. This ensures that we don't overwrite any movie clips previously created.

The `image` variable for each movie clip is determined by taking the remainder between the `objs` counter and the number of images (children in the XML), allowing us to use the image movie clips for multiple mask clips without creating a new image clip for each one. The x, y, and z variables are set by passing the mouse position and a constant to the function.

2. Add this next block of code to the function:

```
for (c=objs-max; c<=objs; c++) {
    if (theScene["obj_"+c]) {
        newPoint = getNewPoint(theScene["obj_"+c].x,theScene
        ➥["obj_"+c].y, theScene["obj_"+c].z, -theScene._ymouse/1000,
        ➥theScene._xmouse/1000);
        theScene["obj_"+c].x = newPoint[0];
        theScene["obj_"+c].y = newPoint[1];
        theScene["obj_"+c].z = newPoint[2];
        depthscale = 1/(1-(Zpos/perspective));
        renderObj(theScene["obj_"+c], (newPoint[0]*depthscale),
        ➥(newPoint[1]*depthscale), 100*(1-(objs-c)/max),
        ➥theScene["obj_"+(c-1)]);
    }
}
```

This sets up a loop that will loop through all of the mask movie clips in theScene and get the new 3D coordinates for each movie clip using our getNewPoint() function. We set the x, y, and z variables of each movie clip based on the result, calculate the depthscale of each movie clip, and call the renderObj() function. The depthscale variable is used to simulate perspective in our movie. Just as objects far away converge to a vanishing point, we want the masks farthest away to appear closer to the center of theScene.

3. Complete the function with the following lines of code:

```
        if (c>max) {
            removeMovieClip(_root.theScene["obj_"+(c-max)]);
        }
    }
```

Last but not least, this checks how many mask movie clips are in theScene, compares the number to max, and removes any extra movie clips.

4. To make the movie stop and start, we'll add an event handler to the root of the movie. Add this function, which will be executed whenever the mouse button is pressed:

```
    this.onMouseDown = function() {
        if (myInt) {
            clearInterval(myInt);
            delete myInt;
        } else {
            myInt = setInterval(run, 33);
        }
    };
```

This function checks to see if the movie is currently running by testing the existence of the variable myInt. This variable is created when we invoke the setInterval() method and contains the ID name of the interval. If myInt exists, we stop the movie from running using the clearInterval() method and delete the variable. If the variable does not exist, we use the setInterval() method to start the movie again. If we do not delete myInt, the if statement will evaluate to true, since clearing the interval does not clear the variable's value.

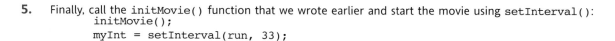

5. Finally, call the `initMovie()` function that we wrote earlier and start the movie using `setInterval()`:
```
initMovie();
myInt = setInterval(run, 33);
```

6. We're done! Go ahead and test the movie (CTRL+ENTER):

 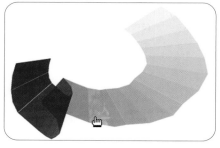 

Okay, that was quite a lot of code so let's recap on what we have just done:

1. We started by initializing our movie, creating the necessary global variables and objects required to make everything work.

2. Next, we used the information in the XML document `imagelist.xml` to create a movie clip for each image and then loaded the images into the movie clips.

3. Then, we wrote a function to create mask movie clips called `createMaskClip()`, taking in several parameters, and we added clip event handlers to the masks to detect user interaction.

4. We used 3D rotation equations to write the `getNewPoint()` function that can rotate a point in space.

5. We wrote the `renderObj()` function to draw a fill in our mask movie clips.

6. And finally, we put all of it together, adding a simple function to pause and start the movie, and also set it running.

If we compare this list with the first one sketched out at the start of this project, the end result isn't all that different from our original list, despite the complexity of the code. Even though we sometimes can't predict every little detail in advance, the plan allows us to see the bigger picture of what we want to accomplish. Possessing it from the beginning helps to keep us on track and force us to really think about how to approach the project. You probably won't understand everything we've just covered, but the more you play with these techniques, the greater your understanding will be.

Beyond the tutorial

So now that you have learned all of these great new techniques and your head is brimming with ideas...what's next? The beauty of these techniques is that they can be applied to any project you work on, in any capacity. You don't have to jump into a project with both feet, foregoing the older drawing methods for the new. Simply try mixing some of the dynamic drawing methods into a typical timeline-based Flash movie. If you don't have a project that would benefit from these new dynamic methods, make one up. The key here is to start playing with these methods because as soon as you have mastered them, applications will start to appear everywhere.

About the Author
David Doull

David is an Australian freelance Flash developer specializing in building applications and games in Flash. Examples of his work and plenty of fun flash games can be found at his business site artifactinteractive.com.au. Within the Flash community, he is best known for his sites

smallblueprinter.com and urbanev.com.

David has been a finalist in the Flash Film Festival three times, and has picked up a Macromedia Site of the Day award for his Flash 3D interactive house plan tool at smallblueprinter.com.

David has contributed to a number for Friends of ED books, including the Flash Usability Guide.

On Flash MX David says...

"What really excites me about working with Flash MX is that you can now create highly interactive multimedia experiences for the web. The days of using Flash for just advertising and animation are gone. You can build real applications in Flash, things that people will experience and use. If you want to build a MP3 jukebox in Flash, then you can do it! If you wanted to build a 3D CAD tool, or an adventure game, or a word processor, or a video clip editor, or just about anything you can think of, it's possible with Flash MX. And the file size will be kept small, so you can put it online and get thousands of people all over the world interacting with it. I can have an idea for a Flash mini-application at the start of the day and can have it online, with people all around the world using it, by the end of the day – that's a pretty amazing experience."

Flash MX MP3 Jukebox
David Doull

About the Effect

Sound has been present in Flash for sometime now, but it's the release of Flash MX that has really revolutionized sound use. Sound files no longer need to be embedded in a SWF file, and can be dynamically loaded into a movie at runtime.

The relative simplicity of this procedure has not transmitted itself through the Flash community easy enough for our liking, hence the need for a comprehensive tutorial on the best MP3 practices within Flash MX.

Sound is now a major part of the successful web experience, and this chapter will show you just how you can bring an every day object in life – the CD player, radio, jukebox – into your online world.

One of the coolest new features of Flash MX is the ability to dynamically load MP3s into your Flash sites. Loading MP3s dynamically means that you don't have to import MP3 files into Flash. Your MP3s can be stored separately to the SWF file and loaded when you want them using ActionScript. In this chapter, we'll make use of this new feature to build a dynamic MP3 jukebox.

Our jukebox will display a list of available MP3 tracks that the user can select to play. The user selects the tracks they want to hear and then clicks the play button to start the playback. It works in the same way as a programmable CD player, or MP3 player, with the user being able to create their own playlist from the tracks available. We'll also make it possible to skip forward and backwards between the selected tracks, pause and stop the playback, and adjust the playback volume. Our track list will be stored in a *very* easy to maintain XML document, which we'll load into the jukebox. To make things fun, we'll give our jukebox a retro look, like it's come straight out of a 1950s diner.

Here's what our final jukebox will look like:

In the download code for this chapter, you'll find a file called `mp3jukebox.fla` – open this file now. This file is our starting point and contains all the graphical elements of the jukebox in its Library. Open up the Library (F11) for this file and you'll see the jukebox interface graphic and eleven buttons (plus a folder containing the graphical assets that make up these symbols).

Six of the buttons are the standard playback controls: previous track, play, pause, stop, next track, and repeat.

There is also a volume button. The final four buttons are for the track selection. Our track list will be made up of two columns and we have different buttons for the left and right columns. For each side, we have a version of the track button that is unselected and a version that is selected.

If you don't wish to download the FLA, you'll need to create your own versions of the eleven buttons and the background graphic.

Now on with the jukebox...

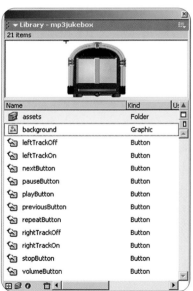

Track selection buttons

If you haven't done so already, start up Flash MX and open the file `mp3jukebox.fla`.

1. Open up the Document Properties window (Modify>Document), and set the Dimensions to 540 pixels by 500 pixels and the frame rate to 20 fps.

   First, we're going to create two movie clips that let us select and de-select tracks for the jukebox to play.

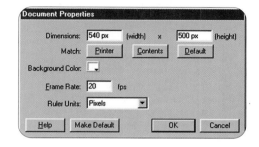

2. Insert a new movie clip symbol (Ctrl+F8) and call it `leftTrackSelection`. Set the name of the default layer in this movie clip to `track Off` and drag the `leftTrackOff` button from the Library (F11) onto this layer.

3. Select the button you've just dragged onto the stage and set its instance name to `trackOff_btn` in the Property inspector. Also set the button's x position to `0` and its y position to `0`.

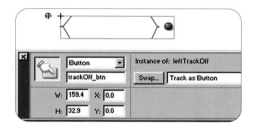

4. Still within the `leftTrackSelection` movie clip, create a new layer (Insert>Layer) and call it `track On`. Drag the `leftTrackOn` button out of the Library and onto this new layer.

5. Select the `leftTrackOn` button and set its instance name to `trackOn_btn`. Then set the button's x position to `0` and its y position to `0`, so that it's positioned exactly on top of the `trackOff_btn` button.

6. Still within the `leftTrackSelection` movie clip, create a new layer (Insert>Layer) and call it `song text box`. Now select the Text tool (T), and within the new layer click on the stage. From the drop-down menu in the Property inspector change the Text type from Static Text to Dynamic Text, and then give the text field the instance name `song`. Adjust the size and position of the text field so that it fills the display area of the button as shown below. Set the font to Arial, the font size to 10, and switch 'off' the Selectable button.

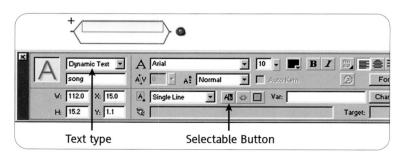

Text type   Selectable Button

7. Create another new layer (Insert>Layer), and this time call it `artist text box`. Create a dynamic text field on this layer in the same way as you did in the previous step, with the only differences being that the instance name is `artist`, and the text field is positioned below the song text field.

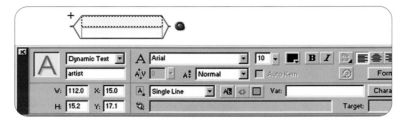

8. Now add a final layer to the `leftTrackSelection` movie clip and call it `Actions`. Open the Actions panel for the first frame of this new layer (F9). Change the Actions panel to Expert Mode (CTRL+SHIFT+E). Don't worry, we don't have to be experts to use this mode, it's just easier for typing in lines of code. Type the following code into the Script pane:

```
selected = false;
trackOn_btn._visible = false;

trackOn_btn.onPress = function() {
    trackOn_btn._visible = false;
    trackOff_btn._visible = true;
    selected = false;
};

trackOff_btn.onPress = function() {
    trackOn_btn._visible = true;
    trackOff_btn._visible = false;
    selected = true;
};
```

Each track in our track list will be unselected by default, and added to the playlist by clicking on the button. A further click will deselect the track again. This is what the above code achieves. The first line creates a variable that defines whether a track is selected for the playlist or not. As the default is unselected, we've set this variable to be `false` initially. For this initial unselected state, we also need to hide the button for the track selected state, which is the `trackOn_btn` instance. This is what the second line of code does.

The rest of the actions consist of two blocks of code, one being the actions for when the selected track button (`trackOn_btn`) is pressed, and the other for when the unselected track button (`trackOff_btn`) is pressed. When `trackOff_btn` is pressed we're making the track selected, so we hide the `trackOff_btn` instance, and make the `trackOn_btn` instance visible. We also change the `selected` variable to `true` to show that the track is selected for the playlist.

The actions for when the `trackOn_btn` instance is pressed are exactly the same, only with the `true`/`false` values reversed to switch the track to unselected.

We have created a toggle switch with the `leftTrackSelection` movie clip. You click it once and the track is selected, click it again and it's deselected.

9. We'll now make a very similar toggle button for the right hand side of the track list. As we've done all the groundwork for this in the `leftTrackSelection` movie clip, the easiest thing to do is duplicate this clip. Open up the Library (F11) and right-click on the `leftTrackSelection` clip. Select Duplicate from the resulting menu.

10. Name the duplicate clip `rightTrackSelection`, and then double-click on the new clip in the Library to go into its edit mode.

11. Delete the button instances from the `track On` and `track Off` layers. Drag a copy of `rightTrackOff` button from the Library onto the `track Off` layer. Give this button the instance name `trackOff_btn` in the Property inspector and then set the button's x position to 0 and its y position to 0. This is exactly the same as we did for the `leftTrackSelection` movie clip.

12. Drag a copy of the `rightTrackOn` button onto the `track On` layer, and give it the instance name `trackOn_btn`. Align this over the `trackOff_btn` instance by setting the x and y positions to 0.

13. The duplicate clip is now finished, except for the fact that we need to move the two text fields across so that they sit comfortably over the button area, as with the `leftTrackSelection` clip. Hold down the Shift key and click on each of the text fields to select them both. With the Shift key still held down, you can now click-drag the text fields across the screen to the right to the desired position. Holding the Shift key down ensures that the movement is horizontal and you don't accidentally move your text fields up or down the screen.

14. Now, return to the main timeline of the movie and open the Library (F11), if it's not currently open.

15. Drag the `background` graphic symbol from the Library onto the default layer of the stage. Set the x and y positions of the graphic to 0 in the Property inspector. Rename the default layer `jukebox background`.

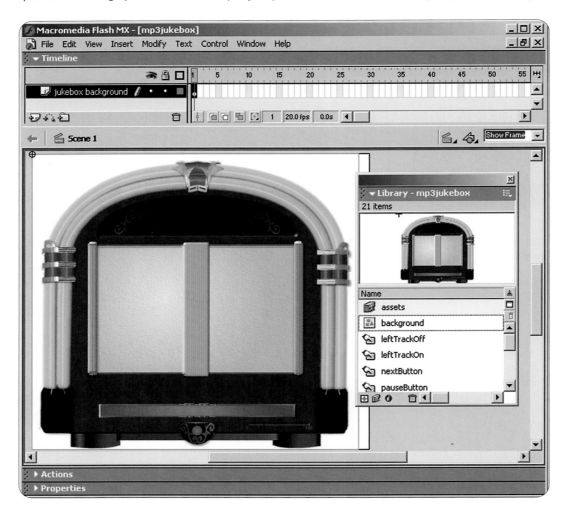

16. With the background graphic still selected, go into the Property inspector and set Alpha to 99% in the Color drop-down menu.

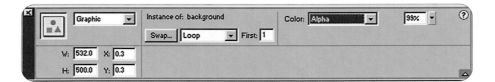

This may seem like a strange thing to do, but it's necessary to fix a bug in how Flash displays bitmapped images. If we left the graphic as normal (100% alpha), then we would notice small distortions in the graphic when we put our buttons on top of the graphic. Setting the alpha to 99% doesn't change how the graphic looks but does 'magically' solve this annoying bug.

17. Create a new layer above the `jukebox background` layer, and name it `left tracks`. Drag five copies of the `leftTrackSelection` movie clip from the Library onto this layer. Position these five movie clips so that they line up on the left column of the jukebox display (as shown below). You might find the Align panel (CTRL+K) useful here. Give each movie clip an instance name starting with `track1`, then `track2` and so on through to `track5` for the final movie clip.

18. Now, still on the main timeline, create a new layer above the `left tracks` layer, and call it `right tracks`. Go into the Library and drag five copies of the `rightTrackSelection` movie clip onto this layer. Position these five movie clips so that they line up on the right column of the jukebox display and give them instance names of `track6` through to `track10`.

Now would be a good time to save your work! You can test out what you've done so far by selecting Control>Test Movie (CTRL+ENTER). You should be able to click on the track buttons to select and de-select the buttons. Admittedly, this isn't all that exciting, but we've taken the first major step towards completing the jukebox.

Top 10 tunes

The next step in building our jukebox will be to create the XML track list. But, before we do so we're going to need some music to play in it. You could spend ages searching for some beautiful vinyl at rare record conventions, but we'll look at the different MP3 resources available on the web to include in your track list.

Where can you find MP3s?

Our jukebox supports ten tracks, so you're going to need ten MP3 files.

There's a wide range of software tools that allow you to convert tracks from your audio CDs to MP3 files. A search for MP3 tools on a software download site such as www.download.com should provide links to many of these tools. Using MP3 files created from your own CD collection in your jukebox will typically not violate any copyright, provided you don't put the jukebox online. You should be aware that, in most cases, putting MP3 files created from audio CDs **online** will be in violation of the artist's copyright. So, if you want to put your jukebox online make sure you use royalty-free MP3 tracks.

A number of companies sell CDs full of royalty-free MP3s. Searching on www.google.com for royalty free MP3s should get you started in finding companies selling these resources.

However, there's an even better option than buying royalty-free CDs – you could have a go at making your own MP3 tracks.

Talent trek

Even if you have no musical knowledge whatsoever and can't play an instrument, you can still make your own music. There are a number of software tools that let you build your own music tracks simply by sequencing together different musical loops.

Some of the more popular tools are:

- eJay (www.ejay.co.uk)

eJay produce a number of products that let you create your own dance and hip hop tracks. The **Dance eJay** product is probably the simplest to use, with absolutely no musical knowledge required. This is like painting with music; you just drag and drop the loop patterns on to the recording tracks and hit play. They also sell royalty-free loop collections and provide a lot of free loops to download.

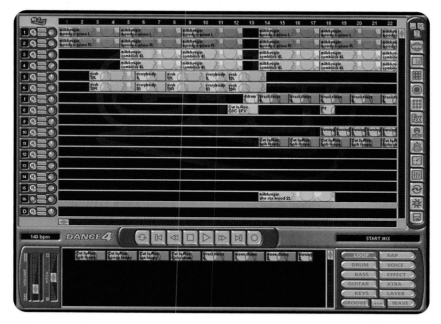

- ACID (www.sonicfoundry.com/products)

Sonic Foundry produce a number of tools for creating your own music. Their ACID Music series of tools are the best place to get started. They also sell royalty-free collections of loops and provide free loops at www.acidplanet.com/loops/8packs.

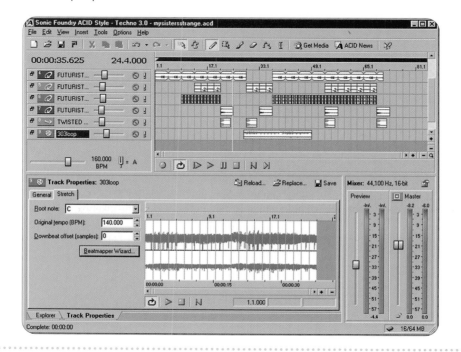

- Fruityloops (www.fruityloops.com)

Fruityloops not only lets you sequence loops together, but also create your own loops by making your own drum and synthesizer patterns.

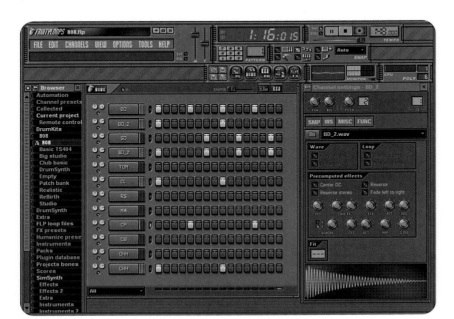

All the companies mentioned above provide demo or trial versions of their products, so you needn't spend any money to give them a go.

Jukebox track list

Let's create the XML track list for our MP3 files. The track list will contain the song title, artist, and file name for each MP3 file, and will be loaded into Flash when we start our jukebox.

1. Copy ten MP3 files to the same folder on your computer that contains your `mp3jukebox.fla`.

Now we'll build the XML document. If you haven't worked with XML before, don't panic, it's really simple. An XML document is just a text file, so we can create our XML track list in *any* text editor, from the basic Windows Notepad (or SimpleText on a Mac), to Macromedia's Dreamweaver MX. XML looks very similar to HTML, with tags such as `<Name>` and `</Name>` indicating the start and end of items of information. The bonus over HTML is that we can actually name our tags, giving them intuitive names to reflect the information that they hold. For example, I want to store the name of my file `file.mp3` in an XML document, so I'll type:

```
<File>file.mp3</File>
```

2. Open up your text editor of choice. Type in the code below, replacing the contents of the tags with the information for your own ten tracks. Name represents the song tile, `File` is the name of the MP3 file (including the MP3 extension), and `Artist` is the name of the artist (as you might have already guessed from the intuitive tag naming).

```
<Playlist>
    <Song>
        <Name>Flash Gordon</Name>
        <File>queen.mp3</File>
        <Artist>Queen</Artist>
    </Song>
    <Song>
        <Name>Flashdance</Name>
        <File>flashdance.mp3</File>
        <Artist>Moroder</Artist>
    </Song>
    <Song>
        <Name>Flash Forward</Name>
        <File>flash_sege.mp3</File>
        <Artist>Serge Gainsbourg</Artist>
    </Song>
    <Song>
        <Name>Flash to the Beat</Name>
        <File>beat.mp3</File>
        <Artist>The Sugarhill Gang</Artist>
    </Song>
    <Song>
        <Name>Flash Light</Name>
        <File>flash_light.mp3</File>
        <Artist>George Clinton</Artist>
    </Song>
    <Song>
        <Name>Flash, Bang, Wallop</Name>
        <File>flashbang.mp3</File>
        <Artist>Half a Sixpence</Artist>
    </Song>
    <Song>
        <Name>Flash in Japan</Name>
        <File>japan.mp3</File>
        <Artist>Eikichi Yazawa</Artist>
    </Song>
    <Song>
        <Name>Flashback</Name>
        <File>flashback_chic.mp3</File>
        <Artist>Chic</Artist>
    </Song>
    <Song>
        <Name>Flash</Name>
        <File>flash-cosmic.mp3</File>
        <Artist>Cosmic Messenger</Artist>
    </Song>
```

```
        <Song>
            <Name>Killing of a flash boy</Name>
            <File>suede_flashboy.mp3</File>
            <Artist>Suede</Artist>
        </Song>
    </Playlist>
```

You'll see from this code that we've got ten pairs of the `Song` tags, one for each of the MP3 tracks. The additional information for each tag (`File`, `Name`, and `Artist`) is contained within the opening and closing `Song` tags to ensure the right information is associated with the right track. All of our songs are for the playlist of our jukebox, so we've put them all inside a `Playlist` tag.

3. Save this file as `tracklist.xml`, making sure you save it in the same folder as the MP3 files and the Flash file. The FLA doesn't have to be in this folder for the jukebox to run, but this is a handy place to keep it because the SWF file, which is required for the jukebox to run, is published to the same folder as the FLA by default.

Loading the track list into Flash

1. Back in Flash MX, create a new layer on the main timeline of your `mp3jukebox.fla`. Call the new layer `Actions` and then open the Actions panel (F9) for the first frame of the `Actions` layer. Type in the following:

```
numberTracks = 10;
tracklist_xml = new XML();
tracklist_xml.onLoad = this.XMLLoaded;
tracklist_xml.ignoreWhite = true;
tracklist_xml.load("tracklist.xml");
```

The first line of code creates a variable called `numberTracks` which stores how many tracks our jukebox will display. The other four lines deal with creating and initializing an XML object. If we want to load an XML file into Flash we need to load it into an XML object, so the second line creates an XML object called `tracklist_xml`.

The rest of the code tells Flash to load the file we just created (`tracklist.xml`) into this XML object and to call a function named `XMLLoaded` when the XML document has finished loading.

2. Now we will create this `XMLLoaded` function. In the Actions panel, directly below the code you just entered, type in the following:

```
function XMLLoaded() {
    for (i=1; i<=numberTracks; i++) {
        item = tracklist_xml.firstChild.childNodes[i-1].firstChild;
        _root["track"+i].song.text = item.firstChild.toString();
        item = item.nextSibling;
        _root["track"+i].file = item.firstChild.toString();
        item = item.nextSibling;
        _root["track"+i].artist.text =item.firstChild.toString();
    }
}
```

The function loops through all the loaded XML data, setting the text fields for song and artist within the track selection movie clips to display the information contained in the XML. The function also creates a new variable called `file` within the track selection movie clips. This variable stores the file name for the MP3 track associated with each track selection clip.

3. You can now test it out. Select Control>Test Movie (CTRL+ENTER). You should see the song names and artists of your MP3 files displayed in the track selection buttons.

Playback buttons

Now we'll add the playback buttons, and finally get some music pumping out of our jukebox!

1. On the main timeline create a new layer (Insert>Layer) called `play back buttons`. Open the Library, if it isn't already open (F11).

2. Drag `nextButton`, `pauseButton`, `playButton`, `previousButton`, `repeatButton` and `stopButton` onto the `play back buttons` layer from the Library. Line up the buttons in a row as shown below. Once again, you might find the Align panel (CTRL+K) useful for this.

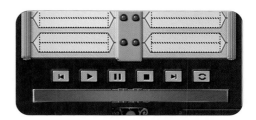

3. Select `previousButton` and set its instance name to `previous_btn`.

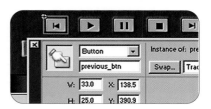

4. Give the other buttons instance names, using the same convention:

Button name	Instance name
playButton	play_btn
pauseButton	pause_btn
stopButton	stop_btn
nextButton	next_btn
repeatButton	repeat_btn

5. In the main timeline, open the Actions panel (F9) for the first frame of the `Actions` layer. Type the following code under the XML-related code you entered earlier:

```
mySound = new Sound(this);

function newSong(songNumber) {
    if (this["track"+songNumber].selected) {
        mySound.loadSound(this["track"+songNumber].file, false);
    } else {
        nextTrack();
    }
}

function playSong() {
    mySound.start();
    paused = false;
}
```

So what does this do? In Flash, if we want to use ActionScript to control any type of sound, we need to use what is known as a **Sound object**. A Sound object is a way of storing a sound or an MP3 within Flash's memory. In the same way that text can be stored in a String and items of data can be stored in an Array, we use Sound objects to store sounds.

The line `mySound = new Sound(this);` creates a new Sound object, which we've called `mySound`. The reference to `this` associates the Sound object with the main timeline.

The remaining lines create two functions that are used to control the Sound object. The first function is called `newSong`. This function checks to see if the track it wishes to play is selected. If it is selected, then it uses the `loadSound` method of our Sound object to load a new MP3 into `mySound`. You can think of the Sound object `mySound` as a being similar to a CD player. It can load, play, and stop sounds, but it can't do anything useful until you load some music into it. So, the `loadSound` method works like loading a CD into a CD player, except that it's loading an MP3 into the Sound object.

The code between the brackets, `(this["track"+songNumber].file, false)`, specifies which MP3 to load, and if the MP3 should stream in (play while it's loading). The term `false` specifies that it won't play the MP3 until it's fully loaded.

If the track isn't selected, then a function called `nextTrack` is called. We'll define this function shortly.

The other function is called `playSong` and it simply starts the MP3 playing, just like pressing the play button on a CD player.

6. Now, still in the Actions panel, directly under the code you just typed, enter the following code:

```
mySound.onLoad = playSong;
mySound.onSoundComplete = nextTrack;
trackNum = 1;
```

The first two lines deal with sound events. When an MP3 has finished loading into `mySound` the `onLoad` event occurs. The `onLoad` event here calls our `playSong` function as soon as the MP3 has finished loading.

The `onSoundComplete` event occurs when the sound has finished playing. Our code tells Flash to run our `nextTrack` function when the sound has completed playing, so when a track has finished it moves to the next track.

The third line creates a variable called `trackNum` and sets it to 1. This variable will store which track is currently being played.

7. After the existing code, type the following:

```
previous_btn.onPress = function() {
    if (trackNum>1) {
        trackNum -= 1;
    }
    while ((_root["track"+trackNum].selected != true) and (trackNum>1)) {
        trackNum -= 1;
    }
    newSong(trackNum);
};
```

This code defines what happens when the previous button is pressed. The `if` test reduces the current track number by one, provided we aren't currently on the first track. We then use a `while` loop to check to see if the new track is selected. The `while` loop will keep reducing the track number until it finds a track that is selected, or reaches the first track. We then call the `newSong` function, which will play the new track.

8. Continue in the Actions panel by typing:

```
play_btn.onPress = function() {
    newSong(trackNum);
};
```

This code defines what happens when the `play_btn` button is pressed. This simply calls the `newSong` function passing the variable `trackNum`, which indicates the currently selected track.

211

9. Now type the code for the pause button:

```
pause_btn.onPress = function() {
    if (paused) {
        paused = false;
        mySound.start(mySound.position/1000);
    } else {
        paused = true;
        mySound.stop();
    }
};
```

The Sound object has a `start` method that allows us to start a sound playing. For the Sound object `mySound` we can start it playing simply by using the code `mySound.start()`. But what if we want to start the sound playing at some point during the sound, rather than at the beginning? All we need to do is pass a number indicating the start point in seconds to the `start` method. For example, if we wanted a sound to start playing from 20 seconds into the track then we would use the code `mySound.start(20)`. We have made use of this functionality to create our pause button.

We have created a variable called `paused` that is either set to `true` or `false`. If it is `true` then the track is currently paused. So, if the pause button is pressed while the track is already paused then `paused` is set to `false` and the track is restarted from the point where it was paused with the line `mySound.start(mySound.position/1000)`. If the track isn't paused, then we pause the track by setting our `pause` variable to `true` and stopping `mySound`.

10. The next button to add the actions for is the stop button:

```
stop_btn.onPress = function() {
    trackNum = 1;
    mySound.stop();
};
```

This simply sets `trackNum` back to the start value of `1` and uses the line `mySound.stop()` to stop the playback of the track currently loaded into `mySound`.

11. Next enter the code for the loop button:

```
loop = false;
repeat_btn.onPress = function() {
    if (loop) {
        loop = false;
        loopDisplay.text = "";
    } else {
        loop = true;
        loopDisplay.text = "L";
    }
};
```

The first line defines a new variable called `loop` that we will use to indicate if the user wants the playback to loop or stop when all selected tracks have finished playing. The remaining code defines what happens when the repeat button is pressed. This simply works like a toggle switch. If the `loop` variable is already true, then it is set to `false`, otherwise it is set to `true`. We also set a text property of a text field called `loopDisplay` to show L if repeat is on and nothing if it is off. We will create this text field shortly.

12. Now the code for the final button, the next track button:

```
next_btn.onPress = nextTrack;

function nextTrack() {
    if (trackNum>=numberTracks) {
        anySelected = false;
        for (j=1; j<=numberTracks; j++) {
            if (this["track"+j].selected) {
                anySelected = true;
            }
        }
        if (loop and anySelected) {
            trackNum = 1;
            newSong(1);
        } else {
            trackNum = 1;
            mySound.stop();
        }
    } else {
        trackNum += 1;
        newSong(trackNum);
    }
}
```

The first line of code defines that when the next button is pressed a function called `nextTrack` will be called. The remaining code defines this `nextTrack` function. The function first checks to see if the current track is the last track. If it isn't the last track, it simply adds one to `trackNum` and plays the next track. However, if it is the last track then things get a little more complicated. The code loops through all the track selection movie clips to see if any are selected. We want to make sure that at least one track has been selected, otherwise we wouldn't have a next track to move to. If even one track is selected then the variable `anySelected` will be set to `true`. If nothing is selected it will be `false`. If there is at least one selected track and the repeat option is on (`loop` is `true`), then the `trackNum` is set back to the start and the first track is played. However, if repeat is off or nothing is selected then the sound is stopped.

13. Now would be a good time to save your work. You can now test out the playback buttons (CTRL+ENTER). You should be able to select tracks and playback your selection, as well as skipping forward, pausing, etc.

Digital display information

Most of our jukebox is now built, but we can improve its usability by adding some playback display information.

1. Close or minimize the Actions panel and create a new layer (Insert>Layer) on the main timeline called `display boxes`.

2. Now select the Text tool (T), and within the new layer click on the stage. Select Dynamic Text from the Text type drop-down menu in the Property inspector. This gives us one dynamic text field; create another four to give us five in total.

3. The first text field should be two characters wide and have the variable name `trackNum`, as shown in the screenshot. The size of a text field can be adjusted easily by typing in the required number of characters and then deleting them, or by click-dragging on the white square at the corner of the editable text field. Position this first text field over the red display area on the jukebox.

4. The second text field should be at least 30 characters wide and have the instance name `songTitle`. Position this text field just to the right of the previous text field, as shown here.

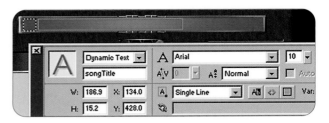

5. The third text field should be at least five characters wide and have the instance name `timePlaying`. Arrange this text field just to the right of the previous text field.

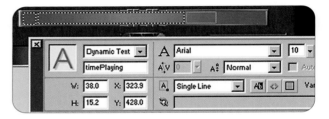

6. The fourth text box should be at least five characters wide and have the instance name `timeTotal`. Position this just to the right of the last text box, as shown.

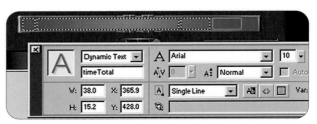

7. The final text field should be one character wide and have the instance name `loopDisplay`. Position this clip at the far right edge of the display.

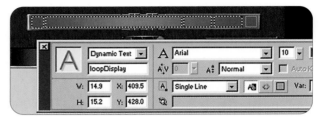

Now we need to add the code for these text fields. We've already added the code to display an `L` if the repeat option is on, but we need to add the code to display the current track title, time elapsed, and total track length.

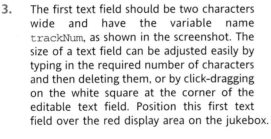
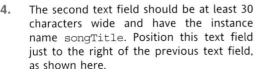
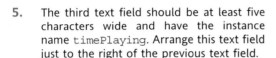
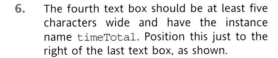
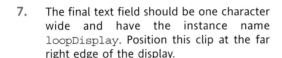

8. Open the Actions panel again (F9), and select frame 1 of the `Actions` layer. Under all the existing code, type the following:

```
this.onEnterFrame = function() {
    timePlayingSeconds = Math.floor((mySound.position/1000)%60);
    if (timePlayingSeconds<10) {
        timePlayingSeconds = "0"+timePlayingSeconds;
    }
    timePlaying.text = Math.floor((mySound.position/1000)/60)+
    ➡":"+timePlayingSeconds;
    timeTotalSeconds = Math.floor((mySound.duration/1000)%60);
    if (timeTotalSeconds<10) {
        timeTotalSeconds = "0"+timeTotalSeconds;
    }
    timeTotal.text = Math.floor((mySound.duration/1000)/60)+
    ➡":"+timeTotalSeconds;
};
```

This code displays the time elapsed and total time for the current track being played on the jukebox. The first line calculates the seconds that have elapsed since the current track started playing. The code then tests to see if this is less than 10 seconds. If the seconds value is less than 10, we add a zero in front of it, so a value such as 9 seconds will appear as 09 in our display.

Next, we calculate the minutes that have elapsed and set the text in the `timePlaying` text box to the minutes and seconds that have elapsed since the current track started playing, separated by a colon. The remaining code calculates and sets the text in the `timeTotal` text box to the total length of the current track, displayed as minutes and seconds.

So why all the math? The property `mySound.position` is the number of milliseconds that have elapsed since the Sound object `mySound` started playing. Similarly, the property `mySound.duration` is the length of the current track loaded into `mySound`. But, a typical MP3 player doesn't display time in milliseconds; it displays time in minutes and seconds, so we divide the values by 1000 to convert them from milliseconds to seconds. We then divide by 60 to get the minutes, add in a : as a separator and calculate the remaining (modulus) seconds. This converts a confusing value like 134034 milliseconds to the more useful 2:14 (2 minutes, 14 seconds).

9. Now, make a change to the code for the `newSong` function. Add the new line highlighted in bold so that the code now reads:

```
function newSong(songNumber) {
    if (this["track"+songNumber].selected) {
        mySound.loadSound(this["track"+songNumber].file, false);
        this.songTitle.text = this["track"+trackNum].song.text;
    } else {
        nextTrack();
    }
}
```

This new line sets the `songTitle` text field to display the name of the song currently playing.

10. Test it out (CTRL+ENTER), and you should have a digital display as shown below.

Turn it up

Our jukebox could really do with a volume control, so let's build one.

1. Create a new movie clip symbol (CTRL+F8) and call it `volumeControl`.

2. Open the Library (F11) and drag the `volumeButton` button onto the default layer of this new movie clip.

3. Still within the `volumeControl` clip, create a new layer (Insert>Layer) and call it `Actions`. Open the Actions panel for the first frame of the `Actions` layer (F9). Enter the following code:

```
this.onPress = function() {
    startDrag(this, false, left, top, right, bottom);
};
this.onRelease = function() {
    stopDrag();
};
```

This code allows the user to drag the volume button, like a standard slider control. `left`, `top`, `right`, and `bottom` are variables that specify the restrictions on how the volume slider can be dragged. We will define the values for these variables in the next step.

4. Directly below the code you just typed, type in the following:

```
top = _y;
bottom = _y;
left = _x-100;
right = _x;

this.onMouseMove = function() {
    _parent.mySound.setVolume((_x-left));
};
```

This code sets up the limits on where the volume slider can be dragged, and sets the volume whenever the slider changes. The first four lines of code set up the values for the variables that control the slider movement, effectively limiting the slider to being dragged left or right, and within a range of 100 pixels.

The `onMouseMove` function is run whenever the mouse moves. This uses the `setVolume` method of our Sound object to set the volume for the sound being played. The volume can be anything between 0 (silent) and 100 (full volume). So, `setVolume(50)` specifies that the volume should be half of the maximum volume.

The slider can only move 100 pixels on the x-axis from its start position, and the start position of the slider is stored in the variable named `left`. The current position of the slider is stored in its `_x` value. So, `_x-left` gives us a number between 0 and 100 representing the location of the slider, which is what we set the volume to.

5. Return to the main timeline of the jukebox and create a new layer called `volume slider`. If it isn't already open, open the Library (F11) and drag the `volumeControl` movie clip onto this new layer. Position the movie clip so that it covers the end of the horizontal ridge at the bottom right corner of the jukebox graphic.

You can now test out the volume control (CTRL+ENTER). You should be able to adjust the playback volume by dragging the volume button to the left.

It's huge

If you've been testing your jukebox on your own computer, then you'll have found that the MP3 tracks load almost instantly. However, MP3 files typically have quite large file sizes and when you put your jukebox online you may find that the MP3 tracks take a little time to load. Therefore, we need to include a loading progress bar, in order to indicate how much of a track has loaded in and how long it will take before playback begins.

1. Create a new movie clip (CTRL+F8) and call it `loadingAnimation`.

2. On the default layer of this new movie clip, draw a black rectangle and set the rectangle's width to 314 pixels and height to 18 pixels as shown.

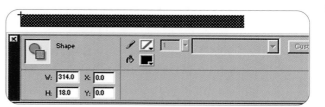

3. Select the black rectangle and copy it (CTRL+C). Create a new layer (Insert>Layer), call it `tween`, and Paste in Place (CTRL+SHIFT+V) the rectangle onto this new layer.

4. Set the fill of the rectangle you have just pasted to red.

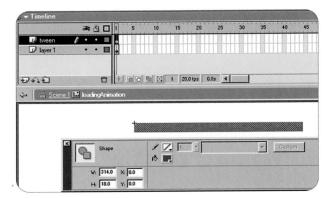

5. Select frame 99 of the `tween` layer and insert a keyframe (F6), then insert a blank keyframe (F7) at frame 100 on this same layer. Select frame 100 of `layer 1` and insert a blank keyframe here.

6. On frame 1, select the red rectangle on the `tween` layer and set its width in this keyframe to 1 pixel.

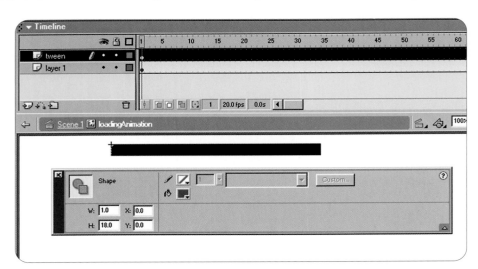

7. Now select frame 1 of the `tween` layer and choose Shape from the Tween drop-down menu in the Property inspector.

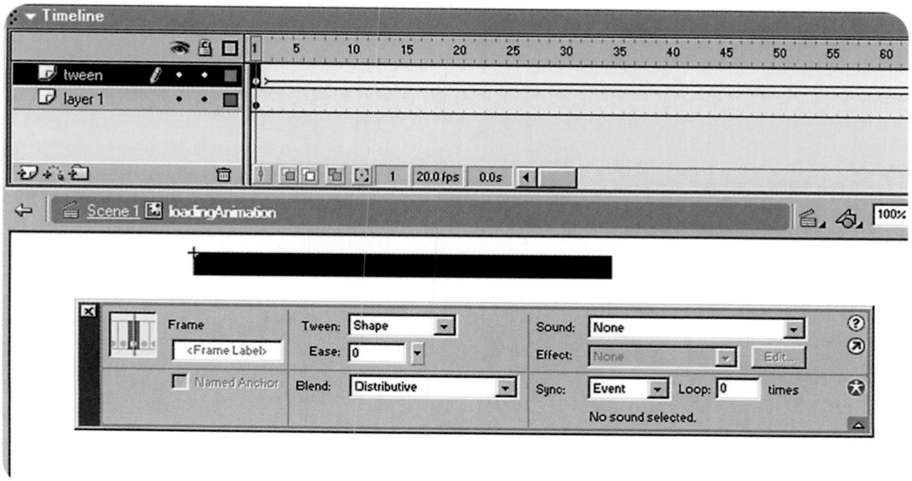

What we have just created is a red rectangle that grows horizontally over 100 frames. This will be our loading progress bar.

8. Now, still in the `loadingAnimation` movie clip, create a new layer (Insert>Layer) and call it `Actions`. Open the Actions panel (F9) and add a `stop` action in frame 1.

9. Now return to the main timeline and create a new layer (Insert>Layer) called `loading`. Open the Library (F11) and drag the `loadingAnimation` movie clip onto the layer, positioning it so that it covers the display bar. Set the movie clip's instance name to `bar`.

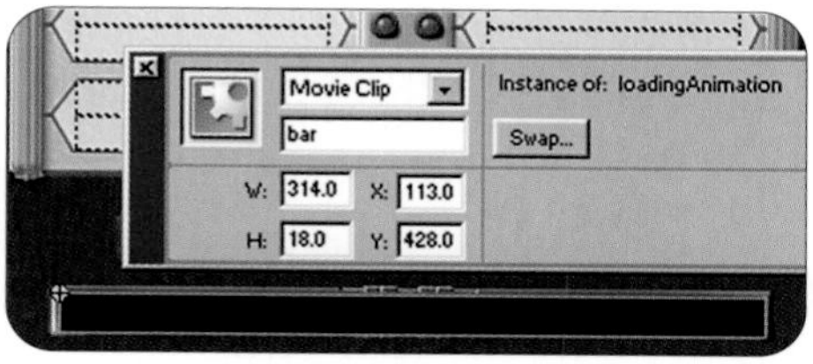

10. Still on the main timeline, open the Actions panel (F9) for the first frame of the `Actions` layer. Add the new line highlighted in bold so that your `onEnterFrame` function now reads:

```
this.onEnterFrame = function() {
    bar.gotoAndStop(Math.floor((mySound.getBytesLoaded()/mySound.getBytes
    ➥Total())*100));
    timePlaying.text = Math.floor((mySound.position/1000)/60)+":"+Math.
    ➥floor((mySound.position/1000)%60);
    timeTotal.text = Math.floor((mySound.duration/1000)/60)+":"+Math.
    ➥floor((mySound.duration/1000)%60);
};
```

This new line calculates what percentage of the MP3 has been loaded and moves the bar animation to the associated frame in the movie clip. So, if 50% has loaded then frame 50 is displayed. If 100% is loaded then frame 100 is displayed. As you will recall, we put blank keyframes on frame 100, so if the MP3 has fully loaded then the blank frames will be shown, which effectively means that the loading bar disappears.

The loading bar is now complete. However, if you wish to see the loading bar in action, you will need to test out the jukebox online, as Flash will load the MP3 files instantly when you try it out on your own computer.

Tips and modifications

Congratulations, your jukebox is now complete. If you test it out you should be able to select tracks, play, pause, skip backwards and forwards, adjust the volume and have a whole lot of fun! Sit back and relax as you listen to your favorite tunes on your new dynamic MP3 jukebox.

Here are a few tips if you had any problems with the MP3 playback and some suggestions on how the jukebox could be modified.

MP3 troubleshooting

- **Same folder**: The MP3s that you're loading should be in the same folder as the Flash file (SWF) and XML file. If you're having trouble with loading MP3s, check that the MP3s are in the same folder as the Flash file.

- **Double speed**: Flash can only play MP3 files with sample rates that are multiples of 11khz. Most MP3s are encoded at 44khz and should play fine in Flash. However, if your MP3s sound speeded up or like they are playing at double speed, it will probably be because they are encoded at a different sample rate, such as 16khz. If this occurs you should re-encode your MP3s at 44khz.

Flash Player versions

The Flash Player that came out with the initial release of Flash MX was version 6,0,21. Since its release, Macromedia has identified some bugs in this version of the player, including some performance issues with the use of sound and video in Flash. Luckily, these bugs have been fixed in an updated release of the player, version 6,0,40 (or higher).

It's quite likely that the Flash Player you use in the authoring application (when you test movies) is still the older version. Even if you have updated the Flash Player in your web browser, the player in the Flash application will still be version 6,0,21. Fortunately, Macromedia have also released an update to the Flash Player used by Flash MX. I strongly recommend that you download and install the **Macromedia Flash Player 6 Update** from www.macromedia.com/support/flash/downloads.html.

Modifying the jukebox

There is nothing stopping you from changing the look and feel of the jukebox to suit your own design taste. The appearance of the background graphic and buttons can be changed without affecting the functionality of the jukebox.

If you want some different playback buttons, have a look in the common libraries that come with Flash MX (Window>Common Libraries>Buttons). The buttons library contains a few collections of playback buttons in the Circle Buttons and Playback folders.

Changing the loading animation

The loading bar is a movie clip animation across 99 frames. In the movie clip we created this animation is just a simple shape tween of a rectangle. However, it needn't be that simple. You could replace this animation with anything you like that stretches across the 99 frames. You could even add the sound of a record changing to add to the authentic 50s style jukebox feel.

More tracks

The current jukebox has ten tracks. However, if you want to change the number of tracks all you need to do is add extra track selection movie clips – add the new tracks to your XML document – and change the `numberTracks = 10;` code on the `Actions` layer of the main timeline to match the new number of tracks you have.

So, if you wanted to have 12 tracks then the first line of the `Actions` layer code on the main timeline would become:

```
numberTracks = 12;
```

The data for the extra two songs would be included in the `tracklist.xml` document. The song information should be in the same form as the current song data:

```
<Song>
    <Name>Adelaide</Name>
    <File>pk_adel.mp3</File>
    <Artist>Paul Kelly</Artist>
</Song>
```

...and should be put after the last `</Song>` tag, but before the `</Playlist>` tag.

Finally, another two track selection movie clips would be added and given the instance names `track11` and `track12`.

To the right is an example of the jukebox with twelve tracks and some changes to the graphics. The appearance of the track selection buttons has been modified slightly, and the playback buttons have been replaced with buttons from the common libraries folder.

About the Author
Keith Peters

Keith Peters is the creator of the Flash experimental site, www.bit-101.com. As an established member of the Flash community, he has committed himself not only to pushing the envelope with Flash, but helping others learn ActionScript as well. As a part of this effort, he has become a moderator in the Flash MX ActionScript forum at www.were-here.com, written a series of ActionScript tutorials which have been translated into Italian, Spanish, Portuguese and possibly several other languages, and contributed to several other books by friends of ED.

He lives north of Boston, with his wife, Kazumi.

"To me, the ultimate use of a computer is to use it to make visual effects with math. Yes, they can be used for many other things, such as national defense, keeping track of inventory and figuring out my paycheck. But to me, all that seems pretty boring compared to making colorful shapes move around the screen in strange, yet somehow familiar patterns.

"I got my first start in computers back in the mid-80s with a Commodore 128 and Amiga 500. Armed with a souped up version of BASIC, I was doing some pretty cool stuff. This is also where I picked up a lot of the basic math and trigonometry required for computer graphics. But what really amazed me back then were the demos done by various elite coder groups, working in machine code, hacking down the most basic level of hardware to produce some of the most mind blowing graphics and animation you could imagine.

"So, I decided I would become a programmer. What I learned then was pretty valuable in terms of basic programming theory and code structure. But I got a bit tired of concatenating text strings, and was itching for the cool graphics stuff. So, I attempted to learn some Windows programming. This was way more than I bargained for, and after a couple of months of banging my head against my monitor trying to figure out OOP, I pretty much gave up the whole programming concept.

"Fast forward – late 90s. A buddy of mine asks me to help him out on a Flash web site he's doing. I download the trial version and play around with it for a couple of nights and tell him, sure, I can help him. We fake our way through it and get paid. A few more deals like that and we are hooked. Then Flash 5 comes out, with this vastly improved ActionScript, and everything suddenly comes together for me.

"People often ask me if I'm a math guru or something, but I have absolutely no formal schooling in math beyond high school algebra (most of which I promptly forgot). All I know is what I need to achieve a particular effect.

"Each new formula I learn (or dream up) is a new tool for me. Most of what I do is just combining these various tools in new ways."

Flash Math Visual Effects

Keith Peters

About the Effect

Code has always been a work to strike fear into many users of Flash. However, the fact that you can easily create amazing effects with nothing on the stage whatsoever is quite mind-blowing.

Code has opened up the world of Flash to mathematical genius, but it's equally accessible to each one of us. While progressing through this chapter, you'll release that math can be a key tool in creating the most awesome effects you'll ever see on a computer screen. You'll also find that the fact you may know little or nothing about code and math will not spoil the fun.

This chapter will provide you with a basic code structure for creating a series of great visual effects, and will also highlight the areas that you can experiment in yourself, just by changing numerical values, and not reinventing trigonometry.

```
Code = fear;
Math = fear;
Flash(Code + Math) = nothing2fear;
```

In this chapter, we'll take a look at highly visual math experiments based on the following themes:

- Grid effects
- Fractal landscapes
- Self-similar fractals
- Color gradients
- Mouse chasers
- Liquid effects

Don't let any of these names scare you – they really are quite fun!

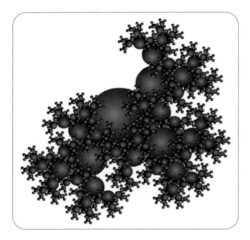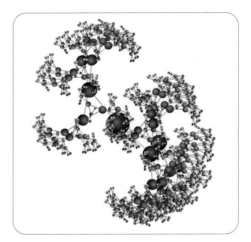

Grid effects

A cool starting point for many Flash math experiments is a grid. All you need is a single movie clip in the Library, a method of attaching it several times in a grid pattern, and the code to give each movie clip the same or similar behavior. Each movie clip functions both on its own, and in conjunction with those surrounding it, which can create some pretty cool effects. There are three basic steps to follow when building a grid effect movie:

- Set up the movie clip.
- Set up the grid formation.
- Create the function that determines each movie clip's behavior.

We'll take these one at a time.

1. Start a new movie (CTRL+N) and save it as `grid01.fla`. First draw a simple graphic and convert it into a movie clip. It can be pretty much any shape, but avoid making it too large or it will overlap its neighbors on the grid. I've drawn a square that's 20 x 20 pixels and called it box. Make sure it is exported from the Library so you can attach it later with ActionScript. You can do this then when converting a shape to a symbol by checking Export for ActionScript (although you'll need to select the Advanced options):

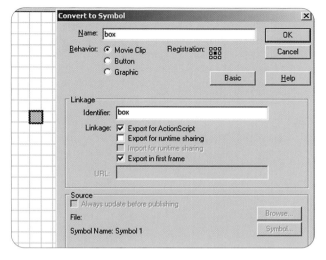

If the symbol you want to use is already in the Library, open up the Library (F11), right-click on the symbol and choose Linkage.... Then, select Export for ActionScript in the Linkage Properties dialog box:

In any case, note the name you exported it as and delete any instances of the movie clip from the stage. Everything will be attached directly from the Library.

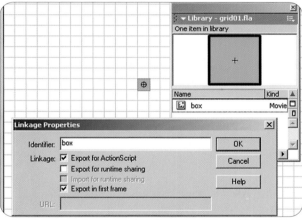

2. Next, we set up the grid formation. Add this code to frame 1 of the main timeline:

```
xMax = 6;
yMax = 6;
xDist = 30;
yDist = 30;
xCenter = Stage.width/2;
yCenter = Stage.height/2;
for (y=0; y<yMax; y++) {
    for (x=0; x<xMax; x++) {
        clip = attachMovie("box", "b"+i, i++);
        clip._x = (x-(xMax-1)/2)*xDist+xCenter;
        clip._y = (y-(yMax-1)/2)*yDist+yCenter;
        // assign additional properties here
    }
}
```

This is a pretty good generic script for creating a grid of any attached movie clips. I'll give you a brief explanation of what it does. First, the two `Max` values determine how many rows and columns are in the grid. Then the `Dist` values tell Flash how much space to put between each row or column. We then find the center of the stage and run two `for` loops – one for the rows, one for the columns. Inside the loops, we attach a movie clip and position it. That complicated looking bit of math in there simply puts an equal number of clips on each side of the center.

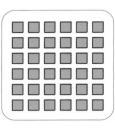

3. Now, before we even get into behaviors, we can add all sorts of effects right here in the grid itself, just by specifying values after we attach the movie clip. For example, the following additional line (highlighted in bold) rotates each square slightly, based on its `x` value:

```
xMax = 6;
yMax = 6;
xDist = 30;
yDist = 30;
xCenter = Stage.width/2;
yCenter = Stage.height/2;
for (y=0; y<yMax; y++) {
    for (x=0; x<xMax; x++) {
        clip = attachMovie("box", "b"+i, i++);
        clip._x = (x-(xMax-1)/2)*xDist+xCenter;
        clip._y = (y-(yMax-1)/2)*yDist+yCenter;
        // assign additional properties here
        clip._rotation = x*10;
    }
}
```

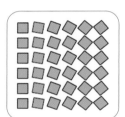

You'll notice that each square's degree of rotation increases the further right it is, and the first square in each row is not rotated at all.

4. We could change that one extra line to make the rotation run down the columns:

```
clip._rotation = y*10;
```

5. We could also use the value of i, which increases throughout the whole loop and never resets to 0:

```
clip._rotation = i*10;
```

6. Or, try playing with some of the other properties, such as scale or alpha. Here are a couple of ideas to get you started:

    ```
    clip._alpha = (36-i)*3;
    clip._xscale = y*15;
    clip._rotation = x*15;
    ```

    If you take a look at the download version of `grid01.fla`, you'll see that we've got these additional properties commented out so that you can quickly add them in to see the effect.

7. Now that we have an interesting *looking* grid, let's make it *do* something interesting. We'll do this by assigning a behavior to each movie clip, which is done by giving it an `onEnterFrame` function. The clearest way to do this is to assign the function inside the loop, and define the function later (this is `grid02.fla` in the download files):

    ```
    xMax = 6;
    yMax = 6;
    xDist = 30;
    yDist = 30;
    xCenter = Stage.width/2;
    yCenter = Stage.height/2;
    for (y=0; y<yMax; y++) {
        for (x=0; x<xMax; x++) {
            clip = attachMovie("box", "b"+i, i++);
            clip._x = (x-(xMax-1)/2)*xDist+xCenter;
            clip._y = (y-(yMax-1)/2)*yDist+yCenter;
            // assign additional properties here
            clip._rotation = x*10;
            clip.onEnterFrame = move;
        }
    }
    function move() {
        // we'll define the behavior in here
        // here's a simple one:
        this._rotation += 3;
    }
    ```

This assigns the function `move` to the `onEnterFrame` handler of each movie clip as it is created. Make sure you type that very carefully with no parentheses! It's `move;` not `move();`. This function merely rotates each movie clip slightly every frame, creating constant rotating motion.

The rest of this section will mainly consist of variations on the `move` function, and changes in the initial properties of the movie clips. First up is a pulsating grid.

Pulsate

Open up `grid02.fla` as a base (if it isn't already open from the last exercise) and save it as `grid_pulsate.fla`. Open the Actions panel (F9) and make the following changes to the code:

```
xMax = 6;
yMax = 6;
xDist = 30;
yDist = 30;
xCenter = Stage.width/2;
yCenter = Stage.height/2;
for (y=0; y<yMax; y++) {
    for (x=0; x<xMax; x++) {
        clip = attachMovie("box", "b"+i, i++);
        clip._x = (x-(xMax-1)/2)*xDist+xCenter;
        clip._y = (y-(yMax-1)/2)*yDist+yCenter;
        // assign additional properties here
        clip.angle = x*.1+y*.1;
        clip.onEnterFrame = move;
    }
}
function move() {
    this._xscale = this._yscale=Math.sin(this.angle += .1)*50+50;
}
```

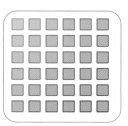
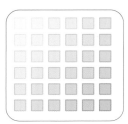

Fading

Now save the previous file as `grid_fading.fla`. All you need to do here to create the fade effect is edit the `move` function:

```
function move() {
    this._alpha = Math.sin(this.angle += .1)*50+50;
}
```

Adding mouse interaction

Here, we'll quickly edit our basic grid movie even further by adding some user interaction code to create different effects.

Fade

Use your previous `grid_fading.fla` movie as a base and save it as `grid_mouse_fade.fla`. Again, we'll only need to change a few lines to create a new effect, like so:

```
xMax = 6;
yMax = 6;
xDist = 30;
yDist = 30;
xCenter = Stage.width/2;
yCenter = Stage.height/2;
for (y=0; y<yMax; y++) {
    for (x=0; x<xMax; x++) {
        clip = attachMovie("box", "b"+i, i++);
        clip._x = (x-(xMax-1)/2)*xDist+xCenter;
        clip._y = (y-(yMax-1)/2)*yDist+yCenter;
        // assign additional properties here
        clip.onEnterFrame = move;
    }
}
function move() {
    var dx = this._x-_xmouse;
    var dy = this._y-_ymouse;
    var dist = Math.sqrt(dx*dx+dy*dy);
    if (dist<100) {
        this._alpha = dist;
    } else {
        this._alpha = 100;
    }
}
```

Here, we use the `_xmouse` and `_ymouse` to work out the mouse position, and affect the `dist` variable's value, and consequently, the alpha value.

 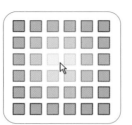 

Scale

This is almost the same as the last file. All you need to change are the contents of the move function:

```
function move() {
    var dx = this._x-_xmouse;
    var dy = this._y-_ymouse;
    var dist = Math.sqrt(dx*dx+dy*dy);
    if (dist<100) {
        this._xscale = this._yscale=110-dist;
    } else {
        this._xscale = this._yscale=10;
    }
}
```

This time the mouse position has been used to affect the scaling of each clip rather than the alpha.

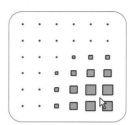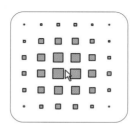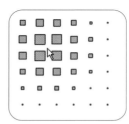

Elastic

Stay in the file from the last exercise and save it as `grid_mouse_elastic.fla`. Make the following changes to the code:

```
xMax = 6;
yMax = 6;
xDist = 30;
yDist = 30;
xCenter = Stage.width/2;
yCenter = Stage.height/2;
for (y=0; y<yMax; y++) {
    for (x=0; x<xMax; x++) {
        clip = attachMovie("box", "b"+i, i++);
        clip._x = clip.xBase=(x-(xMax-1)/2)*xDist+xCenter;
        clip._y = clip.yBase=(y-(yMax-1)/2)*yDist+yCenter;
        // assign additional properties here
        clip.onEnterFrame = move;
    }
}
k = .2;
damp = .9;
maxDist = 100;
function move() {
    var dx = this._x-_xmouse;
    var dy = this._y-_ymouse;
```

```
            var dist = Math.sqrt(dx*dx+dy*dy);
            if (dist<maxDist) {
                // spring towards mouse
                this.vx += (_xmouse-this._x)*k;
                this.vy += (_ymouse-this._y)*k;
            }
            // spring towards base point
            this.vx += (this.xBase-this._x)*k;
            this.vy += (this.yBase-this._y)*k;
            this.vx *= damp;
            this.vy *= damp;
            this._x += this.vx;
            this._y += this.vy;
        }
```

This effect is the most complex so far, using a formula for a spring twice. One springs the movie clip towards the mouse, if the mouse is less than 100 pixels away. The other springs the movie clip towards its original base point.

You can play around with the three variables listed immediately above the move function. This is what they each control:

- `k` controls the 'springiness'.

- `damp` determines how quickly it will settle down.

- `maxDist` is, of course, how close the mouse has to be to the movie clip in order to react.

Advanced elasticity

Use `grid_mouse_elastic.fla` as a base and save it as `grid_mouse_advanced_elastic.fla`. Make the following changes to the code:

```
            xMax = 6;
            yMax = 6;
            xDist = 30;
            yDist = 30;
            xCenter=Stage.width/2;
            yCenter=Stage.height/2;
            for(y=0;y<yMax;y++){
                for(x=0;x<xMax;x++){
                    clip=attachMovie("box", "b"+i, i++);
                    clip._x = clip.xBase = (x-(xMax-1)/2)*xDist + xCenter;
```

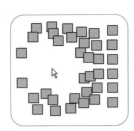
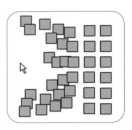
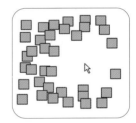

```
                    clip._y = clip.yBase = (y-(yMax-1)/2)*yDist +
                    ➥yCenter;
                    // assign additional properties here
                    clip.onEnterFrame = move;
                }
            }
    offset = 100;
    k = .2;
    damp = .9;
    maxDist = 100;
    function move(){
        var dx = this._x - _xmouse;
        var dy = this._y - _ymouse;
        var dist = Math.sqrt(dx*dx+dy*d7);
        if(dist<maxDist){
            var angle = Math.atan2(dy, dx);
            var tx = _xmouse+Math.cos(angle)*offset;
            var ty = _ymouse+Math.sin(angle)*offset;
            // spring towards mouse
            this.vx += (tx-this._x)*k;
            this.vy += (ty-this._y)*k;
        }
    // spring towards base point
    this.vx += (this.xBase-this._x)*k;
        this.vy += (this.yBase-this._y)*k;
        this.vx *= damp;
        this.vy *= damp;
        this._x += this.vx;
        this._y += this.vy;
    }
```

This file takes it even further. Instead of springing directly towards the mouse, it calculates the angle formed between the point and the mouse and springs toward a point a certain distance away from the mouse, on that angle. You can control that distance with the offset variable. Here, I've set the offset value to be the same as maxDist. This causes the point to remain just out of reach, as if on the edge of an invisible circle around the mouse. You can try making one larger than the other and see what kind of effects you can get.

Waves

Let's take a look at some waves to finish off the grid section. Use grid_mouse_advanced_elastic.fla as a base and save it as grid_mouse_waves.fla, editing the code so it looks like this:

```
xMax = 6;
yMax = 6;
xDist = 30;
yDist = 30;
xCenter=Stage.width/2;
yCenter=Stage.height/2;
for(y=0;y<yMax;y++){
    for(x=0;x<xMax;x++){
        clip=attachMovie("box", "b"+i, i++);
```

```
                    clip.baseX = (x-(xMax-1)/2)*xDist+xCenter;
                    clip.baseY = (y-(yMax-1)/2)*yDist+yCenter;
                    // assign additional properties here
                    clip.onEnterFrame = move;
                    clip.angleX = x*.3+y*3;
                    clip.angleY = x*.15+y*.15;
                }
            }
            function move(){
                this._x = this.baseX+Math.sin(this.angleX += .1)*20;
                this._y = this.baseY+Math.sin(this.angleY += .15)*20;
            }
```

Here, rather than directly assigning an `_x` and `_y` position, we establish a base point and use some basic trigonometry to vary it. Play around with the lines that establish the initial `angleX` and `angleY` values to create different sized wavelengths. In the following line:

```
this._x = this.baseX +
Math.sin(this.angleX+=.1)*10;
```

`.1` is the speed at which the wave moves. The value of `10` controls how much movement back and forth is allowed for each movie clip.

I've tried to give you a few interesting examples, but you could fill a book and more with all the possible permutations for this basic setup. Experimentation is the key – have fun with it.

Fractal landscapes

One of the greatest mathematical concepts to play around with when creating visual effects is **fractals**. The term fractal itself encompasses a wide variety of mathematical concepts. There are Mandelbrot and Julia fractals, strange attractors, self-similar fractals, fractal trees, landscapes... and so on.

I'm going to cover a couple of these concepts here. In this section, we'll build a two-dimensional fractal landscape and then go on to create some self-similar fractals.

The basic theory behind a fractal landscape (or a fractal mountain like the one we'll create) is this: you take a line segment between point A and point B, find the mid-point of that segment, and randomly push it up or down. This now gives you two new line segments. Then, perform the same function on this pair, resulting in four new segments. Repeat this operation a number of times and you'll quickly get a large number of very small lines. This will begin to look eerily like a realistic landscape.

Breaking this down into separate sections that we need to build with ActionScript, there are the following necessary operations to perform:

- Draw lines from the first point through each remaining point.

- Find the mid-point between any two points.

- Randomly move it up or down.

We also need a way to store all the points, and a way to insert new points into the list. Arrays are just the thing here – we can store an object in each element of the array. The object has x and y properties. We can travel from the beginning to the end of the array getting each point, and use the splice method of the Array object to insert new points into the array.

Since this is a little more complex than the last movies, I'll go through the theory of it step-by-step as we build the file. This is mountain01.fla in the download files.

Mountain #1

1. Open a new movie (CTRL+N), and we'll enter the code to create mountain01.fla into the Script pane, a bit at a time. First, we make the array with two elements. Each element contains a generic object. Each object contains an x and y property that corresponds to a point on the center-left of the stage, and also the center-right.

    ```
    points = new Array(2);
    points[0] = {x:50, y:200};
    points[1] = {x:500, y:200};
    ```

2. The line drawing code is pretty simple. We'll keep it in its own function like this:

    ```
    function drawLines() {
        lineStyle(1, 0, 100);
        moveTo(points[0].x, points[0].y);
        for (i=0; i<points.length; i++) {
            lineTo(points[i].x, points[i].y);
        }
    }
    ```

3. The code for inserting points is the toughest. We need to loop through the array and insert a new element between each of the two points. Here's how that function begins:

    ```
    function fractalize() {
        for (i=0; i<points.length-1; i += 2) {
            points.splice(i+1, 0, {});
        }
    }
    ```

    Here, we loop through the array starting at 0, and ending at length-1. (Normally, we'd end at length, but we don't want to add a point *after* the last one.) We also need to increment the array by two each time, since we are inserting a new element, and we want to jump over the new one to the next *old* one.

    Inside the for loop, we use the splice method to insert a new element containing a generic object. Objects are defined with curly brackets in the same way that arrays are defined with square brackets. So, {} creates a new blank object and [] creates a new blank array.

4. Next, we set the x and y properties of this new point. This is done by taking the average values of the two surrounding points and offsetting y by a random value. Add the code into fractalize function:

```
function fractalize() {
    for (i=0; i<points.length-1; i += 2) {
        points.splice(i+1, 0, {});
        points[i+1].x = (points[i].x+points[i+2].x)/2;
        points[i+1].y = (points[i].y+points[i+2].y)/2;
        points[i+1].y += Math.random()*rough-rough/2;
    }
}
```

The value for the variable rough will be determined in the next step.

5. Finally, we need to pull it all together. The game plan is to create the array and initial values, run the fractalize function a number of times to create the mountain, and then draw the lines. As for the rough variable, it should start off large for the first run-through of fractalize but, on each successive run-through, become smaller since we are dealing with smaller and smaller segments. Here's the whole of the code with the relevant additions highlighted:

```
points = new Array(2);
points[0] = {x:50, y:200};
points[1] = {x:500, y:200};
maxCount = 5;
rough = 200;
for (count=0; count<maxCount; count++) {
    fractalize();
    rough *= .5;
}
drawLines();
function drawLines() {
    lineStyle(1, 0, 100);
    moveTo(points[0].x, points[0].y);
    for (i=0; i<points.length; i++) {
        lineTo(points[i].x, points[i].y);
    }
}
function fractalize() {
    for (i=0; i<points.length-1; i += 2) {
        points.splice(i+1, 0, {});
        points[i+1].x = (points[i].x+points[i+2].x)/2;
        points[i+1].y = (points[i].y+points[i+2].y)/2;
        points[i+1].y += Math.random()*rough-rough/2;
    }
}
```

Now, each time you run this file, it will create a new fractal landscape (you can keep pressing CTRL+ENTER to generate new mountains). This is the simple version, to give you a basic understanding of what we're doing.

Mountain #2

Now, let's make it more interesting. The following version (mountain02.fla) draws each successive iteration before moving on to the next one, so you can see the mountain building up before your very eyes. Make the highlighted changes to the code from mountain01.fla:

```
points = new Array(2);
points[0] = {x:50, y:200};
points[1] = {x:500, y:200};
maxCount = 8;
rough = 200;
alpha = 20;
onEnterFrame = function () {
    if (count<maxCount) {
        fractalize();
        drawLines();
        alpha += 50/maxCount;
        rough *= .5;
        count++;
    } else {
        delete onEnterFrame;
    }
};
function drawLines() {
    lineStyle(1, 0, alpha);
    moveTo(points[0].x, points[0].y);
    for (i=0; i<points.length; i++) {
        lineTo(points[i].x, points[i].y);
    }
}
function fractalize() {
    for (i=0; i<points.length-1; i += 2) {
        points.splice(i+1, 0, {});
        points[i+1].x = (points[i].x+points[i+2].x)/2;
        points[i+1].y = (points[i].y+points[i+2].y)/2;
        points[i+1].y += Math.random()*rough-rough/2;
    }
}
```

Here, we have an onEnterFrame function that does all the work of our former for loop. It calls fractalize, then draws the current set of lines, takes care of the roughness and counting, and deletes itself when finished. It also increments an alpha variable that is used in the drawLines function. This causes the initial drawn lines to be quite faint (20%), and get darker with each iteration.

One line to play with is this:

```
rough *= .5;
```

As it is, this `.5` value creates a semi-rough, pretty realistic terrain. If you reduce it down to, say `.2`, the random factor is drastically smaller on each iteration, resulting in a much smoother landscape.

Set it higher, say at `.8`, and you get a very craggy, desolate place. Also very important is the initial `rough` factor. This also has an effect on the overall possible height of hills. By jockeying these two around, you can come up with any number of locales.

Also, of course, `maxCount` will affect how many times your segment is subdivided. Remember that each time you increase `maxCount` by 1, the number of final segments is doubled. So, high `maxCount` values will produce a huge number of segments, and possibly hang up your computer as they are calculated and rendered.

Mountain #3

As a kind of final project for this section, in the following file (`mountain03.fla`), I closed off and filled the shape with a random color, enabled a new shape to be drawn each time you click the mouse, and set up the `rough` factor so it's obtained from the mouse position. Note the code changes used to create this file:

```
onMouseDown = init;
function init() {
    clear();
    col = Math.random()*0xffffff;
    points = new Array(2);
    points[0] = {x:50, y:200};
    points[1] = {x:500, y:200};
    maxCount = 8;
    rough = -(200-_ymouse);
    alpha = 20;
    count = 0;
    onEnterFrame = main;
}
function main() {
    if (count<maxCount) {
        fractalize();
        drawLines();
        alpha += 50/maxCount;
        rough *= .5;
        count++;
    } else {
        delete onEnterFrame;
    }
}
function drawLines() {
    lineStyle(1, 0, 5);
    beginFill(col, 5);
    moveTo(points[0].x, points[0].y);
    for (i=0; i<points.length; i++) {
```

```
            lineTo(points[i].x, points[i].y);
        }
        lineTo(points[0].x, points[0].y);
    }
    function fractalize() {
        for (i=0; i<points.length-1; i += 2) {
            points.splice(i+1, 0, {});
            points[i+1].x = (points[i].x+points[i+2].x)/2;
            points[i+1].y = (points[i].y+points[i+2].y)/2;
            points[i+1].y += Math.random()*rough;
        }
    }
```

Self-similar fractals

As promised, we will now make some self-similar fractals. This is where we take a basic arrangement of shapes and repeat it over and over on smaller and smaller scales. What starts out as a very simple design can become very complex and fascinating after just a few iterations.

Self-similar #1

1. Start a new movie (CTRL+N) and draw a simple shape on the stage. Make it fairly big; say about 100x100 pixels. Convert it to a movie clip (F8) and be sure to check Export for ActionScript in the Advanced settings when doing so. I've called mine unit, and this is the name I use to reference the clip in any subsequent code. Ensure that the registration point of the clip is in the center. Delete any instances of the graphic from the stage, as we'll be attaching them all with ActionScript.

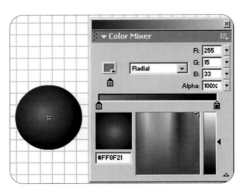

2. Now add the following code to frame 1 of the main timeline:

```
shapes = 3;
iterations = 6;
distance = 80;
scale = 60;
angle0 = 0;
```

```
angle1 = Math.PI*2/3;
angle2 = Math.PI*4/3;
```

All right. So what does all this do? Let's go through it. First, we determine how many shapes will be created on each iteration, then how many iterations there will be in total. This is important because we need to limit the iterations to a small number. If there are three shapes, the number of new shapes triples on each iteration. On the sixth iteration, over 700 shapes are created. If you take it to seven, you'll get up to over 2100! That's not too much for Flash to handle, but you will notice a pause, even on a fast computer.

Next, we set the variables for distance, scale, and three angles. Angles here are measured in **radians** rather than **degrees**. In the above code, the three angles are equivalent to 0, 120, and 240 degrees. The three new shapes will be placed at those angles and that distance from the original shape. They will be scaled to the percentage shown in scale.

3. After this, the next block of code will attach an instance of unit, place it at the center of the screen, and give it a property called uDepth, which keeps track of the number of iterations that have been run.

```
attachMovie("unit", "unit", 0);
unit._x = 275;
unit._y = 200;
unit.uDepth = 0;
```

4. Finally, assign the function fract as the onEnterFrame handler:

```
unit.onEnterFrame = fract;
function fract() {
    if (this.uDepth<iterations) {
        for (var i = 0; i<shapes; i++) {
            clip = this.attachMovie("unit", "u"+i, i);
            clip._x = Math.cos(_root["angle"+i])*distance;
            clip._y = Math.sin(_root["angle"+i])*distance;
            clip._xscale = clip._yscale=scale;
            clip._rotation = _root["angle"+i]*180/Math.PI;
            clip.uDepth = this.uDepth+1;
            clip.onEnterFrame = fract;
            delete this.onEnterFrame;
        }
    }
}
```

Here's a quick run-through of what the fract function does:

1. It checks to see if its uDepth property has surpassed the iterations limit.

2. If not, it loops through and attaches three new instances of unit.

3. For each instance, it uses some basic trigonometry to position it around the original using the defined distance and angles.

4. It scales the new instances down slightly.

5. Then, it rotates the new instances according to the angles.

6. It then increments each new unit's uDepth.

7. It assigns fract as the new movie clip's onEnterFrame handler, which starts the cycle over again at the first step in this list.

8. It then deletes its own onEnterFrame handler. We only need this function to run once. Running once and then deleting is a slightly odd use of onEnterFrame, but it allows for a pause and screen refresh between each iteration. This avoids running into the problem of more than 256 levels of recursion, which will cause the program to fail.

```
Output                                    Options
256 levels of recursion were exceeded in one action list.
This is probably an infinite loop.
Further execution of actions has been disabled in this movie.
```

Anyway, our file is complete so go ahead and test it (CTRL+ENTER).

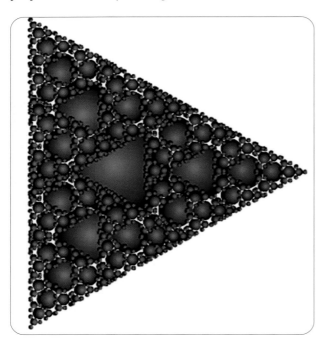

If you're unfamiliar with the 256 levels of recursion problem, type the following code into a new movie (make sure you save everything else first!):

```
recurse();
function recurse() {
    trace(count++);
    recurse();
}
```

Test it and you'll see the error.

The problem is each time recurse is run, it calls recurse again, which of course then calls recurse again. This would continue infinitely, and since it all occurs within one frame, the movie would never update, simply hanging there instead. Flash has had different methods of dealing with this. Flash 4 warned you when any loop had run several thousand times. Flash 5 abandoned this and replaced it with the 15-second rule. If a movie hung for more than 15 seconds, Flash 5 assumed there was a problem and warned you. To this, Flash MX added the 256 levels of recursion rule.

If you want to get a clearer idea of what is happening, change iterations to 1 and run the file.

Now try running it again with `iterations` set to 2.

This is what happens when `iterations` is set 3.

You should start getting the idea. Anyway, the code above is pretty much complete. Now we can start having some fun with it. The way it is structured, the first seven lines are the things you would want to experiment with most. We've pretty much covered what each one does, but here are some ideas to get you started playing with them.

The `shapes` variable controls how many shapes are created on each iteration. As with `iterations`, be careful about setting this too high. For example, on successive iterations a `shapes` value of 3 creates: 3, 9, 27, 81, 243, 729 shapes in total. A value of 5 creates: 5, 25, 125, 625, 3125 and then crashed my PC! As you can see, on recursive programs, things can get out of control very quickly!

`iterations` has been covered pretty well. Just be careful with it.

You may now have a clearer idea of how `distance` fits in. If your original movie clip is 100 pixels in diameter and you set `distance` to 100, each new movie clip will appear a little distance away from the edge of its parent, depending on your `scale` variable. So, generally you want to set it at approximately the same diameter of the original movie clip. If you set it higher, the new movie clips will appear further away from the parent. When closer, they will be caught up inside.

`scale` controls the size of the new movie clip compared to its parent. At 60, each new movie clip will be scaled by 60%. Note that since new movie clips are actually attached *inside* the parent, the next successive level will be 60% of 60%. Therefore, each level continually gets smaller and smaller. This also ends up scaling the distance for each new level, so smaller movie clips are actually closer to their parents, but the same relative distance to their size.

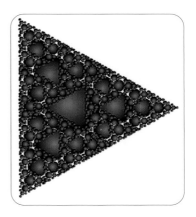

When you run `self_similar_01.fla`, you get a nice triangular shaped cluster of clips. Pretty neat – they're all lined up and organized. But don't get too excited. This is actually pretty boring. That's because the angles are equidistant: 0, 120, and 240. They are each one third of the way around a circle. No variety!

Self-similar #2

First, let's start playing with the angles. To do this a bit more easily, I've altered the last file a little. Since it's a lot easier to think in terms of degrees, I set it up so you could do this, and it would automatically convert into radians for Flash to work with. This is `self_similar_02.fla` with the edited code in bold:

```
shapes = 3;
iterations = 6;
distance = 80;
scale = 60;
degree0 = 120;
degree1 = 300;
degree2 = 350;
angle0 = degree0*Math.PI/180;
angle1 = degree1*Math.PI/180;
angle2 = degree2*Math.PI/180;
attachMovie("unit", "unit", 0);
unit._x = 275;
unit._y = 200;
unit.uDepth = 0;
unit.onEnterFrame = fract;
function fract() {
    if (this.uDepth<iterations) {
        for (var i = 0; i<shapes; i++) {
            clip = this.attachMovie("unit", "u"+i, i);
            clip._x = Math.cos(_root["angle"+i])*distance;
            clip._y = Math.sin(_root["angle"+i])*distance;
            clip._xscale = clip._yscale=scale;
            clip._rotation = _root["angle"+i]*180/Math.PI;
            clip.uDepth = this.uDepth+1;
            clip.onEnterFrame = fract;
            delete this.onEnterFrame;
        }
    }
}
```

Modify the code as above and test the movie to see the effect this new code generates.

Try playing around with the angles to see what other variations you can come up with.

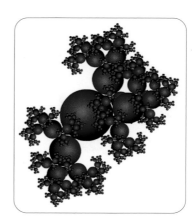

Self-similar #3

In this movie (self_similar_03.fla), I've set the three degree variables to some random numbers between 0 and 360 and got a pretty cool result. You could try some other numbers and get a feel for it.

After a while, you'll probably get pretty tired of closing the test movie down, changing the source code to some other random numbers, and then testing it again. The following code modification takes care of that automatically with a press of a mouse button:

```
onMouseDown = function () {
    shapes = 3;
    iterations = 6;
    distance = 80;
    scale = 60;
    degree0 = Math.random()*360;
    degree1 = Math.random()*360;
    degree2 = Math.random()*360;
    angle0 = degree0*Math.PI/180;
    angle1 = degree1*Math.PI/180;
    angle2 = degree2*Math.PI/180;
    attachMovie("unit", "unit", 0);
    unit._x = 275;
    unit._y = 200;
    unit.uDepth = 0;
    unit.onEnterFrame = fract;
};
```

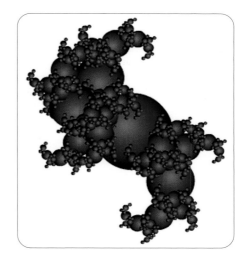

The above listing doesn't show the fract function, as it isn't going to change, so leave it as it is.

The code above takes all the rest of the code that came before the function and puts it in an onMouseDown handler. Now, each time you click, you get a different fractal! Since the original unit clip is the only movie clip on the stage (all others are attached inside it), when we overwrite that one, all the others disappear and we start afresh!

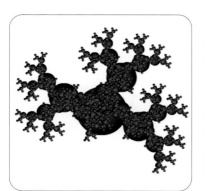
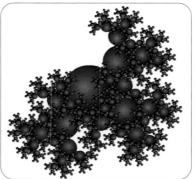

Self-similar #4

We can go even further. No doubt you've already begun experimenting with some of the other numbers, notably `distance` and `scale`. We can randomize those too (`self_similar_04.fla`):

```
onMouseDown = function () {
    shapes = 3;
    iterations = 6;
    distance = Math.random()*100+50;
    scale = Math.random()*80+20;
    degree0 = Math.random()*360;
    degree1 = Math.random()*360;
    degree2 = Math.random()*360;
    angle0 = degree0*Math.PI/180;
    angle1 = degree1*Math.PI/180;
    angle2 = degree2*Math.PI/180;
    attachMovie("unit", "unit", 0);
    unit._x = 275;
    unit._y = 200;
    unit.uDepth = 0;
    unit.onEnterFrame = fract;
};
```

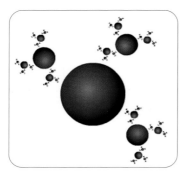

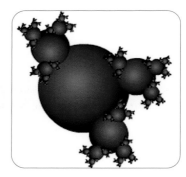

Self-similar #5

In the following file (`self_similar_05.fla`), I edited the original object to make it about half its original size: 50 pixels in diameter. Then, back in the code on the main timeline, I kept the `scale` factor much lower, and increased the distance a little.

```
onMouseDown = function () {
    shapes = 3;
    iterations = 6;
    distance = Math.random()*50+75;
    scale = 70;
    degree0 = Math.random()*360;
    degree1 = Math.random()*360;
    degree2 = Math.random()*360;
    angle0 = degree0*Math.PI/180;
    angle1 = degree1*Math.PI/180;
```

```
        angle2 = degree2*Math.PI/180;
        attachMovie("unit", "unit", 0);
        unit._x = 275;
        unit._y = 200;
        unit.uDepth = 0;
        unit.onEnterFrame = fract;
    };
```

Then, in the `fract` function, I drew a light line between each parent and its three children:

```
function fract() {
    if (this.uDepth<iterations) {
        this.lineStyle(1, 0, 50);
        for (var i = 0; i<shapes; i++) {
            clip = this.attachMovie("unit", "u"+i, i);
            clip._x = Math.cos(_root["angle"+i])*distance;
            clip._y = Math.sin(_root["angle"+i])*distance;
            clip._xscale = clip._yscale=scale;
            clip._rotation = _root["angle"+i]*180/Math.PI;
            clip.uDepth = this.uDepth+1;
            clip.onEnterFrame = fract;
            delete this.onEnterFrame;
            this.moveTo(0, 0);
            this.lineTo(clip._x, clip._y);
        }
    }
}
```

The combination of smaller sizes and higher distances creates a lot of space between the units, and the lines tie them together forming some quite botanical looking structures. Try making the changes and have a play with the variables' values.

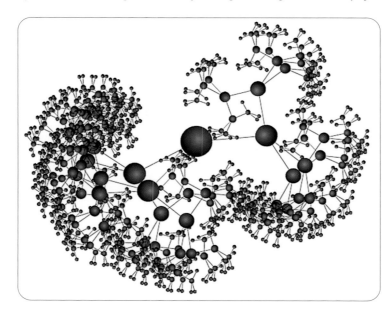

Self-similar #6

1. For a final file (`self_similar_06.fla`), dig into the original `unit` movie clip again. Instead of having it as a single static shape, create a shape tween to change its color over six frames. Also add a `stop` action to the end of the unit's timeline:

2. Then go back into the code on the main timeline and tell each new shape to `gotoAndStop` to the frame associated with its `uDepth`. Therefore, the units will gradually change color, depending on their depth. Here's the new code in bold:

```
onMouseDown = function () {
    shapes = 3;
    iterations = 6;
    distance = Math.random()*50+75;
    scale = 70;
    degree0 = Math.random()*360;
    degree1 = Math.random()*360;
    degree2 = Math.random()*360;
    angle0 = degree0*Math.PI/180;
    angle1 = degree1*Math.PI/180;
    angle2 = degree2*Math.PI/180;
    attachMovie("unit", "unit", 0);
    unit._x = 275;
    unit._y = 200;
    unit.uDepth = 0;
    unit.stop();
    unit.onEnterFrame = fract;
};
function fract() {
    if (this.uDepth<iterations) {
        this.lineStyle(1, 0, 50);
        for (var i = 0; i<shapes; i++) {
            clip = this.attachMovie("unit", "u"+i, i);
            clip._x = Math.cos(_root["angle"+i])*distance;
            clip._y = Math.sin(_root["angle"+i])*distance;
            clip._xscale = clip._yscale=scale;
            clip._rotation = _root["angle"+i]*180/Math.PI;
            clip.uDepth = this.uDepth+1;
            clip.onEnterFrame = fract;
            clip.gotoAndStop(clip.uDepth);
            delete this.onEnterFrame;
```

```
                        this.moveTo(0, 0);
                        this.lineTo(clip._x, clip._y);
                    }
                }
            }
```

3. Go ahead and try it out.

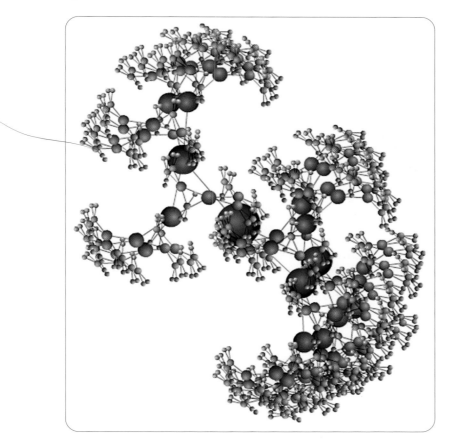

Despite the endless variety here, there is far more you can do with this. I'm sure you're already attempting something I never thought of.

Advanced color gradients

In the next couple of sections, I'm going to try and cover as many useful techniques as possible. There are a lot of one or two liners here that are very useful – and the final files themselves are pretty cool too.

The new gradient fill function in Flash MX is pretty incredible: you can dynamically create linear or radial gradients with any number of colors; specify where the gradient begins and ends; define where each color should appear in the gradient; state how much transparency each color should have; and even rotate the gradient. But let's go crazy with it and create something it was never meant to do!

Color gradient #1

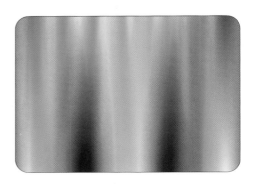

Here's the theory. Rather than make one large gradient fill, we'll make a whole bunch of one-pixel wide 'strips', each with its own individual gradient. We'll change the gradient slightly between one strip and the next, so that they blend nicely (open `color_gradient_01.swf` in the download files to see what we're heading for).

Before we get into the actual construction of the file, we need to first take a look at how to cycle through the color values smoothly.

1. We'll do this with the `Math.sin` function. To give you an idea of how it works, draw a rectangle on the stage with the Rectangle tool (R). The stroke and fill colors of the rectangle aren't important. Select the rectangle and convert it to a movie clip symbol (F8). Give the clip an instance name of `mc1_mc` in the Property inspector. On frame 1 of the main timeline add the following code to the Script pane:

```
col = new Color(mc1_mc);
speed = .1;
_root.onEnterFrame = function() {
    currentColor = Math.sin(angle += speed)*127+128;
    col.setRGB(currentColor << 16);
};
```

If you test this movie, you'll see your movie clip pulse from red to black. The `speed` variable controls how fast it pulsates. So why is it red? It is this color because we used `16` in the fourth line of code. (You can find more data on exactly how this works in the book *Fresh Flash: New Design Ideas with Flash MX* by friends of ED.) If you use a value of `8`, as in the following code:

```
col = new Color(mc1_mc);
speed = .1;
_root.onEnterFrame = function() {
    currentColor = Math.sin(angle += speed)*127+128;
    col.setRGB(currentColor << 8);
};
```

... you'll see it cycle through green. For blue, just leave off the `<<` symbol altogether:

```
col = new Color(mc1_mc);
speed = .1;
_root.onEnterFrame = function() {
    currentColor = Math.sin(angle += speed)*127+128;
    col.setRGB(currentColor);
};
```

2. Back in your file, edit your original code, define `red`, `green`, and `blue` and combine them using '`|`' the bitwise OR operator:

```
col = new Color(mc1_mc);
redSpeed = .1;
greenSpeed = .15;
blueSpeed = .2;
_root.onEnterFrame = function() {
    red = Math.sin(redAngle += redSpeed)*127+128;
    green = Math.sin(greenAngle += greenSpeed)*127+128;
    blue = Math.sin(blueAngle += blueSpeed)*127+128;
    col.setRGB(red << 16 | green << 8 | blue);
};
```

Here, we use three separate speeds with three separate angles in the Math.sin function, to create three separate color components. These are then combined in the last line. Because each component color is cycling at a slightly different speed, you'll get a full range of colors appearing over time.

Okay. That was just a little exercise to understand how to cycle colors. Let's get back to building the main movie.

3. For a gradient, we need at least two colors: one for the start of the gradient and one for the end. So, we'll need two whole sets of rgb components. Each one will cycle as in the example above, and Flash will handle the colors in between the two ends of the gradient. Start a new file (CTRL+N) and save it as color_gradient_01.fla. Type this into frame 1 of the default layer:

```
r1Speed = Math.random()*.1;
g1Speed = Math.random()*.1;
b1Speed = Math.random()*.1;
r2Speed = Math.random()*.1;
g2Speed = Math.random()*.1;
b2Speed = Math.random()*.1;
column = 0;
```

First, there are the speeds, r1Speed through b2Speed. These are set to be random numbers between 0.0 and 0.1. Then, we set a column variable to zero. This keeps track of which gradient strip we are drawing.

4. Underneath the previous lines, type in the following code, which is the start of a function:

```
onEnterFrame = function () {
    red1 = Math.sin(r1 += r1Speed)*127+128;
    green1 = Math.sin(g1 += g1Speed)*127+128;
    blue1 = Math.sin(b1 += b1Speed)*127+128;
    red2 = Math.sin(r2 += r2Speed)*127+128;
    green2 = Math.sin(g2 += g2Speed)*127+128;
    blue2 = Math.sin(b2 += b2Speed)*127+128;
    col1 = red1 << 16 | green1 << 8 | blue1;
    col2 = red2 << 16 | green2 << 8 | blue2;
    colors = [col1, col2];
```

This onEnterFrame function handles all the drawing. What this does is use the exact code we just covered in the example to come up with six color components: red1, green1, and blue1 for the beginning of the gradient, and red2, green2, and blue2 for the end of the gradient. It then combines them into two rgb colors, col1 and col2, and finally packages these into an array called colors.

5.   Now finish off the rest of the function:

```
matrix = {matrixType:"box", x:0, y:0, w:2, h:400, r:Math.PI/2};
line = createEmptyMovieClip("c"+column, column);
line._x = column;
line.beginGradientFill("linear", colors, [100, 100], [0, 255], matrix);
line.lineStyle(0, 0, 0);
line.lineTo(1, 0);
line.lineTo(1, 400);
line.lineTo(0, 400);
line.endFill();
column++;
if (column>550) {
    delete onEnterFrame;
}
};
```

Let's look at what this code does. We've made a matrix that tells Flash how to draw the gradient. Here, the matrix is a "box" type, and the x, y, w and h properties tell it to draw a 1 pixel wide, 400 pixel high, gradient starting at location (0,0). The last property, r, or rotation, is set to Math.PI/2. This is equivalent to 90 degrees. Normally, a linear gradient would be drawn left to right but by rotating it 90 degrees, we draw it from top to bottom.

Next, we create an empty movie clip, position it, and begin to draw a gradient filled shape in it. The other two arrays in the beginGradientFill command, [100, 100] and [0, 255], are for alpha (transparency) and where each color starts and ends. Alpha can be anywhere from 0 (transparent) to 100 (opaque). We'll leave both ends of the gradient fully opaque. The next array can be a little tough to understand. Basically, the numbers can go from 0 to 255. The first number we set at 0. This means that the first color in the colors array will go at the beginning of the gradient. 255 for the second element means the second color goes at the end of the gradient. By making it [255, 0], we could reverse it.

Finally, we draw a 1x400 pixel box. Note that all the lineStyle parameters are set to zero, so we will never see the line, just the fill. Then we increase the value of column, and start over again. When we get to the edge of the screen (550 in this case), we just end off by deleting the onEnterFrame function.

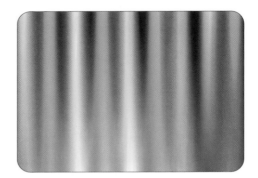

You can run this file and see a pretty amazing rainbow of color gradients.

Each time you run it, you'll get a totally different picture, owing to the random values for the six speeds. If you want to manually play with them, just remove the random lines and put in your own values, anywhere between 0 and 1 generally. Any higher than that and the colors will cycle too fast – but don't let me stop you from experimenting!

Color gradient #2

For the next file (color_gradient_02.fla), I decided to create a three-color gradient. I basically added a third line in each place I previously had something for color 1 and color 2. Note that the various arrays in the beginGradientFill command must all agree in number. If you have three colors, you need three alphas, etc. For the ranges, I put [0, 128, 255]. This causes color 2 to be in the middle of the gradient, and color 3 at the end. Here is the code, with the changes from color_gradient_01.fla highlighted in bold:

```
r1Speed = Math.random()*.1;
g1Speed = Math.random()*.1;
b1Speed = Math.random()*.1;
r2Speed = Math.random()*.1;
g2Speed = Math.random()*.1;
r3Speed = Math.random()*.1;
g3Speed = Math.random()*.1;
b3Speed = Math.random()*.1;
column = 0;
onEnterFrame = function () {
    red1 = Math.sin(r1 += r1Speed)*127+128;
    green1 = Math.sin(g1 += g1Speed)*127+128;
    blue1 = Math.sin(b1 += b1Speed)*127+128;
    red2 = Math.sin(r2 += r2Speed)*127+128;
    green2 = Math.sin(g2 += g2Speed)*127+128;
    blue2 = Math.sin(b2 += b2Speed)*127+128;
    red3 = Math.sin(r3 += r2Speed)*127+128;
    green3 = Math.sin(g3 += g2Speed)*127+128;
    blue3 = Math.sin(b3 += b2Speed)*127+128;
    col1 = red1 << 16 | green1 << 8 | blue1;
    col2 = red2 << 16 | green2 << 8 | blue2;
    col3 = red3 << 16 | green3 << 8 | blue3;
    colors = [col1, col2, col3];
    matrix = {matrixType:"box", x:0, y:0, w:2, h:400, r:Math.PI/2};
    line = createEmptyMovieClip("c"+column, column);
    line.beginGradientFill("linear", colors, [100, 100, 100], [0, 128,
➥255], matrix);
    line.lineStyle(0, 0, 0);
    line.lineTo(1, 0);
    line.lineTo(1, 400);
    line.lineTo(0, 400);
    line.endFill();
    line._x = column;
    column++;
    if (column>550) {
        delete onEnterFrame;
    }
};
```

251

You can continue to add colors to the gradient fill, just as long as you keep the same number of elements in all those arrays.

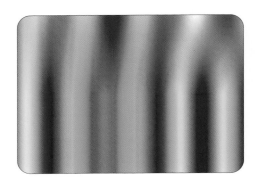 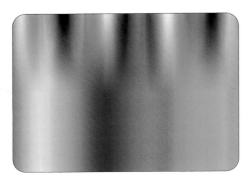

Color gradient #3

For the final file (color_gradient_03.fla), I put all the setup stuff in its own init function and called that function at the beginning of the file. Then, when it reaches the end of the screen, it calls init again, starting over with new speeds. Also, notice the change in the beginGradientFill command. It takes the mid-point value and cycles it up and down plus or minus 100 pixels from 128. This creates an additional bit of randomness in the file. Have fun with it:

```
init();
function init() {
    r1s = Math.random()*.1;
    g1s = Math.random()*.1;
    b1s = Math.random()*.1;
    r2s = Math.random()*.1;
    g2s = Math.random()*.1;
    b2s = Math.random()*.1;
    r3s = Math.random()*.1;
    g3s = Math.random()*.1;
    b3s = Math.random()*.1;
    column = 0;
}
onEnterFrame = function () {
    red1 = Math.sin(r1 += r1s)*127+128;
    green1 = Math.sin(g1 += g1s)*127+128;
    blue1 = Math.sin(b1 += b1s)*127+128;
    red2 = Math.sin(r2 += r2s)*127+128;
    green2 = Math.sin(g2 += g2s)*127+128;
    blue2 = Math.sin(b2 += b2s)*127+128;
    red3 = Math.sin(r3 += r3s)*127+128;
    green3 = Math.sin(g3 += g3s)*127+128;
    blue3 = Math.sin(b3 += b3s)*127+128;
    col1 = red1 << 16 | green1 << 8 | blue1;
    col2 = red2 << 16 | green2 << 8 | blue2;
    col3 = red3 << 16 | green3 << 8 | blue3;
    colors = [col1, col2, col3];
```

```
matrix = {matrixType:"box", x:0, y:0, w:2, h:400, r:Math.PI/2};
line = createEmptyMovieClip("column"+count, count++);
line.beginGradientFill("linear", colors, [100, 100, 100], [0,
➡Math.sin(mid += .05)*100+128, 255], matrix);
line.lineStyle(0, 0, 0);
line.lineTo(1, 0);
line.lineTo(1, 400);
line.lineTo(0, 400);
line.endFill();
line._x = column;
column++;
if (column>550) {
    init();
}
};
```

Mathematical mouse chasers

This project, again, will produce a pretty neat effect, while introducing a lot of important code tidbits that can be used almost anywhere.

The other week, I was driving to work and a flock of sparrows was flying around in the city sky. To me, they were just black dots on the bright blue sky, moving independently, but also as a whole mass. It inspired me to make the following file.

Basically, we'll have a number of 'bugs' starting off at random points on the screen. They will then turn to face the mouse cursor and begin moving towards it, increasing their speed as they approach. This is a bit different from many mouse trailers, which use an easing equation to move towards the mouse. In those examples, the particles will start out moving very quickly and get slower and slower as they approach their target. Here, they will do the opposite and, when they hit the mouse, they will slide past it, turn around and then go back towards it.

I also discovered while building various files like this, that the chasers tend to clump together and move as a unit after a while. For that reason, we'll throw in a little random motion to keep them apart and looking more like individual creatures.

The first useful piece of code we'll tackle will be how to make an object turn to face a particular point, such as the mouse cursor. This is a question that is constantly asked on the discussion boards. The following movie is an exercise on how to do achieve this one task.

Mouse chaser #1: Turn and face

1. First of all, how you draw your movie clip is very important. Normally, you'd think of 0 degrees as facing straight upwards, due north, or 12 o'clock on a clock face. But, in Flash, 0 degrees (or radians, actually) is over at 3 o'clock, due east. So, your original graphic inside the movie clip should be aligned to point to the right. Draw a small shape on the stage, say 20 pixels across, covert it to a movie clip symbol (F8), ensuring a center registration point. Name the instance `bug_mc` in the Property inspector.

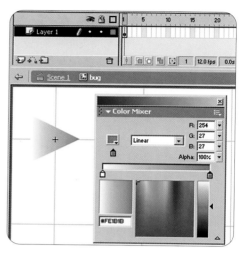

2. Now, get the distance (both x and y) from the target (mouse) to the movie clip. We'll do all this from inside the `onEnterFrame` handler for the movie clip. Insert a new layer called `actions` on the main timeline (Insert>Layer) and type this into the Actions panel (F9) at frame 1:

```
bug_mc.onEnterFrame = function() {
    var dx = _xmouse-this._x;
    var dy = _ymouse-this._y;
};
```

3. Then use those values in the `Math.atan2` function. It's important to note the order that you put them in. The y value goes first! This gives you the angle between the clip and its target.

```
bug_mc.onEnterFrame = function() {
    var dx = _xmouse-this._x;
    var dy = _ymouse-this._y;
    var angle = Math.atan2(dy, dx);
};
```

4. Now, like all Flash math functions, this returns a value in radians but `_rotation` needs degrees. So, we need to convert it, like so:

```
bug_mc.onEnterFrame = function() {
    var dx = _xmouse-this._x;
    var dy = _ymouse-this._y;
    var angle = Math.atan2(dy, dx);
    this._rotation = angle*180/Math.PI;
};
```

5. There you go. Test your movie and you'll see that no matter where you move your mouse, the movie clip will rotate to face it.

Mouse chaser #2: The bugs

Now that we have that down, start a new file for the mouse chaser project.

1. Again, create a movie clip correctly oriented to 3 o'clock, call it bug and be sure to check Export for ActionScript so it has the linkage identifier of bug. Don't leave any instances of it on the stage.

2. Decide how many bugs you want on screen. I chose 20. We'll loop through and attach them to the stage, and then place them at random points, giving them an onEnterFrame handler. Add this code to frame 1 of the main timeline:

    ```
    maxBugs = 20;
    damp = .95;
    for (i=0; i<maxBugs; i++) {
        bug = attachMovie("bug", "b"+i, i);
        bug._x = Math.random()*550;
        bug._y = Math.random()*400;
        bug.speed = Math.random()+1;
        bug.onEnterFrame = bugMove;
    }
    ```

    Right after maxBugs, you'll see a damp variable. This has nothing to do with moisture. This is a value that will act as a kind of friction once things get moving. I also threw in a random speed for each bug, which will end up between 1 and 2. You can change these numbers around to create a higher or more varied speed. Or, you could make all bugs move at the same speed by setting a fixed number instead, like this:

    ```
    bug.speed = 2;
    ```

3. Now, we just need to define what we want the bug to do, inside the bugMove function. We know, first of all, that we want it to rotate to face the mouse, so let's get that out of the way:

    ```
    function bugMove() {
        var dx = _xmouse-this._x;
        var dy = _ymouse-this._y;
        var angle = Math.atan2(dy, dx);
        this._rotation = angle*180/Math.PI;
    }
    ```

If you test your movie now, should have 20 bugs sitting on the screen, carefully watching the mouse. Let's make them move.

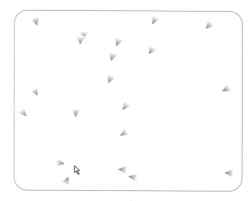

4.   For movement, we need to determine a velocity on x and velocity on y, and add that to the _x and _y properties of the movie clip. The clip should move in the direction it is currently facing and it should move at the speed we randomly determined at the time of creation. We need to use a bit of basic trigonometry to accomplish this. Here it is (the first block of code to create the bugs remains the same for the rest of the section):

```
function bugMove() {
    var dx = _xmouse-this._x;
    var dy = _ymouse-this._y;
    var angle = Math.atan2(dy, dx);
    this._rotation = angle*180/Math.PI;
    this.vx += Math.cos(angle)*this.speed;
    this.vy += Math.sin(angle)*this.speed;
    this.vx *= damp;
    this.vy *= damp;
    this._x += this.vx;
    this._y += this.vy;
}
```

This takes the `angle` we determined, feeds it into `Math.cos` and `Math.sin`, and multiplies by the `speed`. This separates out the `speed` into specific speeds for x and y. I use `vx` and `vy` for velocity x and velocity y. Finally, we add that to the _x and _y properties to get motion.

5.   So far so good. If you test the movie, the bugs should appear, turn to the mouse and begin to follow it around. Still, they seem a bit... lifeless to me. Unlike the flock of sparrows I was watching, these bugs don't really seem to have a life of their own. They clump together. So, we'll give them a bit of independent motion, a bit of random 'wandering' as they pursue their goal. After we determine the vx and vy, we'll just add or subtract a little bit from each:

```
function bugMove() {
    var dx = _xmouse-this._x;
    var dy = _ymouse-this._y;
    var angle = Math.atan2(dy, dx);
    this._rotation = angle*180/Math.PI;
    this.vx += Math.cos(angle)*this.speed;
    this.vy += Math.sin(angle)*this.speed;
    this.vx += Math.random()*4-2;
    this.vy += Math.random()*4-2;
    this.vx *= damp;
    this.vy *= damp;
    this._x += this.vx;
    this._y += this.vy;
}
```

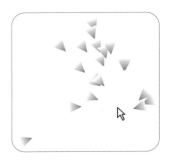

Changing the 4 and 2 will give you a more or less erratically flying bug. Just remember that the second number should always be one half of the first, such as this code for a more erratic bug:

```
this.vx += Math.random()*8-4;
```

or for a more stable, goal-oriented, bug try:

```
this.vx += Math.random()*2-1;
```

6. There's one more tidbit I want to throw in there, which should also be useful for you. Sometimes, it is very important to know the actual distance between two points. We have the x distance and y distance as dx and dy. To find the actual distance from there, we square each of them, add them together and find the square root. In ActionScript this looks like:

```
dist = Math.sqrt(dx*dx+dy*dy);
```

7. Now, what can we do with that? Pretty much anything we want. We could, for instance, *only* have the bug move if it was within a certain distance, such as:

```
function bugMove() {
    var dx = _xmouse-this._x;
    var dy = _ymouse-this._y;
    var angle = Math.atan2(dy, dx);
    this._rotation = angle*180/Math.PI;
    var dist = Math.sqrt(dx*dx+dy*dy);
    if (dist<200) {
        this.vx += Math.cos(angle)*this.speed;
        this.vy += Math.sin(angle)*this.speed;
        this.vx += Math.random()*4-2;
        this.vy += Math.random()*4-2;
        this.vx *= damp;
        this.vy *= damp;
        this._x += this.vx;
        this._y += this.vy;
    }
}
```

Here, the code for moving the bug will only occur if it is within 200 pixels of the mouse. Note that since the rotation code is outside the `if` block, it will continue to turn to face the mouse, no matter how great the distance. You could easily move that line inside the block to make that stop as well.

Or, rather than having a black and white decision like that, you can vary some property based on the distance. The following code changes the alpha based on the distance. It divides the distance by 200, giving a range of values from 0 when the distance is 0, and 1, when the distance is 200. (Or slightly higher than 1, if the distance goes above 200.) It then multiplies that by 100, giving us 0 to 100. We then subtract that value from 100, which reverses it, giving us from 100 to 0. So, the alpha of the movie clip will be close to 100 when the distance is very small, and closer to 0 as the distance approaches 200.

```
function bugMove() {
    var dx = _xmouse-this._x;
    var dy = _ymouse-this._y;
    var angle = Math.atan2(dy, dx);
    this._rotation = angle*180/Math.PI;
    var dist = Math.sqrt(dx*dx+dy*dy);
    this._alpha = 100-(dist/200)*100;
    this.vx += Math.cos(angle);
```

```
        this.vy += Math.sin(angle);
        this.vx += Math.random()*4-2;
        this.vy += Math.random()*4-2;
        this.vx *= damp;
        this.vy *= damp;
        this._x += this.vx;
        this._y += this.vy;
    }
```

It kind of feels like the bugs are flying in and out of a thick fog. You can change that value of 200 to make the fog thicker or lighter.

As with most of the files in this chapter, this is just a beginning. Please experiment with it. Try using _xscale and _yscale instead of _alpha, and combine other techniques you have learned. Have fun with it.

Slimy liquid

What better way to end off the chapter than with some slime? Actually, in this section we'll create some organic, reactive, liquid shapes that could be water, slime, Jell-O, or pretty much any similar matter. I've even used it for blood.

We'll be using the curveTo method extensively here to create nice, smooth shapes. The curves will be drawn using a set of points stored in an array. We'll constantly update the position of the points, thus changing our shape. Once we have the basic point creation and curve-drawing engine sorted, all kinds of effects can be created by manipulating points in different ways.

Point creation

1. OK, onto the code. First we'll create the array, and fill each element with a point. A point is simply a generic object with an x and a y property. We'll arrange them from left to right across the upper portion of the stage. Please keep maxPoints as an even number, for reasons we'll soon see. Start a new movie and add this code to frame 1 of the default layer:

```
maxPoints = 20;
points = new Array();
for (i=0; i<maxPoints; i++) {
    points[i] = {x:i*500/(maxPoints-1), y:Math.random()*50+25};
}
```

Now, you won't see anything here, because objects are invisible! We'll need to draw something using these points' values. We'll do that in an onEnterFrame function, so that when we start moving them around, we'll be able to see it.

2. Add this function underneath your previous code and then test the movie:

```
maxPoints = 20;
points = new Array();
for (i=0; i<maxPoints; i++) {
    points[i] = {x:i*500/(maxPoints-1), y:Math.random()*50+25};
}
onEnterFrame = function () {
    clear();
    lineStyle(1, 0, 100);
    moveTo(points[0].x, points[0].y);
    for (i=1; i<points.length; i++) {
        lineTo(points[i].x, points[i].y);
    }
};
```

Now, that is hardly organic or slimy. In fact, it looks more like our old fractal landscape than slime, but it shows that those points do indeed exist as values we can use. As I said, we'll use `curveTo` to make some curves, but we're going to go a step beyond that.

3. To show you one of the downfalls of simply using `curveTo`, use the following code instead of the above `onEnterFrame`:

```
onEnterFrame=function(){
    clear();
    lineStyle(1,0,100);
    moveTo(points[0].x, points[0].y);
    for(i=1;i<points.length-1;i+=2){
        curveTo(points[i].x, points[i].y, points[i+1].x, points[i+1].y);
    }
}
```

In this code, we jump over two points in each loop with the `i+=2` in the `for` statement. We use the first point, `points[i]`, as the control point of the `curveTo`, and the next point, `points[i+1]`, as the end point.

Now, when you test this file, you'll see the problem I'm talking about. While each individual curve is just fine, there is a sharp corner where each curve joins the next one. Still hardly slime-like.

To get a nice smooth curve between curves, there's a little trick we'll use. Basically, we'll find a mid-point between each existing point. We'll use those mid-points as the beginning and end points for the curve, and the existing points as the control points. I have no doubt that I just completely confused you, so here's a drawing that will hopefully help a bit.

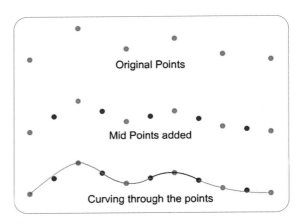

For a far more in-depth explanation of how this technique works, check Lifaros' chapter in Fresh Flash, by friends of ED.

4. Here's the code we'll use to accomplish this:

```
maxPoints = 20;
points = new Array();
midPoints = new Array();
for (i=0; i<maxPoints; i++) {
    points[i] = {x:i*550/(maxPoints-1), y:Math.random()*50+25};
}
for (i=0; i<maxPoints-1; i++) {
    midPoints[i] = {x:0, y:0};
}
onEnterFrame = function () {
    for (i=0; i<points.length-1; i++) {
        midpoints[i].x = (points[i].x+points[i+1].x)/2;
        midpoints[i].y = (points[i].y+points[i+1].y)/2;
    }
    clear();
    lineStyle(1, 0, 100);
    moveTo(points[0].x, points[0].y);
    for (i=1; i<points.length-2; i++) {
        curveTo(points[i].x, points[i].y, midPoints[i].x, midPoints[i].y);
    }
    curveTo(points[i].x, points[i].y, points[i+1].x, points[i+1].y);
};
```

This gets pretty complex, but let's go through it. First, we make an array called `midPoints`. We populate it with points. The value of the points isn't important, since they will be set later. So, we'll just stick zeros in there to hold the place.

In the beginning of the `onEnterFrame` function, we loop through all the points, finding the average of each pair. This average becomes the value for that mid-point.

The complex part comes in the line drawing code. Here, we actually end up skipping the first and last `midPoints`, as you can actually see in the previous drawing.

This could be coded differently for efficiency, but it would become even more complicated. I've gone for clarity at this point. This is how the line looks when you test it:

Well, there we have our basic drawing function. Now we can start making it move.

5. The first thing we could try is some simple gravity. We'll pull each point down at a slightly different rate. To do this, we'll give each point a slightly different `vy` property (remember, velocity y?), and add that to its value on each frame:

```
maxPoints = 20;
points = new Array();
midPoints = new Array();
for (i=0; i<maxPoints; i++) {
    points[i] = {x:i*550/(maxPoints-1), y:Math.random()*50+25,vy:Math.
    ➥random()*2+1};
}
for (i=0; i<maxPoints-1; i++) {
    midPoints[i] = {x:0, y:0};
}
onEnterFrame = function () {
    for (i=0; i<points.length; i++) {
        points[i].y += points[i].vy;
    }
    for (i=0; i<points.length-1; i++) {
        midpoints[i].x = (points[i].x+points[i+1].x)/2;
        midpoints[i].y = (points[i].y+points[i+1].y)/2;
    }
    clear();
    lineStyle(1, 0, 100);
    moveTo(points[0].x, points[0].y);
    for (i=1; i<points.length-2; i++) {
        curveTo(points[i].x, points[i].y, midPoints[i].x, midPoints[i].y);
    }
    curveTo(points[i].x, points[i].y, points[i+1].x, points[i+1].y);
};
```

Again, this could be done in a much more efficient way, but this keeps what we are doing very clear . Test it and you'll see the line softly falling down the stage with a liquid-like motion.

6. With a few extra lines in the drawing code, we can have some dripping slime!

```
maxPoints = 20;
points = new Array();
midPoints = new Array();
for (i=0; i<maxPoints; i++) {
    points[i] = {x:i*550/(maxPoints-1), y:Math.random()*50+25, vy:Math.
    ➥random()*2+1};
}
for (i=0; i<maxPoints-1; i++) {
    midPoints[i] = {x:0, y:0};
}
onEnterFrame = function () {
    for (i=0; i<points.length; i++) {
        points[i].y += points[i].vy;
    }
    for (i=0; i<points.length-1; i++) {
        midpoints[i].x = (points[i].x+points[i+1].x)/2;
        midpoints[i].y = (points[i].y+points[i+1].y)/2;
    }
    clear();
    lineStyle(1, 0, 0);
    beginFill(0x00ff00, 100);
    moveTo(points[0].x, points[0].y);
    for (i=1; i<points.length-2; i++) {
        curveTo(points[i].x, points[i].y, midPoints[i].x, midPoints[i].y);
    }
    curveTo(points[i].x, points[i].y, points[i+1].x, points[i+1].y);
    lineTo(550, 0);
    lineTo(0, 0);
    lineto(points[0].x, points[0].y);
    endFill();
};
```

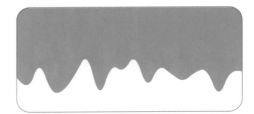

Of course, if you don't like slime, you could change it to dripping blood by making the fill color 0xFF0000! Once again, consider this as a launching pad to your own creations. Try more points, or maybe a gradient fill, or have the points rise up rather than fall. Over to you.

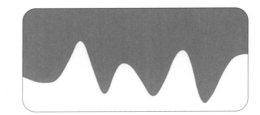

Further information

One of the most amazing things about Flash is the community that has built up around it. In addition to whole sections in the bookstore, there's a ton of online resources – tutorials, open source, forums.

The following web sites contain forums specifically dedicated to Flash Math and Physics:

- www.bit-101.com

- www.were-here.com

- www.flashkit.com

- www.ultrashock.com

There are some amazing minds on those boards who are more than willing to answer your toughest questions. Much of the math I have learned and used in Flash came from there. Also, most have tutorials and loads of open source files to play with and learn from.

As far as inspiration, the list would be too long. There are three particularly that I would like to mention as personal sources of inspiration that had a very large impact on what I decided to do:

- Yugo Nakamura: www.yugop.com

- Joshua Davis: www.praystation.com

- Jared Tarbell: www.levitated.net

What struck me about these sites, and made me want to imitate them, was the following three points:

1. The sheer "wow" factor of what they were doing.

2. The fact that the pieces they were doing were not portfolio pieces of commercial work, scientific visualizations or even viable games. They were simply cool little pieces of motion graphics. The main reason these things existed was because the authors apparently enjoyed creating them.

3. The fact that these sites were live. You could check back from time to time and see all the old stuff as well as some new things – sometimes weekly or even daily. You could often watch an idea develop in the author's mind.

All of these things were points I implemented in creating my own experimental site, www.bit-101.com.

Here's some suggested reading for Flash math and physics:

- Flash Math Creativity, friends of ED

- Flash MX Studio, friends of ED

- Fresh Flash, friends of ED

Index

The index is arranged hierarchically, in alphabetical order, with symbols preceding the letter A. Many second-level entries also occur as first-level entries. This is to ensure that you will find the information you require however you choose to search for it.

friends of ED particularly welcomes feedback on the layout and structure of this index. If you have any comments or criticisms, please contact: feedback@friendsofED.com

DESIGNER TO DESIGNER™

friends of ED writes books for you. Any suggestions, or ideas about how you want information given in your ideal book will be studied by our team. Your comments are always valued at friends of ED.

For technical support please contact support@friendsofed.com.

Free phone in USA:	800.873.9769
Fax:	312.893.8001
UK Telephone:	0121.258.8858
Fax:	0121.258.8868

Registration Code : 09427G8FID90C201

Flash MX Most Wanted Effects & Movies: Fast & Fun Design Dynamite – Registration Card

Name ....

Address ....

City ....State/Region ....

Country ....Postcode/Zip ....

E-mail ....

Profession: design student ☐ freelance designer ☐
part of an agency ☐ inhouse designer ☐
other (please specify) ....

Age: Under 20 ☐ 20-24 ☐ 25-29 ☐ 30-40 ☐ over 40 ☐

Do you use: mac ☐ pc ☐ both ☐

How did you hear about this book?...................................
☐ Book review (name)..
☐ Advertisement (name) ....
☐ Recommendation ....
☐ Catalog ....
☐ Other ....

Where did you buy this book? ....
☐ Bookstore (name) ....City...................
☐ Computer Store (name)..
☐ Mail Order...
☐ Other...

How did you rate the overall content of this book?
Excellent ☐   Good ☐
Average ☐   Poor ☐

What applications/technologies do you intend to learn in the near future?...
....

What did you find most useful about this book? ....
....

What did you find the least useful about this book? ....
....

Please add any additional comments ....
....

What other subjects will you buy a computer book on soon?
....

What is the best computer book you have used this year?
....

Note: This information will only be used to keep you updated about new friends of ED titles and will not be used for any other purpose or passed to any other third party.

ISBN: 1903450942

friendsof

D E S I G N E R   T O   D E S I G N E R ™

N.B. If you post the bounce back card below in the UK, please send it to:

friends of ED Ltd.,
30 Lincoln Road, Olton,
Birmingham, B27 6PA. UK.

BUSINESS REPLY MAIL
*FIRST CLASS MAIL   PERMIT*64   CHICAGO,IL*

POSTAGE WILL BE PAID BY ADDRESSEE

**friends of ED.
29 S. LA SALLE ST.
SUITE 520
CHICAGO IL 60603-USA**